CHAPTER 1

WHO IS JESUS?

I HAD TO GO TO THE GOSPELS to see Jesus and then to know Him. I used to spend a lot of time, as I was growing up, thinking about His conception and His birth, His life as a baby, as a child, as a boy, a teenager, and then a man.

Although Jesus's life and ministry fulfilled all the Old Testament prophecies for the first coming of the Messiah, the details are always astounding and unpredictable. The prophecy said that the Messiah would be born in Bethlehem, but no one could have guessed exactly how the King of kings would arrive on the scene.

> But thou, Bethlehem Ephratah, though thou be little among the thousands of Judah, yet out of thee shall he come forth unto me that is to be ruler in Israel; whose goings forth have been from of old, from everlasting.
>
> MICAH 5:2

> Now the birth of Jesus Christ was on this wise: When as his mother Mary was espoused to Joseph, before they came together, she was found with child of the Holy Ghost. Then Joseph her husband, being a just man, and not willing to make her a public example, was minded

to put her away privily. But while he thought on these things, behold, the angel of the Lord appeared unto him in a dream, saying, Joseph, thou son of David, fear not to take unto thee Mary thy wife: for that which is conceived in her is of the Holy Ghost.

MATTHEW 1:18-20

Something really hit me when I first read this. How would you like to be Joseph or Mary?

"Joseph, I'm pregnant, okay? Now listen, I know this is going to sound crazy…and I love you with all my heart, but I have not allowed another man to touch me. I'm a virgin, but I'm pregnant. Oh, and the angel of the Lord told me that God was the father."

Joseph's not married and his lady, Mary, is pregnant. Talk about embarrassing! How in the world do you explain to your family and friends how your girlfriend got pregnant if you say you haven't done anything? "Mary's pregnant, and I know we're not married yet, but this is different. This is not what you think it is."

"You're not even married, you haven't had marital relations, and she's pregnant? Yeah, right. Don't lie to us, Joseph."

Do you understand what we're dealing with here? These are not saints; they are normal, everyday people. So Joseph came to the only conclusion that he could. He was going to have to break off his engagement to Mary. I mean, who's going to believe he didn't touch her—and just forget that crazy story about the angel of the Lord? But then the angel of the Lord spoke to Joseph in a dream and said: "Don't break off your engagement with Mary! This whole thing is of God." Now Joseph can say for sure, "No, I am not lying! I'm telling you the truth! I never touched Mary and neither has anyone else. An angel came to me and said that the baby was conceived by the power of the Holy Spirit." But can you imagine the frustration? This has never happened before. This is a unique, one-of-a-kind event. Who will believe him? What will family and friends say about this?

Thank God for the Word of the Lord that came to Joseph through the angel. Knowing that this was done by the hand of God was the only reason he and Mary could endure the shame and reproach. I guarantee you that there were family members, close friends, and neighbors who said: "Yeah, we know what Joseph and Mary have been doing!"

"But we didn't do it! The Holy Ghost did it! The angel of the Lord spoke the Word and that's it. We promise you, before God, we did not do anything."

For me, this is where it all begins: Jesus's supernatural conception. He was born of a *virgin*. Jesus entered humanity in controversy, as the rock of offense, the stumbling block—because the whole thing was *supernatural*.

WHO IS JESUS?

> And she shall bring forth a son, and thou shalt call his name JESUS: for he shall save his people from their sins. Now all this was done, that it might be fulfilled which was spoken of the Lord by the Prophet, saying, Behold, a virgin shall be with child, and shall bring forth a son, and they shall call his name Emmanuel, which being interpreted is, God with us.
>
> MATTHEW 1:21-23

Thank God, Joseph and Mary could go back to the Word of God and say: "It says that a virgin shall be with child, and shall bring forth a son." And this description of Jesus by the angel showed us who Jesus is—Emmanuel, God with us, God manifested in the flesh.

> Then Joseph being raised from sleep did as the angel of the Lord had bidden him, and took unto him his wife: And knew her not till she had brought forth her firstborn son: and he called his name Jesus.
>
> MATTHEW 1:24-25

Now in John 1:1 we read, *"In the beginning was the Word and the Word was with God, and the Word was God."* This "Word" was Jesus prior to His coming on the scene in human flesh. Jesus didn't come into existence the day He was born. He preexisted with the Father and the Holy Spirit, the "three in one."

The Father said to the Son: "You need to become a man and pay the price for man's sin."

The Son said: "I will go. I will become a man."

3

The Word was spoken as a seed into the womb of Mary—not a seed from a natural man—but the Word of God was spoken into the womb of Mary. And she conceived and brought forth Jesus the God-man, who was without sin, without spot, and without blemish.

Why did God have to do it that way? Ever since Adam sinned in the Garden of Eden, man had been separated from God by his sin. So God needed a *sinless* man to pay the price for sinful mankind. Only a man who was without sin could pay the penalty for sinful man. God and man came together in one person—Jesus Christ—in order to cut an unbreakable covenant between God and man.

Jesus said that He would give Himself. "I'm the one. I will become a man and pay the price for man's sin so man can have the choice to come back to the Father." So the Word came into the womb of a virgin, and nine months later Jesus came forth just like a regular baby. Now, the baby Jesus didn't fly around the crib, you know! He had diapers. He had to cut His baby teeth. He did all this and everything any other child would do.

Just think about Jesus's boyhood. What was it like for Him growing up in an ordinary family with brothers and sisters and a mother and father? What was it like for them and for Him, knowing that He had a supernatural mission, that He came from Heaven to the earth to die for the sin of mankind?

When Jesus was a young man, twelve years of age, He and His family went to the temple in Jerusalem to pay their taxes. Joseph and Mary were already heading home when they realized He was missing. So, they went back to Jerusalem. They found Him in the temple, discussing the things of God with the priests. When they discovered Him, they were angry, and asked Him where He had been. He said: "Did you not know that I must be about My Father's business?"

> And he said unto them, How is it that ye sought me? wist ye not that I must be about my Father's business?
>
> LUKE 2:49

Jesus knew what His mission was. Even as a young boy, He knew He had to be about His heavenly Father's business. Somebody would say, "But Your father's business is working in the carpentry shop. What do You mean, You're about Your Father's business?" The young Jesus had to live like a regular human among regular people—all the while knowing He was different—VERY—different!

What was it like for Him as a teenager? Imagine all the pressures of growing up and coming to adulthood that teenagers have. There must have been pressure that He faced when the young girls showed interest in Him. The Bible tells us that Jesus was tempted in all the ways that we are, yet He was without sin. If you look at history you will find that the Jews during this time period would get married young. Many of the young boys were trained in the family business by the age of thirteen, and some of them had their wives chosen for them by their parents years in advance.

> For we have not an high priest which cannot be touched with the feeling of our infirmities; but was in all points tempted like as we are, yet without sin.
>
> HEBREWS 4:15

You wonder what other people were thinking about Jesus. "Maybe there is something wrong with Him. He shows no interest in women." When He was twenty-nine years old and not married, you can understand why people might have thought there was something wrong with Him!

On top of that, Jesus kept talking about the fact that His kingdom was not on this earth. Where did He come from? Was He from another planet? He was not interested in political things and didn't really care who was in power. He had no hatred for anyone, including the government of the day.

He could have grown up with a chip on His shoulder because, when He was just a toddler, all the little Hebrew boys in Bethlehem, two years old and younger, had been slaughtered by Herod—who was trying to kill the "King of the Jews." Yet Jesus never said: "I'll overthrow these Jewish traitors and Roman dogs. We'll raise up an army and take them out." Not once did He ever mention it. He must have seemed odd, different in many ways from His brothers and sisters, and He was not interested in following His earthly father's footsteps either.

5

But all these pressures were forming Him and shaping Him, preparing Him for the greatest mission ever known to man. Jesus's eternal purpose was greater than just what was happening at that time. God does not see things the way we see them. Those things which we think are so important often are not an issue to Him, as He sits in eternity.

Finally, the day came when Jesus came to the Jordan to be baptized. John the Baptist baptized Jesus and God Himself spoke from Heaven and proclaimed Him to be His own beloved Son. Jesus was led by the Spirit into the wilderness, where He fasted for forty days and forty nights and was tempted by the devil. But He soundly defeated Satan with the Word of God. When Jesus came out of the wilderness, the power of the Holy Spirit was all over Him to preach, teach, heal, and deliver.

And Jesus being full of the Holy Ghost returned from Jordan, and was led by the Spirit into the wilderness, Being forty days tempted of the devil. And in those days he did eat nothing: and when they were ended, he afterward hungered. And the devil said unto him, If thou be the Son of God, command this stone that it be made bread. And Jesus answered him, saying, It is written, That man shall not live by bread alone, but by every word of God. And the devil, taking him up into an high mountain, shewed unto him all the kingdoms of the world in a moment of time. And the devil said unto him, All this power will I give thee, and the glory of them: for that is delivered unto me; and to whomsoever I will I give it. If thou therefore wilt worship me, all shall be thine. And Jesus answered and said unto him, Get thee behind me, Satan: for it is written, Thou shalt worship the Lord thy God, and him only shalt thou serve. And he brought him to Jerusalem, and set him on a pinnacle of the temple, and said unto him, If thou be the Son of God, cast thyself down from hence: For it is written, He shall give his angels charge over thee, to keep thee: And in their hands they shall bear thee up, lest at any time thou dash thy foot against a stone. And Jesus answering said unto him, It is said, Thou shalt not tempt the Lord thy God. And when the devil had ended all the temptation, he departed from him for a season. And

Jesus returned in the power of the Spirit into Galilee: and there went out a fame of him through all the region round about. And he taught in their synagogues, being glorified of all.

LUKE 4:1-15

Everywhere Jesus went during His earthly ministry, He left a trail of people who were set free and healed, who went away walking and leaping and praising God. We count three people raised from the dead.

The widow's boy outside the city of Nain:

And it came to pass the day after, that he went into a city called Nain; and many of his disciples went with him, and much people. Now when he came nigh to the gate of the city, behold, there was a dead man carried out, the only son of his mother, and she was a widow: and much people of the city was with her. And when the Lord saw her, he had compassion on her, and said unto her, Weep not. And he came and touched the bier: and they that bare him stood still. And he said, Young man, I say unto thee, Arise. And he that was dead sat up, and began to speak. And he delivered him to his mother. And there came a fear on all: and they glorified God, saying, That a great prophet is risen up among us; and, That God hath visited his people.

LUKE 7:11-16

Jairus' daughter:

While he yet spake, there cometh one from the ruler of the synagogue's house, saying to him, Thy daughter is dead; trouble not the Master. But when Jesus heard it, he answered him, saying, Fear not: believe only, and she shall be made whole. And when he came into the house, he suffered no man to go in, save Peter, and James, and John, and the father and the mother of the maiden. And all wept, and bewailed her: but he said, Weep not; she is not dead, but sleepeth. And they laughed him to scorn, knowing that she was dead. And he put them all out, and took her by the hand, and called, saying, Maid, arise. And her spirit came again, and she arose straightway: and he commanded to give her meat. And her parents were astonished: but he charged them that they should tell no man what was done.

LUKE 8:49-56

Lazarus:

And when he thus had spoken, he cried with a loud voice, Lazarus, come forth. And he that was dead came forth, bound hand and foot with graveclothes: and his face was bound about with a napkin. Jesus saith unto them, Loose him, and let him go. Then many of the Jews which came to Mary, and had seen the things which Jesus did, believed on him.

JOHN 11:43-45

What's more, at the end of his Gospel, John said:

And there are also many other things which Jesus did, the which, if they should be written every one, I suppose that even the world itself could not contain the books that should be written. Amen.

JOHN 21:25

Miracles were not the only unusual occurrences in Jesus's ministry, however. He habitually hung out with the despised tax collectors and sinners. He didn't act like them, but He didn't condemn them or make them feel inferior either. That's why they loved to be around Him, because they felt He accepted them as they were. Then, when He looked at them with eyes of love and taught them the truth about God, they wanted to get rid of their sin to get closer to Him.

Jesus has never been repulsive like religion can be. When you see Hollywood's idea of what they think God and God's people are like—condemning, mean, angry, and uncompassionate—you know that they get it straight from religion. Religion focuses on your sin and condemns you for it; Jesus focuses on setting you free. His love and goodness lead you to repent and give you the power to overcome the sin in your life. Religion locks you into sin; Jesus is the lover of your soul who sets you free from sin.

For God so loved the world, that he gave his only begotten Son, that whosoever believeth in him should not perish, but have everlasting life. For God sent not his Son into the world to condemn the world; but that the world through him might be saved.

JOHN 3:16-17

That was His whole mission. There was never a time that Jesus did not keep in mind the divine purpose and plan for His life. He came with one goal, and that was to pay the price at Calvary for your sin and my sin. He was born to die—in a remarkable, unparalleled act of love.

Yet if you listen to some preachers today, you'd think that God only sent His Son into the world to tell the world, "You are sinners and I am angry with you. I want you to burn in the flames of hell." Somehow they think that this is the Gospel of Jesus Christ. Jesus never came with a message of condemnation. Jesus came with a message of love and forgiveness. We can see this demonstrated through the story of the woman who was caught in adultery:

And the scribes and Pharisees brought unto him a woman taken in adultery; and when they had set her in the midst, They said unto him, Master, this woman was taken in adultery, in the very act. Now Moses in the law commanded us, that such should be stoned: but what sayest thou? This they said, tempting him, that they might have to accuse him. But Jesus stooped down, and with his finger wrote on the ground, as though he heard them not. So when they continued asking him, he lifted up himself, and said unto them, He that is without sin among you, let him first cast a stone at her. And again he stooped down, and wrote on the ground. And they which heard it, being convicted by their own conscience, went out one by one, beginning at the eldest, even unto the last: and Jesus was left alone, and the woman standing in the midst. When Jesus had lifted up himself, and saw none but the woman, he said unto her, Woman, where are those thine accusers? Hath no man condemned thee? She said, No man, Lord. And Jesus said unto her, Neither do I condemn thee: go, and sin no more.

JOHN 8:3-11

Jesus said: *"Go, and sin no more."* He released her from her sin, and He is still releasing people from their sin today. He does not condone sin, but He has compassion on and forgives sinners. He releases people from their guilt and condemnation.

But religion does not release you from guilt and condemnation. Religion has to make you feel guilty in order to survive, because religion is a parasite that thrives on your guilt. As long as you're guilty, you're caught in religion's trap. You'll go through all the rituals and try to keep all the laws, and when you can't do it, you'll be even more guilty and condemned. It's a vicious cycle that only Jesus can break.

When you're released from your guilt and sin by receiving Jesus as your Lord and Savior, you're free from religion's control. The power of God is not only working on the inside of you, but works through you. You can cast out devils, heal the sick, and raise the dead just like Jesus did! Religion does not want you to do that.

That's why Jesus was a total oddity to the religious world. He came in total opposition to the religious system of the day and wreaked havoc. The religious people were the ones who put Him on the cross. They were the ones who said: "We've got to get rid of Him." Jesus had a power that they did not understand—the power of unconditional love which sets men and women free and allows them to know God personally, for themselves.

But religion says,

"Do what we say and *we'll* tell you what God says."

The history of Jesus is greater than any James Bond 007 movie. Jesus the God/Man came to the earth and took on human flesh for the purpose of paying the price and becoming the eternal sacrifice for man's sin. God-and-man-in-one did it, so that all we have to do is say, "I believe!" and salvation becomes ours.

Jesus speaks to me. His body speaks to me of the fact that He is a human being and understands everything I'm going through. The beatings He endured speak to me that by His stripes He bore my sicknesses and carried my diseases. His blood shed on the cross speaks to me that He washed away my sin. And His resurrection speaks to me that because

He lives, I can also live—really live! I'm talking about eternal life! I'm talking about everlasting life!

> Wherefore in all things it behoved him to be made like unto his brethren, that he might be a merciful and faithful high priest in things pertaining to God, to make reconciliation for the sins of the people. For in that he himself hath suffered being tempted, he is able to succour them that are tempted.
>
> HEBREWS 2:17-18

> But he was wounded for our transgressions, he was bruised for our iniquities: the chastisement of our peace was upon him; and with his stripes we are healed.
>
> ISAIAH 53:5

> I am crucified with Christ: nevertheless I live; yet not I, but Christ liveth in me: and the life which I now live in the flesh I live by the faith of the Son of God, who loved me, and gave himself for me.
>
> GALATIANS 2:20

We know that Jesus could have walked away at any time. Even on the cross, He could have called thousands of angels to help Him. But He gladly laid His life down for us. Heaven's court of justice was waiting to be satisfied, the price for sin had to be paid, and Jesus did it—for you and me.

> Thinkest thou that I cannot now pray to my Father, and he shall presently give me more than twelve legions of angels?
>
> MATTHEW 26:53

WHO IS JESUS?

He is the God/Man who paid the price for our sin so that we could know God and be set free from sin and all religious bondage. Hallelujah!

CHAPTER 2

SEEING JESUS CLEARLY

When Jesus came into the coasts of Caesarea Philippi, he asked his disciples, saying, Whom do men say that I the Son of man am? And they said, Some say that thou art John the Baptist: some, Elias; and others, Jeremiah, or one of the prophets. He saith unto them, But whom say ye that I am?

MATTHEW 16:13-15

Jesus asked the disciples two questions. "Whom do men say that I am?" And then, "Whom do you say that I am?" I believe that these two questions will be asked of you as you read this book. Jesus wanted to know who His disciples thought He was, and now He wants to know who you think He is.

And Simon Peter answered and said, Thou art the Christ, the Son of the living God. And Jesus answered and said unto him, Blessed art thou, Simon Barjona: for flesh and blood hath not revealed it unto thee, but my Father which is in heaven. And I say also unto thee, That thou art Peter, and upon this rock I will build my church; and the gates of hell will not prevail against it.

MATTHEW 16:16-18

I want you to notice something. Peter saw something that day. His eyes were opened and he saw who Jesus really was. As we step into this new millennium, what the world needs more than anything is to see Jesus clearly. Unfortunately, most people see Jesus through the eyes of religion and tradition.

When we went to Disney World to see their Christmas production one year, we saw people put out their cigarettes and stand there with tears rolling down their cheeks, singing about the babe who was born in Bethlehem. Everybody can get tearful about a baby. If you keep Him as a baby, you don't have to accept Him as the Lord of your life.

Jesus is born at Christmas and He dies at Easter. At Easter, Jesus is on the cross. The world again stands with tears rolling down their cheeks, this time about the fact that Jesus died. But you know what? They still don't make Him their Lord. To be born again and make Heaven their home, they have to invite the risen Lord Jesus to come and make His home on the inside of them. They have to see, and believe, that the tomb is empty.

The world says that Jesus was just a good man. Some say that He was a prophet in a long line of prophets. Others say that He was an eccentric. Some say that He was a martyr. And others say that He was a fairy tale. Children are raised to believe in the tooth fairy, the Easter bunny, Santa Claus, and Jesus Christ. We've put Jesus in there with the fairy tales, and when children eventually find out the fairy tales are not real, they start to wonder about Jesus too. But Jesus is not a fairy tale; He's a living reality.

What is very interesting is that every year is marked on the calendar as the year of our Lord. 2000 AD. Anno Domini—AD—is Latin for "year of our Lord." You don't see it written down as "Year of Buddha 2000," or "2000 Mohammed," or "2000 Confucius." One man split the time of a whole planet, and His name is Jesus. It's more than just coincidence.

Jesus came to earth as a human being. He was born of a virgin and lived a sinless life. He went to the cross of Calvary and paid the price for our sin. Then He rose from the dead, sat down at the right hand of the Father, and sent the Holy Ghost to live in the hearts of those who believe. So now you and I can come and simply surrender our lives to Him, and the Holy Ghost can come into our hearts and give us a new life. I thank God for the reality of the risen, resurrected Lord Jesus Christ.

If you want to see Jesus clearly, take your Bible and read through the Gospels of Matthew, Mark, Luke, and John. Underline everything He did and everything He said. Put yourself in every verse. I've been at the pool of Bethesda. "When did you go there?" you might ask. I went there in the pages of the Word of God!

> Now there is at Jerusalem by the sheep market a pool, which is called in the Hebrew tongue Bethesda, having five porches. In these lay a great multitude of impotent folk, of blind, halt, withered, waiting for the moving of the water.
>
> JOHN 5:2-3

I've been there. I've seen it in the Spirit! When you walk through the pages of the Word of God, Jesus will walk right off the pages of the Gospel and into your heart. The living reality of the resurrected Lord will walk up and down in your heart. The Bible says: *"Jesus saith unto him, Thomas, because thou hast seen me, thou hast believed: blessed are they that have not seen, and yet have believed"* (John 20:29). I haven't seen, but I believe. I haven't seen with my natural eye, but I've seen Him with the eye of my spirit in the pages of the Word of God.

The Word says: *"Then said I, Lo, I come (in the volume of the book it is written of me) to do thy will, O God"* (Hebrews 10:7). We must see Him as He really is—not through the eyes of religious tradition, but through the eyes of the Holy Spirit and God's Word. Religious people don't want to be around sinners, and they didn't like Jesus because He convicted them of their hard-heartedness.

Jesus was not a barefoot, scrawny, weak-kneed individual with a lamb under His arm who spoke in Elizabethan English, "For yea, as thou hast gathered here this day." That's not Jesus; that is religion and tradition. If you read the Bible, you'll see that the reputation Jesus had among the religious people was that of a gluttonous man and a winebibber, because He hung around with the sinners. Religious people don't want to be around sinners, and they didn't like Jesus because He convicted them of their hard-heartedness.

Jesus was also a man's man. If He walked in the door, your head would turn, and when He spoke, He would get your attention. People sometimes say to me, "Rodney just be nice. Just be like Jesus." I say, "Man, you haven't read about Jesus!" He was straight; He was right down the line with His message. There was no gray area with Him; it was either white or black. He was merciful to sinners, but to religious people His words cut like a knife.

For example, we see His incredible mercy in the Garden of Gethsemane when Peter chopped off the ear of Malchus, the high priest's servant. Malchus was trying to arrest Jesus. But rather than treating him as an enemy, Jesus bent right down, picked up the ear, stuck it back on, and healed him.

On the other hand, when He was dealing with religious people—the Pharisees and the Sadducees, the "wouldn't sees" and the "couldn't sees"— He was extremely blunt. In Matthew 23, He called them a *"generation of vipers."* He called them *"blind guides"* (v. 24) and *"whited sepulchers…full of dead men's bones"* (v. 27). He said, *"If you make any converts,"* (which He doubted) *"you're gonna make them twice the devils of hell that you are"* (Matthew 23:27, author's paraphrase). That's Jesus!

> Then spake Jesus to the multitude, and to his disciples, Saying The scribes and the Pharisees sit in Moses' seat: All therefore whatsoever they bid you observe, that observe and do; but do not ye after their works: for they say, and do not. For they bind heavy burdens and grievous to be borne, and lay them on men's shoulders; but they themselves will not move them with one of their fingers. But all their works they do for to be seen of men: they make broad their phylacteries, and enlarge the borders of their garments, And love the uppermost rooms at feasts, and the chief seats in the synagogues, And greetings in the markets, and to be called of men, Rabbi, Rabbi. But be not ye called Rabbi: for one is your Master, even Christ; and all ye

are brethren. And call no man your father upon the earth: for one is your Father, which is in heaven. Neither be ye called masters: for one is your Master, even Christ. But he that is greatest among you shall be your servant. And whosoever shall exalt himself shall be abased; and he that shall humble himself shall be exalted. But woe unto you, scribes and Pharisees, hypocrites! for ye shut up the kingdom of heaven against men: for ye neither go in yourselves, neither suffer ye them that are entering to go in. Woe unto you, scribes and Pharisees, hypocrites! for ye devour widows' houses, and for a pretence make long prayer: therefore ye shall receive the greater damnation. Woe unto you, scribes and Pharisees, hypocrites! for ye compass sea and land to make one proselyte, and when he is made, ye make him twofold more the child of hell than yourselves. Woe unto you, ye blind guides, which say, Whosoever shall swear by the temple, it is nothing; but whosoever shall swear by the gold of the temple, he is a debtor! Ye fools and blind: for whether is greater, the gold, or the temple that sanctifieth the gold? And, Whosoever shall swear by the altar, it is nothing; but whosoever sweareth by the gift that is upon it, he is guilty. Ye fools and blind: for whether is greater, the gift, or the altar that sanctifieth the gift? Whoso therefore shall swear by the altar, sweareth by it, and by all things thereon. And whoso shall swear by the temple, sweareth by it, and by him that dwelleth therein. And he that shall swear by heaven, sweareth by the throne of God, and by him that sitteth thereon. Woe unto you, scribes and Pharisees, hypocrites! for ye pay tithe of mint and anise and cummin, and have omitted the weightier matters of the law, judgment, mercy, and faith: these ought ye to have done, and not to leave the other undone. Ye blind guides, which strain at a gnat, and swallow a camel. Woe unto you, scribes and Pharisees, hypocrites! for ye make clean the outside of the cup and of the platter, but within they are full of extortion and excess. Thou blind Pharisee, cleanse first that which is within the cup and platter, that the outside of them may be clean also. Woe unto you, scribes and Pharisees, hypocrites! for ye are like unto whited sepulchres, which indeed appear beautiful outward, but are within full of dead men's bones, and of all uncleanness. Even so ye also outwardly appear righteous unto men, but within ye are full of hypocrisy and iniquity. Woe unto you, scribes and Pharisees, hypocrites! because ye build the tombs of the prophets, and garnish the sepulchres of the righteous, And say, If we had been in the days of our fathers, we would not have been partakers with them in the blood of the prophets. Wherefore ye be witnesses unto yourselves, that ye are the children of them which killed the prophets. Fill ye up then the measure of your fathers. Ye serpents, ye generation of vipers, how can ye escape the damnation of hell? Wherefore, behold, I send unto you prophets, and wise men, and scribes: and some of them ye shall kill and crucify; and some of them shall ye scourge in your synagogues, and persecute them from city to city: That upon you may come all the righteous blood shed upon the earth, from the blood of righteous Abel unto the blood of Zacharias son of Barachias, whom ye slew between the temple and the altar. Verily I say unto you, All these things shall come upon this generation. O Jerusalem, Jerusalem, thou that killest the prophets, and stonest them which are sent unto thee, how often would I have gathered thy children together, even as a hen gathereth her chickens under her wings, and ye would not! Behold, your house is left unto you desolate. For I say unto you, Ye shall not see me henceforth, till ye shall say, Blessed is he that cometh in the name of the Lord.

MATTHEW 23

We have this religious idea of what we think Jesus is like. But as you go through the Gospels, you begin to see Him as He really is! If He walked the earth today, He would run cross-grain with religious tradition. Religious tradition tries to keep Him on the cross or in the crib. Jesus would be persecuted by many of today's religious leaders.

Take, for example, casting out demons. The religious Pharisees and Sadducees told Jesus that He was of the devil and that He cast out devils by the devil. Religious people are still saying that today. So you're in good company when people accuse you of the same thing!

Many churches make the world think that whenever you come around God, you've got to be morbid and sad. Too many religious, traditional churches put people off from serving Jesus because they have no life, no joy. But Jesus said: *"I am come that they might have life, and that they might have it more abundantly"* (John 10:10). That's the Jesus of the Gospels; in fact, that's the Jesus of the whole Bible!

Let's go on a journey through the Bible, from Genesis to Revelation, and let's see how Jesus is portrayed through the Word of God.[1]

In Genesis, He is the Seed of the Woman.

In Exodus, He is the Passover Lamb.

In Leviticus, He is our High Priest.

In Numbers, He's our Pillar of Cloud by day and our Pillar of Fire by night.

In Deuteronomy, He is the Prophet like unto Moses.

In Joshua, He is the Captain of our Salvation.

In Judges, He is our Lawgiver.

In Ruth, He is our Kinsman Redeemer.

In First and Second Samuel, He's our Trusted Prophet.

In Kings and Chronicles, He is our Reigning King.

In Ezra, He's our Faithful Scribe.

In Nehemiah, He's the Rebuilder of the broken walls.

In Esther, He's our Advocate.

In Job, He's our Ever-Living Redeemer.

In Psalms, He is the Lord, our Shepherd, so we shall not want.

In Proverbs, He is our Wisdom.

In Ecclesiastes, He is our Goal!

In the Song of Solomon, He is our Lover and our Bridegroom.

In Isaiah, He's the Prince of Peace.

In Jeremiah and Lamentations, He is the Weeping Prophet.

---

1   This is from a message I heard as a boy, which had a great impact on my life, "The Fourth Man," by Oral Roberts.

In Ezekiel, He's the Wonderful Four-faced Man.

In Daniel, He's the Fourth Man in the burning, fiery furnace.

In Hosea, He's the Eternal Husband, forever married to the backslider.

In Joel, He's the Baptizer in the Holy Ghost.

In Amos, He's our Burden-bearer.

In Obadiah, He's our Savior.

In Jonah, He's the Great Foreign Missionary.

In Micah, He's the Messenger with beautiful feet.

In Nahum, He's our Avenger.

In Habakkuk, He's the Evangelist pleading for revival.

In Zephaniah, He's the Lord, mighty to save.

In Haggai, He's the Restorer of the lost heritage.

In Zechariah, He's the Fountain springing up with everlasting life.

In Malachi, He's the Son of Righteousness, rising with healing in His wings.

In Matthew, He's the Messiah.

In Mark, He's the Wonder Worker.

In Luke, He's the Son of Man.

In John, He's the Son of God.

In Acts, He's the Holy Ghost, moving among men.

In Romans, He's the Justifier.

In First and Second Corinthians, He's the Sanctifier.

In Galatians, He's the Redeemer from the curse of the law.

In Ephesians, He is the Christ of unsearchable riches.

In Philippians, He's the God who supplies ALL of our needs.

In Colossians, He's the fullness of the godhead bodily.

In First and Second Thessalonians, He's our Soon-coming King.

In First and Second Timothy, He's the Mediator between God and man.

In Titus, He is the Faithful Pastor.

In Philemon, He's the Friend of the oppressed.

In Hebrews, He's the Blood of the everlasting covenant.

In James, He is the Lord who raises the sick.

In First and Second Peter, He's the Chief Shepherd, who shall soon appear.

In First, Second, and Third John, He is Love.

In Jude, He's the Lord coming with ten thousand of His saints.

In Revelation, He is King of kings and Lord of lords.

Jesus is Abel's sacrifice and Noah's rainbow. He's Abraham's ram and Isaac's well. He's Jacob's ladder and Ezekiel's burden. He's Judah's scepter, Moses' rod, David's slingshot, and Hezekiah's sundial. He's the Church's Head and is risen from the dead. He is a Husband to the widow and a Father to the orphan.

To those traveling by night, He's the Bright and the Morning Star. To those in the lonesome valley, He's the Lily of the Valley, the Rose of Sharon, the Honey in the Rock and the Staff of Life. He's the Pearl of Great Price. He's the Rock in the weary land. He's the Counselor. He's the Everlasting Father. The government is upon His shoulders. He's Peter's shadow, John's pearly white city. He's Jesus of Nazareth, the Son of the Living God.

He's the One who owns the cattle on a thousand hills. He's the One who split the Red Sea. He's the One who took the children of Israel out of Egypt into the Promised Land. He's the One who humbled Himself, came to earth, healed the sick, raised the dead, cleansed the lepers, opened the eyes of the blind, and turned the water into wine.

He's the One who fed the five thousand, walked on water, and cast out devils. He's the One who humbled Himself, once again, and became obedient unto death—even the death of the cross. He's the One who died on the cross, rose from the dead, ascended to the right hand of the Father, and ever liveth to make intercession for us. And He's coming back very, very soon. He is Jesus Christ of Nazareth, King of kings and Lord of lords.

Jesus said: *"I and my Father are one"* (John 10:30). He said: *"If you've seen Me, you've seen the Father." "Jesus saith unto him, Have I been so long time with you, and yet hast thou not known me, Philip? he that hath seen me hath seen the Father; and how sayest thou then, Show us the Father"* (John 14:9)? Jesus was God manifest in the flesh.

> I am Alpha and Omega, the first and the last...And I turned to see the voice that spake with me. And being turned, I saw seven golden candlesticks. And in the midst of the seven candlesticks one like unto the Son of man, clothed with a garment down to the foot, and girt about the paps with a golden girdle. His head and his hairs were white like wool, as white as snow; and his eyes were as flames of fire; And his feet like unto fine brass, as if they burned in a furnace; and his voice as the sound aof many waters. And he bad in his right hand seven stars: and out of his mouth went a sharp twoedged sword: and his countenance was as the sun shineth in his strength. And when I saw him, I fell at his feet as dead. And he laid his right hand upon me, saying unto me, Fear not; I am the first and the last: I am he that liveth, and was dead; and behold, I am alive for evermore, Amen; and have the keys of hell and of death.
>
> REVELATION 1:11-18

CHAPTER 3

WHAT HAPPENS WHEN JESUS SHOWS UP?

The Spirit of the Lord is upon me, because be hath anointed me to preach the Gospel to the poor; he hath sent me to heal the broken-hearted, to preach deliverance to the captives, and recovering of sight to the blind, to set at liberty them that are bruised, To preach the acceptable year of the Lord.

LUKE 4:18-19

This is the message that Jesus declared all during His earthly ministry: *"The Spirit of the Lord is upon me, because he hath anointed me to preach the Gospel."* And the Gospel is *Good News!* There are too many *bad news* preachers in the earth today. All they want to do is bring doom and gloom. Some people seem to think that they're Old Testament prophets, called to rail out against sin. But thank God we're under a new covenant. The message of this new covenant is the same message that Jesus proclaimed: the Spirit of the Lord is upon *me*, and He has anointed *me* to preach the Gospel, the Good News.

The Gospel is Good News, my dear friend. Good News! I bring you Good News! I bring you glad tidings. *I bring you Good News! Hallelujah!*

I get happy just thinking about the Good News!

We all know that the world is full of bad news. You can turn on a television and all you hear is bad news. The last thing you need is a preacher bringing you more bad news. We need to hear the Good News of the Gospel: that Jesus still saves, Jesus still heals, Jesus still sets free, and that Jesus is coming again. That's the Gospel!

The problem is that many Christians are confused. They have a little bit of the old covenant, a little bit of the new covenant, and they've made up their own covenant. Their own covenant brings them under condemnation and bondage one minute, and it sets them free the next. In their confusion, they think God is blessing them one moment and the next moment He is saying, "I'm going to kill you." They walk around waiting for God to beat them and hurt them for reasons known only to Him.

That's not the Good News! The Good News is the same as it was when Jesus walked the earth. Do you know why it's still the same? Because Jesus is still the same. Jesus has not changed!

The question I pose to you is, "What happens when Jesus shows up?" What happens when Jesus walks in the door? I want you to know that when Jesus walks in the door, the very atmosphere of the room changes. When Jesus walks in the door, sickness and death and poverty and the curse of hell go out the back door, saying, "It's time for us to leave."

When Jesus walks in the door, you will know that He is there. You can see His nature and His character in Matthew, Mark, Luke, and John. What happens when He shows up? Jesus answered that Himself.

> The thief cometh not, but for to steal, and to kill, and to destroy: I am come that they might have life, and that they might have it more abundantly.
>
> JOHN 10:10

> He that committeth sin is of the devil; for the devil sinneth from the beginning. For this purpose the Son of God was manifested, that he might destroy the works of the devil.
>
> 1 JOHN 3:8

How God anointed Jesus of Nazareth with the Holy Ghost and with power: who went about doing good, and healing all that were oppressed of the devil for God was with him.

ACTS 10:38

I have good news for you: God is *good*; Jesus is *good*. God wants to bless you! Jesus wants to bless you! People ask me, "What's all this joy in your meetings? Why joy? What is the purpose? Don't you know it's the *Holy* Spirit, not the *joy* spirit?"

Joy is a fruit of the Spirit, although it is not the only fruit of the Spirit. When the Holy Spirit does His work in your life, you will have all nine fruits of the Spirit: love, joy, peace, patience, kindness, goodness, faithfulness, gentleness, and self-control. Joy is noticeable, however, because it is very much an outward expression that others can see.

But the fruit of the Spirit is love, joy, peace, forbearance, kindness, goodness, faithfulness, gentleness and self-control. Against such things there is no law.

GALATIANS 5:22-23 NIV

Jesus brings joy. When Jesus shows up, He says to you, "Be of good cheer." When Jesus shows up, He says: "Rejoice! Rejoice! Rejoice!" When Jesus shows up, He says: "Be strong."

In the book of Acts, chapter 8, we see that when Philip went down to the city of Samaria and preached Jesus Christ to them, there was great joy in the city. What happens when Jesus shows up? There is great joy!

And Saul was consenting unto his death. And at that time there was a great persecution against the church which was at Jerusalem; and they were all scattered abroad throughout the regions of Judaea and Samaria, except the apostles. And devout men carried Stephen to his burial, and made great lamentation over him. As for Saul, he made havock of the church, entering into every house, and haling men and women committed them to prison. Therefore they that were scattered abroad went every where preaching the word. Then Philip went down to the city of Samaria, and preached Christ unto them. And the people with one accord gave heed unto those things which Philip spake, hearing and seeing the miracles which he did. For unclean spirits, crying with loud voice, came out of many that were possessed with them: and many taken with palsies, and that were lame, were healed. And there was great joy in that city. But there was a certain man, called Simon, which beforetime in the same city used sorcery, and bewitched the people of Samaria, giving out that himself was some great one: To whom they all gave heed, from the least to the greatest, saying, This man is the great power of God. And to him they had regard, because that of long time he had bewitched them with sorceries. But when they believed Philip preaching the things concerning the kingdom of God, and the name of Jesus Christ, they were baptized, both men and women. Then Simon himself believed also: and when he was baptized, he continued with Philip, and wondered, beholding the miracles and signs which were done. Now when the apostles which were at Jerusalem heard that Samaria had received the word of God, they sent unto them Peter and John: Who, when they were come down, prayed for them, that they might receive the Holy Ghost: (For as yet he was fallen upon none of them: only they were baptized in the name of the Lord Jesus.) Then laid they their hands on them, and they received the Holy Ghost. And when Simon saw that through laying on of the apostles' hands the Holy Ghost was given, he offered them money, Saying, Give me also this power, that on whomsoever I lay hands, he may receive the Holy Ghost. But Peter said unto him, Thy money perish with thee, because thou hast thought that the gift of God may be purchased with money. Thou hast neither part nor lot in this matter: for thy heart is not right in the sight of God. Repent therefore of this thy wickedness, and pray God, if perhaps the thought of thine heart may be forgiven thee. For I perceive that thou art in the gall of bitterness, and in the bond of iniquity. Then answered Simon, and said, Pray ye to the LORD for me, that none of these things which ye have spoken come upon me. And they, when they had testified and preached the word of the Lord, returned to Jerusalem, and preached the Gospel in many villages of the Samaritans. And the angel of the Lord spake unto Philip, saying, Arise, and go toward the south unto the way that goeth down from Jerusalem unto Gaza, which is desert. And he arose and went: and, behold, a man of Ethiopia, an eunuch of great authority under Candace queen of the Ethiopians, who had the charge of all her treasure, and had come to Jerusalem for to worship, Was returning, and sitting in his chariot read Esaias the prophet. Then the Spirit said unto Philip, Go near, and join thyself to this chariot. And Philip ran thither to him, and heard him read the prophet Esaias, and said, Understandest thou what thou readest? And he said, How can I, except some man should guide me? And he desired Philip that he would come up and sit with him. The place of the scripture which he read was this, He was led as a sheep to the slaughter; and like a lamb dumb before his shearer, so opened he not his mouth: In his humiliation his judgment was taken away: and who shall declare his generation? for his life is taken from the earth. And the eunuch answered Philip, and said, I pray thee, of whom speaketh the prophet this? of himself, or of some other man? Then Philip opened his mouth, and began at the same scripture, and preached unto him Jesus. And as they went on their way, they came unto a certain water: and the eunuch said, See, here is water; what doth hinder me to be baptized? And Philip said, If thou believest with all thine heart, thou mayest. And he answered and said, I believe that Jesus Christ is the Son of God. And he commanded the chariot to stand still: and they went down both into the water, both Philip and the eunuch; and he baptized him. And when they were come up out of the water, the Spirit of the Lord caught away Philip, that the eunuch saw him no more: and he went on his way rejoicing. But Philip was found at Azotus: and passing through he preached in all the cities, till he came to Caesarea.

ACTS 8

A glad heart makes a cheerful countenance.

PROVERBS 15:13A AMPC

Someone wrote, "But Rodney, Jesus didn't jump up and down, do cartwheels, and run around the place." Maybe Jesus didn't, but people He touched did. They went around walking and leaping and praising God! Oh, hallelujah!

Another person said: "You don't have to get so emotional." I'm telling you right now, when Jesus touches you, you want to shout it from the rooftops! If you say that you had an encounter with the Living God and are not stirred in your heart all the way through your emotions—then I question whether you had a real touch. Only people who have not had a personal encounter with the power and presence of God tell us that we should not have an emotional response to the reality of the touch of God in and on our lives. God is real, Jesus is real, the Holy Spirit is real, and if I meet them face-to-face—I am going to know about it and so is everybody else!

If you can have an emotional response to something other than the Lord, such as a spouse, a child, a sporting event, a great triumph, or a great tragedy—then it's only logical that your emotions would respond to the love and power of God in your life. Emotions are not all bad. Emotions which come out of your carnal nature, such as bitterness and lust, should be controlled and eliminated by the power of God. Our emotions, like the other areas of our life, should be controlled by our spirit and the Holy Spirit—not by our flesh and our sin. But to express good emotions is normal and healthy.

And my language and my message were not set forth in persuasive (enticing and plausible) words of wisdom, but they were in demonstration of the [Holy] Spirit and power [a proof by the Spirit and power of God, operating on me and stirring in the minds of my hearers the most holy emotions and thus persuading them].

1 CORINTHIANS 2:4 AMPC

According to the Gospel, when Jesus walks in the door, He meets your every need. As the Holy Spirit moves on people in our meetings, many times they are filled with joy. Critics have said: "Well, it doesn't really seem there's any purpose in what's happening in your meetings, because nobody's life depends upon receiving joy."

The problem is that people are always looking for some great significance and reading other things into everything Jesus did. But the desire of Jesus's heart was simply to meet people's needs, whatever they might be; to show us that God has provided for us in every situation.

Jesus walked into the wedding in Cana of Galilee and what did they need there? They had run out of wine. His turning the water into wine was a miracle, to be sure, but it wasn't essential. Nobody's life depended upon the miracle. He was just showing His glory. He was manifesting His power.

> This beginning of miracles did Jesus in Cana of Galilee, and manifested forth his glory; and his disciples believed on him.
>
> JOHN 2:11

You ask, "What is Jesus doing in the meetings you conduct?" Quite simply, He's doing what He's always done. He's just showing forth His glory and meeting the needs—big and small—of the people. Jesus walked into that wedding feast and was pushed into that miracle by His mother. He turned the water into wine to manifest His glory and meet the need.

What does that tell you? It tells you that Jesus wants to bless you. He is interested in the smallest details of your life. He wants to take care of you. He wants to meet your every need, just like He did for the disciples in Mark 4:35-41. Jesus is sleeping in the back of the boat as He and His disciples are taking a cruise across the lake. Alas, a storm arises and the waves roll and the winds howl. The disciples are afraid and they run back and awaken Jesus.

What happened when Jesus showed up? He commanded, *"Peace, be still!"* and the wind obeyed.

I want you to know, He can still calm the storms in your life! It doesn't matter what your storm looks like. It doesn't matter what you're facing. Jesus still calms the storm for you.

You might think, "Well, maybe He's sleeping in the back of the boat. Then why don't you just go lie down at the back of the boat with Him and take a nap too? As long as He's sleeping, you can rest too. He'll calm the storm for you.

Jesus also casts out demons. After calming the storm, Jesus and the disciples came to the country of the Gadarenes where a man with an unclean spirit met Him. The devils possessing the man took one look at Jesus and said: "Uh-oh, we have to go! We can't stay here anymore! Where can we go? Oh, there's a bunch of swine; let's go into those swine." The devils know they can't stay around when Jesus walks in the door.

> And they came over unto the other side of the sea, into the country of the Gadarenes. And when he was come out of the ship, immediately there met him out of the tombs a man with an unclean spirit, Who had his dwelling among the tombs; and no man could bind him, no, not with chains: Because that he had been often bound with fetters and chains, and the chains had been plucked asunder by him, and the fetters broken in pieces: neither could any man tame him. And always, night and day, he was in the mountains, and in the tombs, crying, and cutting himself with stones. But when he saw Jesus afar off, he ran and worshipped him.
>
> MARK 5:1-6

What's more, Jesus forgives sin. In Matthew 9:2-8, He walked up to a man with palsy and said: "Your sins are forgiven you," and he was healed. When Jesus shows up, it's the absolute opposite of when the Pharisees show up. When the Pharisees and the Sadducees and the wouldn't-sees and couldn't-sees show up, they bring rocks! They're ready to stone you to death for your sins. When Jesus shows up, He forgives sin! It's easy for Him to forgive sin and heal the sick because it's His nature and His purpose to forgive.

And, behold, they brought to him a man sick of the palsy, lying on a bed: and Jesus seeing their faith said unto the sick of the palsy; Son, be of good cheer; thy sins be forgiven thee. And, behold, certain of the scribes said within themselves, This man blasphemeth. And Jesus knowing their thoughts said, Wherefore think ye evil in your hearts? For whether is easier, to say, Thy sins be forgiven thee; or to say, Arise, and walk? But that ye may know that the Son of man hath power on earth to forgive sins, (then saith he to the sick of the palsy,) Arise, take up thy bed, and go unto thine house. And he arose, and departed to his house. But when the multitudes saw it, they marvelled, and glorified God, which had given such power unto men.

MATTHEW 9:2-8

Jesus heals sickness. In Mark 5:25-34, a woman had been sick for twelve years with an issue of blood. She had spent all that she had on medical doctors, who were unable to help her. When she heard that Jesus was going to pass by, she said: "If I can just touch the hem of His garment, I'm going to be made whole."

And a certain woman, which had an issue of blood twelve years, And had suffered many things of many physicians, and had spent all that she had, and was nothing bettered, but rather grew worse, When she had heard of Jesus, came in the press behind, and touched his garment. For she said, If I may touch but his clothes, I shall be whole. And straightway the fountain of her blood was dried up; and she felt in her body that she was healed of that plague. And Jesus, immediately knowing in himself that virtue had gone out of him, turned him about in the press, and said, Who touched my clothes? And his disciples said unto him, Thou seest the multitude thronging thee, and sayest thou, Who touched me? And he looked round about to see her that had done this thing. But the woman fearing and trembling, knowing what was done in her, came and fell down before him, and told him all the truth. And he said unto her, Daughter, thy faith hath made thee whole; go in peace, and be whole of thy plague.

MARK 5:25-34

As the woman touched the hem of Jesus's garment, the power of God, the anointing of the Holy Spirit that was on the life and the ministry of Jesus, flowed out of Him into her, and she was made whole. He said to her: *"Go in peace, and be whole of thy plague"* (Mark 5:34).

When Jesus shows up, He'll heal you. It doesn't matter what you're facing. You might have an incurable disease right now, a disease that has been diagnosed as terminal. I want you to know that Jesus still heals today. Hallelujah! He's the same yesterday, today, and forever.

> Jesus Christ the same yesterday, and today, and for ever.
>
> HEBREWS 13:8

Jesus provides for us. In Matthew 14:15-21, Jesus had been followed into a desert place by a multitude of people who didn't have anything to eat. He took a little boy's lunch, blessed it, and multiplied it. Then He fed thousands with five loaves and two fishes. That's what happens when Jesus shows up!

> And when it was evening, his disciples came to him, saying, This is a desert place, and the time is now past; send the multitude away, that they may go into the villages, and buy themselves victuals. But Jesus said unto them, They need not depart; give ye them to eat. And they say unto him, We have here but five loaves, and two fishes. He said, Bring them hither to me. And he commanded the multitude to sit down on the grass, and took the five loaves, and the two fishes, and looking up to heaven, he blessed, and brake, and gave the loaves to his disciples, and the disciples to the multitude. And they did all eat, and were filled: and they took up of the fragments that remained twelve baskets full. And they that had eaten were about five thousand men, beside women and children.
>
> MATTHEW 14:15-21

Jesus shows mercy to sinners. Luke 19:2-9 tells the story of Jesus meeting a sinner. As He walked along a road, He saw a man named Zacchaeus sitting up in a tree. He said: "Come down, Zacchaeus. Let's go to your house." You might feel stuck way up in a tree right now, but I want you to know that Jesus will show up and say, "Come on down; let's go to your house." And believe me, when you experience Jesus's uncon-ditional love and compassion, you will do what Zacchaeus did—drop everything and go with Jesus!

> And, behold, there was a man named Zacchaeus, which was the chief among the publicans, and he was rich. And he sought to see Jesus who he was; and could not for the press, because he was little of stature. And he ran before, and climbed up into a sycomore tree to see him: for he was to pass that way. And when Jesus came to the place, he looked up, and saw him, and said unto him, Zacchaeus, make haste, and come down; for to day I must abide at thy house. And he made haste, and came down, and received him joyfully. And when they saw it, they all murmured, saying, That he was gone to be guest with a man that is a sinner. And Zacchaeus stood, and said unto the Lord: Behold, Lord, the half of my goods I give to the poor; and if I have taken any thing from any man by false accusation, I restore him fourfold. And Jesus said unto him, This day is salvation come to this house, forsomuch as he also is a son of Abraham.
>
> LUKE 19:2-9

Jesus will raise us from the dead. In Mark 5:22-34 and 35-43, Jairus, one of the rulers of the synagogue, fell down in the dusty road at Jesus's feet and said: "My daughter is sick at home." Jesus went with Jairus to his home, but before they got there, they heard that she had died. Jesus told Jairus to continue believing, and because He walked into that house, the young girl was raised from the dead. When Jesus shows up, He brings new life!

> And, behold, there cometh one of the rulers of the synagogue, Jairus by name; and when he saw him, he fell at his feet, And besought him greatly, saying, My little daughter lieth at the point of death: I pray thee, come and lay thy hands on her, that she may be healed; and she shall live. And Jesus went with him; and much people followed him, and thronged him.
>
> MARK 5:22-24

While he yet spake, there came from the ruler of the synagogue's house certain which said, Thy daughter is dead: why troublest thou the Master any further? As soon as Jesus heard the word that was spoken, he saith unto the ruler of the synagogue, Be not afraid, only believe. And he suffered no man to follow him, save Peter, and James, and John the brother of James. And he cometh to the house of the ruler of the synagogue, and seeth the tumult, and them that wept and wailed greatly. And when he was come in, he saith unto them, Why make ye this ado, and weep? the damsel is not dead, but sleepeth. And they laughed him to scorn. But when he had put them all out, he taketh the father and the mother of the damsel, and them that were with him, and entereth in where the damsel was lying. And he took the damsel by the hand, and said unto her, Talitha cumi; which is, being interpreted, Damsel, I say unto thee, arise. And straightway the damsel arose, and walked; for she was of the age of twelve years. And they were astonished with a great astonishment. And he charged them straitly that no man should know it; and commanded that something should be given her to eat.

MARK 5:35-43

Jesus found a funeral procession outside the city of Nain. He called the boy right up out of the coffin and gave him back to his mother. When Jesus shows up, He'll raise the dead!

He came to the tomb where His dear friend Lazarus had been dead for four days. Lazarus' sisters were grieving. "Master," they said: "if You'd come earlier, this would not have happened. He's dead now and stinketh." But what happened when Jesus showed up? He said: "Roll away the stone." And then He said: "Lazarus, come forth!" And he did!

And it came to pass the day after, that he went into a city called Nain; and many of his disciples went with him, and much people. Now when he came nigh to the gate of the city, behold, there was a dead man carried out, the only son of his mother, and she was a widow: and much people of the city was with her. And when the Lord saw

her, he had compassion on her, and said unto her, Weep not. And he
came and touched the bier: and they that bare him stood still. And
he said, Young man, I say unto thee, Arise. And he that was dead sat
up, and began to speak. And he delivered him to his mother.

LUKE 7:11-15

You might be right in the middle of a situation where you have no
hope. The things that you've been believing and trusting God for look
dead. They look like they're buried in the tomb, stinking. But I want
you to know that the same Jesus who walked the shores of Galilee two
thousand years ago comes to you and says: "Roll away the stone and come
forth!" Hallelujah! He brings life!

It doesn't matter what your circumstances are. When Jesus comes on
the scene, impossible situations can be turned around. It doesn't matter
what the devil says. It doesn't matter what other people say. When Jesus
walks in the door, everything changes. When Jesus walks in the door,
there's no more argument. There's no more question, for *He is the Answer.*
How can there be a question remaining when He is the Answer?

When Jesus walks in the door, there's no more loss of direction. How
can there be a loss of direction when He *is the Way?* When He walks in
the door, there are no more lies. How can there be lies when He *is the
Truth?* When He walks in the door, there's no more death. How can there
be death when He *is the Life?*

Jesus saith unto him, I am the way, the truth, and the life: no man
cometh unto the Father, but by me.

JOHN 14:6

What happens when you've been in your boat all night fishing, but
have caught nothing? You've fished and you've fished—and you know
how to fish because you're a fisherman by trade—but you've caught
absolutely nothing. Then Jesus shows up and gives you clear direction:
"Cast your nets on the other side."

After these things Jesus shewed himself again to the disciples at the sea
of Tiberias; and on this wise shewed he himself. There were together

Simon Peter, and Thomas called Didymus, and Nathanael of Cana in Galilee, and the sons of Zebedee, and two other of his disciples. Simon Peter saith unto them, I go a fishing. They say unto him, We also go with thee. They went forth, and entered into a ship immediately; and that night they caught nothing. But when the morning was now come, Jesus stood on the shore: but the disciples knew not that it was Jesus. Then Jesus saith unto them, Children, have ye any meat? They answered him, No. And he said unto them, Cast the net on the right side of the ship, and ye shall find. They cast therefore, and now they were not able to draw it for the multitude of fishes.

JOHN 21:1-6

You might be a minister of the Gospel and you've been fishing for souls all your life. You've been fishing for years in Podunk Hollow but you've caught no fish. Jesus comes to you now and says: "Cast your nets on the other side." Watch in wonder as hundreds of fish jump into your net!

Your first thought might be to say, "Rodney, you can't be serious. Surely Jesus won't meet every need—not *every single* need. Some He'll meet, yes, but surely not every need."

Yes! He'll meet every need, every one! Some people think His power is only for life and death situations. But that's not true. In fact, Jesus used His power not only to touch people in every area of their lives, but to meet the needs of His own ministry as well. When the disciples needed tax money, for instance, Jesus said to Peter: "Go down and catch the first fish. The money you need is in his mouth."

And when they were come to Capernaum, they that received tribute money came to Peter, and said, Doth not your master pay tribute? He saith, Yes. And when he was come into the house, Jesus prevented him, saying, What thinkest thou, Simon? of whom do the kings of the earth take custom or tribute? of their own children, or of strangers? Peter saith unto him, Of strangers. Jesus saith unto him, Then are the children free. Notwithstanding, lest we should offend them, go thou to the sea, and cast an hook, and take up the fish that first cometh up; and when thou hast opened his mouth, thou shalt find a piece of money: that take, and give unto them for me and thee.

MATTHEW 17:24-27

When you have a need, no matter how simple or how complicated it is, when Jesus shows up, He's going to meet that need. That is the Gospel! *It's Good News!*

Jesus is also our Miracle Worker. Think about this for a moment: Jesus walked on water. Nobody benefited from that miracle except Him. So why, then, did He walk on water? He walked on water because He needed to get to the other side! He sent the disciples on across the lake because when you're in ministry, you need to get away from people and pray sometimes. Then he walked on the water to catch up with them. When Jesus walked on water, it did not seem like a necessity, but a luxury. He could have waited for another boat!

If the Pharisees had gotten hold of Jesus, they would have said: "You're abusing God's power! How dare You walk on water for Your own benefit? Who do You think You are? From now on, please refrain from walking on water and always take a boat like everyone else. Look at You, taking God's power and using it for Yourself."

I believe that Jesus walked on water to show us that He had control over the elements as a sign and a wonder. But I also believe that He did it to show us that if we are obeying and serving God, we can trust Him to make a way for us where there is no way. Most of the time we have no faith for the supernatural, but God wants us to know that His supernatural power is there for us when we need it.

And Jesus looking upon them saith, with men it is impossible, but not with God: for with God all things are possible.

MARK 10:27

We could go on and on telling what happens when Jesus shows up. He showed up at the Pool of Bethesda, around which lay a great multitude of blind, crippled, maimed, and withered people. What happened when Jesus showed up? He found a man who had been there for a long time because he didn't have anybody to help him get into the pool. Jesus tells you the same thing He told that man, *"Rise, take up thy bed, and walk."*

> Jesus saith unto him, Rise, take up thy bed, and walk.
>
> JOHN 5:8

Do you realize that all we need in our churches, all we need in America, is for Jesus to show up? When He walks in the door, He is going to make a difference.

The problem is that some people are waiting for Prophet Doodad to show up; they're waiting for Evangelist Dingaling or Apostle Bucketmouth to come along. "Oh, if only he would come to our town, if only he would come and hold a crusade, it would be so wonderful." But you don't need any man; you need Jesus Christ, the Son of the Living God.

You say: "Rodney; I would love for Jesus to show up in my house. I would love for Jesus to show up in my church. I would love for Jesus to show up in my town."

Well, the truth is that if you are born-again, Jesus will show up when you show up, because He's in you! He is in you and *"greater is he that is in you, than he that is in the world!"*

> Ye are of God, little children, and have overcome them: because greater is he that is in you, than he that is in the world.
>
> 1 JOHN 4:4

Jesus also gives you power. He said to His disciples: *"Behold, I give unto you power to tread on serpents and scorpions, and over all the power of the enemy"* (Luke 10:19). When Jesus shows up, He gives you power and authority, the same power and authority that He walked in on the earth.

You're waiting for Jesus to show up and He's waiting for you to show up. He already did show up. Jesus has done everything He can do to bring you everything you need. He is waiting for you to believe it, to receive it for your life, and to see it manifested. Jesus is here right now, visiting your house! Just receive your need as being met as it would have been if Jesus had come to your house during His earthly ministry. You have a better covenant. The new covenant is better than the old. The only thing standing in your way is doubt and unbelief.

> Jesus replied, Have I been with all of you for so long a time, and do you not recognize and know Me yet, Philip? Anyone who has seen Me has seen the Father: How can you say then, Show us the Father? Do you not believe that I am in the Father, and that the Father is in Me? What I am telling you I do not say on My own authority and of My own accord; but the Father Who lives continually in Me does the (His) works (His own miracles, deeds of power). Believe Me that I am in the Father and the Father in Me; or else believe Me for the sake of the [very] works themselves.

> [If you cannot trust Me, at least let these works that I do in My Father's name convince you.] I assure you, most solemnly I tell you, if anyone steadfastly believes in Me, he will himself be able to do the things that I do; and he will do even greater things than these, because I go to the Father.

> JOHN 14:9-12 AMPC

If Jesus lives in us, we can do the same things that He did. He even said that we would do greater works. All we have to do is to take Him at His Word and believe it. When we show up, Jesus shows up! And when Jesus shows up, all of Heaven's power is on the scene to save, heal, deliver, and set free!

CHAPTER 4

JESUS AND HIS METHODS

ONE OF THE THINGS that really intrigued me about the ministry of Jesus was the methods He used to reach people. Whatever method He used, He was always led by the Holy Spirit. In the Gospels, we see that Jesus was anointed by the Holy Spirit to minister to people. Everything He did was by the prompting and the leading of the Holy Spirit.

> And Jesus, when he was baptized, went up straightway out of the water: and, lo, the heavens were opened unto him, and he saw the Spirit of God descending like a dove, and lighting upon him.
>
> MATTHEW 3:16

> How God anointed Jesus of Nazareth with the Holy Ghost and with power: who went about doing good, and healing all that were oppressed of the devil; for God was with him.
>
> ACTS 10:38

God anointed Jesus with the Holy Ghost to do everything He did. To study Jesus's methods and the anointing He operated under, I want us to look at the ministry of Jesus through the eyes of a religious person or a skeptic—someone who does not believe. This might sound strange, but let's pretend that we don't know Him at all. We don't know who He really is. We're hearing about Him for the first time. Would His methods be acceptable in our day and time?

I am positive that if Jesus were here today in the flesh, He would be kicked out of most churches and would not be invited to speak at most conferences because of His methods. If His methods were put under scrutiny, many would not receive Him today, just as they did not receive Him yesterday.

Let's look at some of the methods Jesus used that would cause a problem today.

1. He was constantly with sinners and was accused of being a gluttonous man and a winebibber (a drunk). *"The Son of man came eating and drinking, and they say, Behold a man gluttonous, and a winebibber, a friend of publicans and sinners. But wisdom is justified of her children."* MATTHEW 11:19

2. He healed on the Sabbath day. *"And the ruler of the synagogue answered with indignation, because that Jesus had healed on the sabbath day, and said unto the people, There are six days in which men ought to work: in them therefore come and be healed, and not on the sabbath day. The Lord then answered him, and said, Thou hypocrite, doth not each one of you on the sabbath loose his ox or his ass from the stall, and lead him away to watering? And ought not this woman, being a daughter of Abraham, whom Satan hath bound, lo, these eighteen years, be loosed from this bond on the sabbath day? And when he had said these things, all his adversaries were ashamed: and all the people rejoiced for all the glorious things that were done by him."* LUKE 13:14-17

3. His disciples did not wash their hands when they ate, which was against Jewish law. *"Why do thy disciples transgress the tradition of the elders? for they wash not their hands when they eat bread."* MATTHEW 15:2

4. His disciples did not keep the traditions of the elders. *"Then the Pharisees and scribes asked him, Why walk not thy disciples according to the tradition of the elders, but eat bread with unwashen hands?"* MARK 7:5

5. He and His disciples harvested food to eat on the Sabbath. *"At that time Jesus went on the sabbath day through the corn; and his disciples were an hungred, and began to pluck the ears of corn and to eat."* MATTHEW 12:1

6. He walked on water when He could have taken a boat. *"And in the fourth watch of the night Jesus went unto them, walking on the sea. And when the disciples saw him walking on the sea, they were troubled, saying, It is a spirit; and they cried out for fear. But straightway Jesus spake unto them, saying, Be of good cheer; it is I; be not afraid. And Peter answered him and said, Lord, if it be thou, bid me come unto thee on the water. And he said, Come. And when Peter was come down out of the ship, he walked on the water, to go to Jesus. But when he saw the wind boisterous, he was afraid; and beginning to sink, he cried, saying, Lord, save me. And immediately Jesus stretched forth his hand, and caught him, and said unto him, O thou of little faith, wherefore didst thou doubt? And when they were come into the ship, the wind ceased."* MATTHEW 14:25-32

7. He went over to the country of the Gadarenes and cast demons out of a man, which resulted in a whole herd of swine running down a hill into the sea and drowning. The local people, who made their living by raising pigs, then begged Him to leave their country. *"And they came over unto the other side of the sea, into the country of the Gadarenes. And when he was come out of the ship, immediately there met him out of the tombs a man with an unclean spirit. Who had his dwelling among the tombs; and no man could bind him, no, not with chains: Because that he had been often bound with fetters and chains, and the chains had been*

plucked asunder by him, and the fetters broken in pieces: neither could any man tame him. And always, night and day, he was in the mountains, and in the tombs, crying, and cutting himself with stones. But when he saw Jesus afar off, he ran and worshipped him, And cried with a loud voice, and said, What have I to do with thee, Jesus, thou Son of the most high God? I adjure thee by God, that thou torment me not. For he said unto him, Come out of the man, thou unclean spirit. And he asked him, What is thy name? And he answered, saying, My name is Legion: for we are many. And he besought him much that he would not send them away out of the country. Now there was there nigh unto the mountains a great herd of swine feeding. And all the devils besought him, saying, Send us into the swine, that we may enter into them. And forthwith Jesus gave them leave. And the unclean spirits went out, and entered into the swine: and the herd ran violently down a steep place into the sea, (they were about two thousand;) and were choked in the sea. And they that fed the swine fled, and told it in the city, and in the country. And they went out to see what it was that was done. And they come to Jesus, and see him that was possessed with the devil, and had the legion, sitting, and clothed, and in his right mind: and they were afraid. And they that saw it told them how it befell to him that was possessed with the devil, and also concerning the swine. And they began to pray him to depart out of their coasts. And when he was come into the ship, he that had been possessed with the devil prayed him that he might be with him. Howbeit Jesus suffered him not, but saith unto him, Go home to thy friends, and tell them how great things the Lord hath done for thee, and hath had compassion on thee. And he departed, and began to publish in Decapolis how great things Jesus had done for him: and all men did marvel." MARK 5:1-20

8. When they needed tax money, He told His closest followers to go fishing and get the money out of the fish's mouth. *"And when they were come to Capernaum, they that received tribute money*

came to Peter, and said, Doth not your master pay tribute? He saith, Yes. And when he was come into the house, Jesus prevented him, saying, What thinkest thou, Simon? of whom do the kings of the earth take custom or tribute? of their own children, or of strangers? Peter saith unto him, Of strangers. Jesus saith unto him, Then are the children free. Notwithstanding, lest we should offend them, go thou to the sea, and cast an hook, and take up the fish that first cometh up; and when thou hast opened his mouth, thou shalt find a piece of money: that take, and give unto them for me and thee."
MATTHEW 17:24-27

9. He stopped a funeral procession and raised a boy from the dead. *"Now when he came nigh to the gate of the city, behold, there was a dead man carried out, the only son of his mother, and she was a widow: and much people of the city was with her. And when the Lord saw her, he had compassion on her, and said unto her, Weep not. And he came and touched the bier: and they that bare him stood still. And he said, Young man, I say unto thee, Arise. And he that was dead sat up, and began to speak. And he delivered him to his mother."* LUKE 7:12-15

10. He spat on the ground and made clay, put it on a blind man's eyes, and told him to go wash in the pool of Siloam. *"And as Jesus passed by, he saw a man which was blind from his birth. And his disciples asked him, saying, Master, who did sin, this man, or his parents, that he was born blind? Jesus answered, Neither hath this man sinned, nor his parents: but that the works of God should be made manifest in him. I must work the works of him that sent me, while it is day: the night cometh, when no man can work. As long as I am in the world, I am the light of the world. When he had thus spoken, he spat on the ground, and made clay of the spittle, and he anointed the eyes of the blind man with the clay, And said unto him, Go, wash in the pool of Siloam, (which is by interpretation, Sent.) He went his way therefore, and washed, and came seeing."* JOHN 9:1-7

11. He called a Syrophenician woman a dog. And as Jesus passed
by, he saw a man which was blind from his birth. *"For a certain woman, whose young daughter had an unclean spirit, heard
of him, and came and fell at his feet: The woman was a Greek, a
Syrophenician by nation; and she besought him that he would cast
forth the devil out of her daughter. But Jesus said unto her, Let the
children first be filled: for it is not meet to take the children's bread,
and to cast it unto the dogs. And she answered and said unto him, Yes,
Lord: yet the dogs under the table eat of the children's crumbs. And
he said unto her, For this saying go thy way; the devil is gone out of
thy daughter. And when she was come to her house, she found the
devil gone out, and her daughter laid upon the bed."* MARK 7:25-30

12. He got angry and cursed a fig tree. *"And on the morrow, when they
were come from Bethany, he was hungry: And seeing a fig tree afar
off having leaves, he came, if haply he might find any thing thereon:
and when he came to it, he found nothing but leaves; for the time
of figs was not yet. And Jesus answered and said unto it, No man
eat fruit of thee hereafter for ever. And his disciples heard it. And in
the morning, as they passed by, they saw the fig tree dried up from
the roots. And Peter calling to remembrance saith unto him, Master,
behold, the fig tree which thou cursedst is withered away."* MARK
11:12-14, 20-21

13. He got angry in the temple, overturned the moneychangers'
tables, and beat the moneychangers with whips. *"And Jesus went
into the temple of God, and cast out all them that sold and bought in
the temple, and overthrew the tables of the moneychangers, and the
seats of them that sold doves, And said unto them, It is written, My
house shall be called the house of prayer; but ye have made it a den
of thieves."* MATTHEW 21:12-13

14. At one of His meetings, His followers got out of order and
ripped the roof off a house to lower a crippled man down

through the hole—and He didn't mind! *"And straightway many were gathered together, insomuch that there was no room to receive them, no, not so much as about the door: and he preached the word unto them. And they come unto him, bringing one sick of the palsy, which was borne of four. And when they could not come nigh unto him for the press, they uncovered the roof where he was: and when they had broken it up, they let down the bed wherein the sick of the palsy lay. When Jesus saw their faith, he said unto the sick of the palsy, Son, thy sins be forgiven thee."* MARK 2:2-5

15. He made strong statements like: "Unless you eat of My flesh and drink of My blood you have no life in you." *"Then Jesus said unto them, Verily, verily, I say unto you, Except ye eat the flesh of the Son of man, and drink his blood, ye have no life in you."* JOHN 6:53

16. He told a man who wanted to follow Him—when he wanted to go home and bury his father—"Let the dead bury the dead." *"And another of his disciples said unto him, Lord, suffer me first to go and bury my father. But Jesus said unto him, Follow me; and let the dead bury their dead."* MATTHEW 8:21-22

17. He stood by the offering, watched it being taken up, and called His disciples to come and observe. *"And Jesus sat over against the treasury, and beheld how the people cast money into the treasury: and many that were rich cast in much. And there came a certain poor widow, and she threw in two mites, which make a farthing. And he called unto him his disciples, and saith unto them, Verily I say unto you, That this poor widow hath cast more in, than all they which have cast into the treasury: For all they did cast in of their abundance; but she of her want did cast in all that she had, even all her living."* MARK 12:41-44

18. He allowed people to go walking and leaping and praising God in His services. *"And when he was come nigh, even now at the descent of the mount of Olives, the whole multitude of the disciples*

began to rejoice and praise God with a loud voice for all the mighty works that they had seen; Saying, Blessed be the King that cometh in the name of the Lord: peace in heaven, and glory in the highest. And some of the Pharisees from among the multitude said unto him, Master, rebuke thy disciples. And he answered and said unto them, I tell you that, if these should hold their peace, the stones would immediately cry out." LUKE 19:37-40

19. He allowed a woman to pour expensive perfume on His head when the money could have been given to the poor. *"There came unto him a woman having an alabaster box of very precious ointment, and poured it on his head, as he sat at meat. But when his disciples saw it, they had indignation, saying, To what purpose is this waste? For this ointment might have been sold for much, and given to the poor. When Jesus understood it, he said unto them, Why trouble ye the woman? for she hath wrought a good work upon me. For ye have the poor always with you; but me ye have not always. For in that she hath poured this ointment on my body, she did it for my burial. Verily I say unto you, Wheresoever this Gospel shall be preached in the whole world, there shall also this, that this woman hath done, be told for a memorial of her."* MATTHEW 26:7-13

20. He didn't show up to attend the funeral of Lazarus, a dear friend, and waited four days before raising him from the dead. *"Now a certain man was sick, named Lazarus, of Bethany, the town of Mary and her sister Martha. (It was that Mary which anointed the Lord with ointment, and wiped his feet with her hair, whose brother Lazarus was sick.) Therefore his sisters sent unto him, saying, Lord, behold, he whom thou lovest is sick. When Jesus heard that, he said, This sickness is not unto death, but for the glory of God, that the Son of God might be glorified thereby. Now Jesus loved Martha, and her sister, and Lazarus. When he had heard therefore that he was sick, he abode two days still in the same place where he was. Then after that saith he to his disciples, Let us go into Judaea again. His disciples say*

unto him, Master, the Jews of late sought to stone thee; and goest thou thither again? Jesus answered, Are there not twelve hours in the day? If any man walk in the day, he stumbleth not, because he seeth the light of this world. But if a man walk in the night, he stumbleth, because there is no light in him. These things said he: and after that he saith unto them, Our friend Lazarus sleepeth; but I go, that I may awake him out of sleep. Then said his disciples, Lord, if he sleep, he shall do well. Howbeit Jesus spake of his death: but they thought that he had spoken of taking of rest in sleep. Then said Jesus unto them plainly, Lazarus is dead. And I am glad for your sakes that I was not there, to the intent ye may believe; nevertheless let us go unto him. Then said Thomas, which is called Didymus, unto his fellow disciples, Let us also go, that we may die with him. Then when Jesus came, he found that he had lain in the grave four days already. Now Bethany was nigh unto Jerusalem, about fifteen furlongs off: And many of the Jews came to Martha and Mary, to comfort them concerning their brother. Then Martha, as soon as she heard that Jesus was coming, went and met him: but Mary sat still in the house. Then said Martha unto Jesus, Lord, if thou hadst been here, my brother had not died. But I know, that even now, whatsoever thou wilt ask of God, God will give it thee. Jesus saith unto her, Thy brother shall rise again. Martha saith unto him, I know that he shall rise again in the resurrection at the last day. Jesus said unto her, I am the resurrection, and the life: he that believeth in me, though he were dead, yet shall he live: And whosoever liveth and believeth in me shall never die. Believest thou this? She saith unto him, Yea, Lord: I believe that thou art the Christ, the Son of God, which should come into the world. And when she had so said, she went her way, and called Mary her sister secretly, saying, The Master is come, and calleth for thee. As soon as she heard that, she arose quickly, and came unto him. Now Jesus was not yet come into the town, but was in that place where Martha met him. The Jews then which were with her in the house, and comforted her, when they saw Mary, that she rose up hastily and went out, followed her, saying,

She goeth unto the grave to weep there. Then when Mary was come where Jesus was, and saw him, she fell down at his feet, saying unto him, Lord, if thou hadst been here, my brother had not died. When Jesus therefore saw her weeping, and the Jews also weeping which came with her, he groaned in the spirit, and was troubled. And said, Where have ye laid him? They said unto him, Lord, come and see. Jesus wept. Then said the Jews, Behold how he loved him! And some of them said, Could not this man, which opened the eyes of the blind, have caused that even this man should not have died? Jesus therefore again groaning in himself cometh to the grave. It was a cave, and a stone lay upon it. Jesus said, Take ye away the stone. Martha, the sister of him that was dead, saith unto him, Lord, by this time he stinketh: for he hath been dead four days. Jesus saith unto her, Said I not unto thee, that, if thou wouldest believe, thou shouldest see the glory of God? Then they took away the stone from the place where the dead was laid. And Jesus lifted up his eyes, and said, Father, I thank thee that thou hast heard me. And I knew that thou hearest me always: but because of the people which stand by I said it, that they may believe that thou hast sent me. And when he thus had spoken, he cried with a loud voice, Lazarus, come forth. And he that was dead came forth, bound hand and foot with graveclothes: and his face was bound about with a napkin. Jesus saith unto them, Loose him, and let him go. Then many of the Jews which came to Mary, and had seen the things which Jesus did, believed on him. " JOHN 11:1-45

21. He called respected religious leaders the "blind leading the blind," and "white-washed sepulchres of dead men's bones." He called them a "generation of vipers" and said that they were of "their father the devil." *"Then came his disciples, and said unto him, Knowest thou that the Pharisees were offended, after they heard this saying? But he answered and said, Every plant, which my heavenly Father hath not planted, shall be rooted up. Let them alone: they be blind leaders of the blind. And if the blind lead the blind, both shall fall into the ditch."* MATTHEW 15:12-14

"Woe unto you, scribes and Pharisees, hypocrites! for ye are like unto whited sepulchres, which indeed appear beautiful outward, but are within full of dead men's bones, and of all uncleanness." MATTHEW 23:27

"Ye serpents, ye generation of vipers, how can ye escape the damnation of hell?" MATTHEW 23:33

"Ye are of your father the devil, and the lusts of your father ye will do. He was a murderer from the beginning, and abode not in the truth, because there is no truth in him. When he speaketh a lie, he speaketh of his own: for he is a liar, and the father of it." JOHN 8:44

22. He caused unclean spirits to cry out with loud voices in the synagogue. *"And in the synagogue there was a man, which had a spirit of an unclean devil, and cried out with a loud voice, Saying, Let us alone; what have we to do with thee, thou Jesus of Nazareth? art thou come to destroy us? I know thee who thou art; the Holy One of God."* LUKE 4:33-34

23. He let a woman who was caught in adultery go when she should have been stoned. *"Jesus went unto the mount of Olives. And early in the morning he came again into the temple, and all the people came unto him; and he sat down, and taught them. And the scribes and Pharisees brought unto him a woman taken in adultery; and when they had set her in the midst, They say unto him, Master, this woman was taken in adultery, in the very act. Now Moses in the law commanded us, that such should be stoned: but what sayest thou? This they said, tempting him, that they might have to accuse him. But Jesus stooped down, and with his finger wrote on the ground, as though he heard them not. So when they continued asking him, he lifted up himself, and said unto them, He that is without sin among you, let him first cast a stone at her. And again he stooped down, and wrote on the ground. And they which heard it, being convicted by their own conscience, went out one by one, beginning at the eldest, even unto the*

last: and Jesus was left alone, and the woman standing in the midst. When Jesus had lifted up himself, and saw none but the woman, he said unto her, Woman, where are those thine accusers? hath no man condemned thee? She said, No man, Lord. And Jesus said unto her, Neither do I condemn thee: go, and sin no more." JOHN 8:1-11

24. He offended a rich young ruler by telling him to sell all he had and give it to the poor. *"And a certain ruler asked him, saying, Good Master, what shall I do to inherit eternal life? And Jesus said unto him, Why callest thou me good? none is good, save one, that is, God. Thou knowest the commandments, Do not commit adultery, Do not kill, Do not steal, Do not bear false witness, Honour thy father and thy mother. And he said, All these have I kept from my youth up. Now when Jesus heard these things, he said unto him, Yet lackest thou one thing: sell all that thou hast, and distribute unto the poor, and thou shalt have treasure in heaven: and come, follow me. And when he heard this, he was very sorrowful: for he was very rich."* LUKE 18:18-23

25. He forgave a man of his sin and healed him—then said that both were easy. *"And, behold, they brought to him a man sick of the palsy, lying on a bed: and Jesus seeing their faith said unto the sick of the palsy; Son, be of good cheer; thy sins be forgiven thee. And, behold, certain of the scribes said within themselves, This man blasphemeth. And Jesus knowing their thoughts said, Wherefore think ye evil in your hearts? For whether is easier, to say, Thy sins be forgiven thee; or to say, Arise, and walk? But that ye may know that the Son of man hath power on earth to forgive sins, (then saith he to the sick of the palsy,) Arise, take up thy bed, and go unto thine house."* MATTHEW 9:2-6

26. He accepted people just as they were. *"And, behold, there was a man named Zacchaeus, which was the chief among the publicans, and he was rich. And he sought to see Jesus who he was; and could not for the press, because he was little of stature. And he ran before,*

and climbed up into a sycomore tree to see him: for he was to pass that way. And when Jesus came to the place, he looked up, and saw him, and said unto him, Zacchaeus, make haste, and come down; for to day I must abide at thy house. And he made haste, and came down, and received him joyfully. And when they saw it, they all murmured, saying, That he was gone to be guest with a man that is a sinner. And Zacchaeus stood, and said unto the Lord: Behold, Lord, the half of my goods I give to the poor; and if I have taken any thing from any man by false accusation, I restore him fourfold. And Jesus said unto him, This day is salvation come to this house, forsomuch as he also is a son of Abraham. For the Son of man is come to seek and to save that which was lost." LUKE 19:2-10

"Jesus went unto the mount of Olives. And early in the morning he came again into the temple, and all the people came unto him; and he sat down, and taught them. And the scribes and Pharisees brought unto him a woman taken in adultery; and when they had set her in the midst, They say unto him, Master, this woman was taken in adultery, in the very act. Now Moses in the law commanded us, that such should be stoned: but what sayest thou? This they said, tempting him, that they might have to accuse him. But Jesus stooped down, and with his finger wrote on the ground, as though he heard them not. So when they continued asking him, he lifted up himself, and said unto them, He that is without sin among you, let him first cast a stone at her. And again he stooped down, and wrote on the ground. And they which heard it, being convicted by their own conscience, went out one by one, beginning at the eldest, even unto the last: and Jesus was left alone, and the woman standing in the midst. When Jesus had lifted up himself, and saw none but the woman, he said unto her, Woman, where are those thine accusers? hath no man condemned thee? She said, No man, Lord. And Jesus said unto her, Neither do I condemn thee: go, and sin no more." JOHN 8:1-11

"There cometh a woman of Samaria to draw water: Jesus saith unto her, Give me to drink. (For his disciples were gone away unto the city to buy meat.) Then saith the woman of Samaria unto him, How is it that thou, being a Jew, askest drink of me, which am a woman of Samaria? for the Jews have no dealings with the Samaritans. Jesus answered and said unto her, If thou knewest the gift of God, and who it is that saith to thee, Give me to drink; thou wouldest have asked of him, and he would have given thee living water. The woman saith unto him, Sir, thou hast nothing to draw with, and the well is deep: from whence then hast thou that living water? Art thou greater than our father Jacob, which gave us the well, and drank thereof himself, and his children, and his cattle? Jesus answered and said unto her, Whosoever drinketh of this water shall thirst again: But whosoever drinketh of the water that I shall give him shall never thirst; but the water that I shall give him shall be in him a well of water springing up into everlasting life. The woman saith unto him, Sir, give me this water, that I thirst not, neither come hither to draw. Jesus saith unto her, Go, call thy husband, and come hither. The woman answered and said, I have no husband. Jesus said unto her, Thou hast well said, I have no husband: For thou hast had five husbands; and he whom thou now hast is not thy husband: in that saidst thou truly. The woman saith unto him, Sir, I perceive that thou art a prophet. Our fathers worshipped in this mountain; and ye say, that in Jerusalem is the place where men ought to worship. Jesus saith unto her, Woman, believe me, the hour cometh, when ye shall neither in this mountain, nor yet at Jerusalem, worship the Father. Ye worship ye know not what: we know what we worship: for salvation is of the Jews. But the hour cometh, and now is, when the true worshippers shall worship the Father in spirit and in truth: for the Father seeketh such to worship him. God is a Spirit: and they that worship him must worship him in spirit and in truth. The woman saith unto him, I know that Messias cometh, which is called Christ: when he is come, he will tell us all things. Jesus saith unto

her, I that speak unto thee am he. And upon this came his disciples, and marvelled that he talked with the woman: yet no man said, What seekest thou? or, Why talkest thou with her? The woman then left her waterpot, and went her way into the city, and saith to the men, Come, see a man, which told me all things that ever I did: is not this the Christ? Then they went out of the city, and came unto him." JOHN 4:7-30

27. He breathed on His disciples and said: "Receive ye the Holy Ghost." *"And when he had said this, he breathed on them, and saith unto them, Receive ye the Holy Ghost."* JOHN 20:22

28. He spat on His hands, touched a deaf boy's tongue and ears, and healed him. *"And they bring unto him one that was deaf, and had an impediment in his speech; and they beseech him to put his hand upon him. And he took him aside from the multitude, and put his fingers into his ears, and he spit, and touched his tongue; And looking up to heaven, he sighed, and saith unto him, Ephphatha, that is, Be opened. And straightway his ears were opened, and the string of his tongue was loosed, and he spake plain."* MARK 7:32-35

29. He wasn't "polite" enough to His mother when He said: "Woman, what have I to do with thee?" *"Jesus saith unto her, Woman, what have I to do with thee? mine hour is not yet come."* JOHN 2:4

These methods would get Him kicked out of most churches today; He would not be accepted in the religious world.

Jesus was radical.

CHAPTER 5

WHAT DID JESUS DO?

HAVE YOU SEEN THE W.W.J.D. WRISTBANDS that everybody's wearing? What Would Jesus Do? It's a craze that's gone across America. There are probably millions of people wearing those wristbands. W.W.J.D? is a question that many people ask today. We could sit and speculate for hours over what Jesus would do. But I want to come from the angle of what Jesus *did* do. W.D.J.D.—What Did Jesus Do?

At the end of the book of John, the Bible says: *"Jesus did many other things as well. If every one of them were written down, I suppose that even the whole world would not have room for the books that would be written"* (John 21:25 NIV). What did He do? He did a bunch of things, and they all had to do with God's relationship with mankind, because He loves mankind so much.

If you look at religion and you look at Jesus, you get two totally different pictures. Religion is rigid, argumentative, and judgmental. But Jesus is loving and forgiving. He always comes with compassion, with arms wide open, and He never holds anything against anybody.

Because of His compassion for people, Jesus had to destroy the works of the devil. In 1 John 3:8, it says: *"For this purpose was the Son of God manifested, that he might destroy the works of the devil."* Jesus hates the devil and the devil hates Him. Two thousand years ago on the cross of Calvary, Jesus totally destroyed the works of the devil. There He paid the price for our sin, for our sickness, for our disease, for our mental turmoil, for our anguish, poverty, and lack.

It is evident from looking at the Gospels of Matthew, Mark, Luke, and John that Jesus's whole ministry was directly opposed to the devil and to his works. Most importantly, He stripped the devil of any authority that he had over man by paying the price for the sin of man. When Adam fell from grace in the Garden of Eden and exiled himself and all mankind from the presence of God, it was only Jesus who could come and pay the price to bring man back into the presence of God.

Can you imagine what it was like for Adam to be in the presence of God—to not know a day of sin in his life, to know God's provision, to know God's plan, and to know His joy and His peace—and then suddenly, because of his own disobedience, he is cut off? Suddenly He's on the outside looking in, cast away from the presence of God.

Thank God Jesus reversed what Adam did. My Bible tells me: *"For God so loved the world, that he gave his only begotten Son, that whosoever believeth in him should not perish"* (John 3:16). And that's the Good News. Jesus came to buy us back so that we can come back into the presence of God. Jesus says:

> Come unto me, all ye that labour and are heavy laden, and I will give you rest. Take my yoke upon you, and learn of me.... for my yoke is easy, and my burden is light.
>
> MATTHEW 11:28-30

The yoke of religious tradition is hard and its burden is heavy. If you are finding that serving God is hard, you need to jettison religion and discover Jesus afresh. Jesus's message today is, "I love you. I forgive you. Come to Me. You're tired, you're bruised, you're battered, you're weary, you're torn. Come unto Me and I'll give you rest. I'll give you what you need."

People are always looking for the latest fix, the latest joy, the latest thrill. They try to escape from reality through movies, computer games, virtual reality, drugs, sex, or alcohol, but they are wasting their time. The only true joy, the only true satisfaction, comes from Jesus and knowing Him as your personal Lord and Savior.

When Jesus comes into your life, He changes you, He sets you free, and He breaks the yoke of sin and bondage off you. God never made you to be a slave to sin. God made you to be lord and master of the sin. The Bible says that when you're bought with a price, when you're washed in the blood of Jesus, when you become a new creation in Christ Jesus, sin shall no longer have dominion over you.

> For sin shall not have dominion over you: for ye are not under the law, but under grace.
>
> ROMANS 6:14

How wonderful it is to be a new creature. Aren't you glad that you're a new creature today? Oh, Hallelujah! The Bible says old things are passed away. Behold, all things are become new.

> Therefore if any man be in Christ, he is a new creature: old things are passed away; behold, all things are become new.
>
> 2 CORINTHIANS 5:17

If you have given your life to Jesus, if you have been born-again and washed in the blood of Jesus, you should not spend any time talking about the past. Don't allow people to say, "Hey, do you remember what we did ten years ago? You know how bad...."

Just look at them with a puzzled look on your face and say, "What are you talking about? That person's dead. Yeah, I used to do those things, but then Jesus came. He touched me. My life will never be the same again. Who are you talking about?"

"Well, you remember we robbed the bank. Remember, we used to deal drugs. Remember, we used to do this and that."

"Sorry, I don't know who you're talking about. That person's dead. That person's gone. I'm a new creature in Christ Jesus. I've been washed in the blood of Jesus. I've been cleansed by the blood of Jesus."

The apostle Paul said: *"Receive us because we've wronged no man, we have corrupted no man, we have defrauded no man"* (2 Corinthians 7:2). If you study the life of Paul before he was converted, when he was still Saul of Tarsus, you'll see how Saul threatened the Church and slaughtered the people of God. Yet Paul boldly wrote, "Receive us for we've wronged nobody."

How could he say that? It's because he was a new man. He knew that he'd had an encounter with God. He knew that the old man had died on the road to Damascus. When he had a head-on collision with Jesus of Nazareth, his name changed from Saul to Paul, and his name was written down in the Lamb's Book of Life. He knew on that day he was crucified with Christ. That's why he could say:

> I am crucified with Christ; nevertheless I live; yet not I, but Christ liveth in me; and the life which I now live in the flesh I live by the faith of the Son of God, who love me, and gave himself for me.
>
> GALATIANS 2:20

"Receive us," Paul said, "because we've wronged nobody." Someone said: "Oh, I know you."

"No, you don't."

"Oh yeah, I know you. I know what you were like."

"No, you don't. All you know is somebody who died." How can I say that? It's all because of what *Jesus did do*. Adam was cast out of the presence of God, but Jesus came as a second Adam to make us welcome there. He opened the door. He made a way and said: "Come."

Not only did Jesus pay the price for our sin on the cross, but He also paid the price for our sickness and disease. Sickness and disease don't come from Heaven. I've never heard of a heavenly flu, have you? I've heard of Asian flu, I've heard of swine flu, I've heard of Hong Kong flu, but none of them are mine because I'm a citizen of Heaven!

That's one area where the reality of Jesus conflicts with religious tradition. There are people in the religious world who believe that sickness and disease are God's plan for His people. What kind of a god is sitting in Heaven trying to teach mankind a lesson, trying to bring them closer to him by afflicting mankind with sickness and disease? That's a lie from the pit of hell!

I want you to know that Jesus is the Healer as well as the Savior. Why would He save you from hell only to make you live in hell all your life on earth? No, He came to save you, heal you, and set you free!

There are many people bound by sickness and disease who believe that God put that on them. And that's a lie of the devil; God's not a monster and His idea of abundant life is not a life filled with pain and suffering. If our earthly parents did to us what we accuse God of doing, the authorities would lock them away for life. God's not a child molester; God's not a child abuser. There is one who is abusing and his name is Satan. Jesus came to destroy the works of the devil and to pay the price so that you and I could go free.

> Who his own self bare our sins in his own body on the tree, that we, being dead to sins, should live unto righteousness: by whose stripes ye were healed.
>
> 1 PETER 2:24

Two thousand years ago, Jesus bore the stripes upon His back so that today you could have health. Today you can have divine healing. It doesn't matter what sickness or disease is coming against you right now. The name of Jesus is greater than any cancer, greater than any arthritis, greater than any tumor, greater than any heart condition, greater than any lung problem that you might ever face. The name of Jesus!

At the mention of His name, sickness and disease have to bow. Why? Because Jesus paid the price on the cross of Calvary. That's why the cross was so powerful. That's the finished work of the cross. When Jesus hung on the cross, He said: "It is finished." He didn't say: "There's still more that has to be done." No! He said: "It is finished. This is it. I've paid the price. You can go free. This is the year of jubilee. Shout it from the mountaintops! Shout it from the rooftops!" Tell the world the Good News! He saves, He heals, He delivers!

Jesus also paid the price for our peace. Watch people who don't believe. They're tormented. They can't sleep at night and have to take special tablets to go to sleep. The Bible says: *"He gives his beloved sleep."* And yet, people are worried—worried about tomorrow, worried about the future, worried about the close of the millennium. But the Prince of Peace has come and paid the price so that you and I can have peace of mind.

> It is vain for you to rise up early, to sit up late, to eat the bread of sorrows: for so he giveth his beloved sleep."
>
> PSALM 127:2

Do you remember the day that the war stopped in your head? Before you met Jesus, there was a battle going on in your mind constantly, but the day that He came, you had peace. It was not a peace that the world gives, but the peace that He gives you. Now you can lie down at night and sleep, and you don't have to be afraid. You don't have to worry about a thing because you know that He's with you. You know that you dwell in the secret place of the Most High. You know you abide in the shadow of the Almighty. You know that He's your shepherd.

> He that dwelleth in the secret place of the most High shall abide under the shadow of the Almighty. I will say of the LORD, He is my refuge and my fortress: my God; in him will I trust.
>
> PSALM 91:1-2

> The LORD is my shepherd; I shall not want.
>
> PSALM 23:1

Not only did Jesus pay the price for our sin, our sickness, and our fears, but also for our poverty. Poverty's not a blessing. Poverty is a stinking curse! Heaven's not in a state of poverty. God's not sitting in the middle of a rubbish dump with flies hanging around the throne and angels slipping on rotten banana peels. No, we're going to a city where the roses never fade and where the streets are lined with crystal-clear gold.

Poverty is a curse, and since you are no longer under the curse, poverty's not for you. It's not your inheritance. You don't have to have it in your life. You have to resist poverty just like you would sickness and sin. You have to say, "No, poverty! I'm not going to allow you to come. You've come this far, but no further. You're not coming into my house. You're not going to dictate to my family. You're not going to dictate to my life. I come against you in the name of Jesus." You just have to make the decision. In Deuteronomy 30:19, God said:

> I call heaven and earth to record this day against you, that I set before you life and death, blessing and cursing: therefore choose life, that both thou and thy seed may live.

The choice is yours. Somebody said: "Well, we can't choose. It's just whatever will be, will be. *Que sera, sera.*" I want you to know, the choice is ours to choose life. We can make a decision. Fathers, you can make a decision for your house. As for me and my house, we are going to serve the Lord. As for me and my house—it's time to draw a line in the sand. It's time to tell the devil, "You've come this far and you're coming no further. I rebuke sickness and disease, poverty, lack, depression and oppression, fear, bondage, and all that hell has to offer." And you tell him to get the hell out of your life! You can tell the devil to get the *hell* out and then you can let the Heaven in. Hallelujah!

When Heaven comes down, everything begins to change. Sin says, "I can't hang around here any longer; I need to leave."

Sickness and disease say, "Uh-oh, I can't stay. I have to leave."

Poverty says, "I can't hang around. I've got to go."

Fear says, "I can't hang around anymore. I must leave."

Torment says, "I can't stay; I've got to go."

Why? Because Jesus is here, and He paid the price on Calvary two thousand years ago so that you and I could go free.

What did Jesus do? He acted like His Father. Jesus said: *"I can of mine own self do nothing: as I hear, I judge: and my judgment is just; because I seek not mine own will, but the will of the Father which hath sent me."* (John 5:30). He said: *"I and my Father are one"* (John 10:30). *"Jesus saith unto him, Have I been so long time with you, and yet hast thou not known me, Philip? he that hath seen me hath seen the Father; and how sayest thou then, Show us the Father"* (John 14:9)? So if we read about Jesus in Matthew, Mark, Luke, and John, we're going to get a portrayal of what the Father's like.

Over 70 percent of the life and ministry of Jesus was healing the sick, casting out devils, and setting the captives free. If Jesus dedicated 70 percent of His ministry to it, I would say it's important, wouldn't you? Our job is to get people saved, but once we get them saved, we want to get them healed. Once we get them healed, we want to get them free and walking in the blessings of Heaven.

Salvation is an all-inclusive term. It comes from the Greek word *sozo*, which means soundness, wholeness, healing, preservation, deliverance, blessing, and provision—all of the goodness of God wrapped up in the finished work of the cross of Calvary (See W.E. Vine's *Expository Dictionary of Biblical Words,* "save," Thomas Nelson Publishers, 1985). And it's all yours for the taking. You just have to say, "Thank You, Lord! I take it now. I take it by faith. Jesus is my Savior, Jesus is my Healer, Jesus is my Prince of Peace, Jesus is my Provider."

You could be saved, yet still be walking in anguish because you haven't taken Him as your Prince of Peace. You could be saved, yet still be walking in sickness because you haven't taken Him as your Healer. You could be saved, yet still be walking in poverty because you haven't taken Him as your Provider. But you know what? I want *all* that Jesus has for me. You know why? Because I've found out *what Jesus did.*

Somebody said: "Where did you find out what He did?" I found out in the pages of Matthew, Mark, Luke, and John. Jesus was the expressed will of the Father. He was God manifest in the flesh. He didn't do anything that He didn't first see His Father do. In other words, the Father loves—Jesus loves. The Father saves—Jesus saves. The Father forgives—Jesus forgives. The Father heals—Jesus heals. The Father delivers—Jesus delivers. He never did anything other than what His Father wanted Him to do.

And His will has not changed. I know that's true because my Bible says in Hebrews 13:8 (NIV): *"Jesus Christ is the same yesterday and today and forever."* You have to settle that in your heart, because religion and tradition will try to distract you away from the truth. You have to make a decision in your heart to receive and accept the Word of God. God doesn't lie. I'm going to stand upon the Word of God, because everything else will fade away, but the Word will not.

What did Jesus do? He was born of a virgin, lived a sinless life, took our place at the cross of Calvary where you and I should have died for our sin. He died that you and I might live. He rose from the dead to be the head of His body, the Church. Then He gave us His resurrection power—the power of the Holy Spirit—to do His works. Now, when I've found out what Jesus did do, that puts a responsibility on me to go and do what Jesus did.

But I can still avoid taking responsibility if I keep asking, "What would Jesus do?"

"Well, I don't know what He would do. Who knows what He would do?"

"We don't know. Do you know?"

We're just speculating. So whenever we come across a sick person, if we don't know what Jesus did, we'll say, "If it be Thy will, Lord, save this dear brother. Looooord! If it be Thy will, please heal Sister Bucketmouth. Lord, if it be Thy will, please provide for Brother Doodad."

But if you know exactly what Jesus *did* do, you know what His will is. You know what He *would* do. He's mighty to save, mighty to heal, mighty to deliver, mighty to forgive. So then, what must we do? We must take responsibility for what we know and do what He did—and what He told us to do. He said:

> Go ye into all the world, and preach the Gospel to every creature. And these signs shall follow them that believe; In my name shall they cast out devils; they shall speak with new tongues; They shall take up serpents; and if they drink any deadly thing, it shall not hurt them; they shall lay hands on the sick, and they shall recover.
>
> MARK 16:15, 17-20

We have the same commission He had. *"For this purpose the Son of God was manifested, that he might destroy the works of the devil"* (1 John 3:8). For this purpose are you and I made manifest, that we might destroy the works of the devil, set the captives free, destroy the yokes of bondage, and break the chains that have bound people for years. Hallelujah!

So with the knowledge of what Jesus did do, there's a responsibility that comes to me. I can't wander in the Land of Questions anymore because I have the Answer, and His name is Jesus, the solution to every problem. He gave us the power to do His works. He told us to go into all the world. Go. Two-thirds of God's name is "go." The other two-thirds of His name is "do."

What would Jesus do? Well, what did He do? He did it all. A lot of the things people think Jesus would do are nonessentials, but what He did do, eternity depends upon. We're not going to be held responsible for some myth of what we *think* Jesus would do. We'll be held responsible for what He *did* do.

Somebody said: "Why do you want the Holy Ghost in your life?" Because Jesus told the disciples to tarry at Jerusalem until they were endued with power from on high. And we can assume that if He said that, He knew that it was important. So that's what I want to do—I want Him to pour out His power upon me. I want Him to empower me and anoint me to go and reach the lost. He said: *"Ye shall receive power, after that the Holy Ghost is come upon you; and ye shall be witnesses"* (Acts 1:8).

Being a witness isn't running around with a T-shirt with a fish on it or having a "Honk if you love Jesus" sticker on your car. Being a witness is showing people there's something different about your life even when you say nothing. They can see Jesus in your eyes. They can hear Jesus in your voice. They can feel Jesus in your touch. The world is waiting to see Him made manifest in these last days.

It's time to do it. What would Jesus do? Matthew, Mark, Luke, and John tell us. Then it's not, What Would Jesus Do; it's what will you do? What are you going to do? He's waiting. He will do it when you do it.

We say, "Oh God, please do it."

God's saying, "I have already done My part in Jesus. It's your move now. You move and I will meet you at your point of faith."

I remember when I was praying, "Lord, if I were You, I'd do more than what I'm doing." The Lord said to me, "Son, if I were you, I'd do more than what I'm doing."

I said: "Lord, I'm waiting for You."

He said: "Son, I'm waiting for you."

"You mean that, Lord?"

"Yes. Get up and go. Do it."

"Lord, can I wait for conditions to be right?"

"No."

"Oh God, there's opposition."

"Good, then I'll be with you."

"Oh God, there's persecution."

"Good. Now you know what I faced. Count it all joy. Rejoice!"

What must we do? What Jesus did: heal the sick, raise the dead, cast out devils, and preach the Good News of the Lord Jesus Christ everywhere we go. That commission doesn't leave any gray areas. People come upon a car wreck or somebody just had a heart attack and everybody runs around like a chicken with its head chopped off. What would Jesus do? He'd walk right in there and say, "Arise, in Jesus's name."

Somebody might say, "Well, you're just bold." No, it's got nothing to do with being naturally bold. If you've seen Him do it, you can do it. As you obey, He will make you supernaturally bold. Somebody might say, "But I'm not some great preacher." You don't have to be! Are you born-again? Are you washed in the blood of Jesus? Is your name written in the Lamb's Book of Life? Have you accepted Him as your Lord and Savior? Then He lives on the inside of you and His Holy Spirit is right there to lead you and empower you.

What did Jesus do? Go do it!

It's time to rise up and do what Jesus would want us to do in the circumstances of life. The world is dying and needs a solution, and that

WHAT DID JESUS DO?

solution is Jesus. You know He wants to save people more than we want them to be saved. He wants to heal people more than we want them to be healed. He wants to deliver people more than we want them to be delivered. He wants revival in America more than we want revival in America. He wants to shake whole cities in this nation more than we want to see whole cities shaken.

He's waiting for us while we're waiting for Him. He's waiting for us to get with the program, to say: "Oh, all right, Lord, whatever You want to do. I'll be the glove if You'll put Your hand in me, then do whatever You want to do. Whatever You want me to do, I'll do it. Wherever You want me to go, I'll go."

Jesus wants the Holy Spirit to live big on the inside of you. When you wake up and realize what you have on the inside, it's going to be explosive. You're going to say: "Blessed be the name of the Lord God forevermore! He's put His power and anointing on the inside of me! I might not have the education. I might not even know how to speak properly. But I know God lives on the inside of me. What would Jesus do? Just watch. I'm going to show you what He would do. Take up your bed and walk. Be healed. Be forgiven. Be free. I'll show you what He would do."

What would Jesus do? A friend of mine, someone in the ministry whom I really respect, was preaching out West many years ago. While he was preaching, a person in the meeting had a heart attack and died. The moment he heard that, he prayed, "Don't expect me to do something about that. I mean the person's dead, You know. It's time to die. They needed to die." You know how people start reasoning.

But the Lord said to him: "What would Peter do if he was here right now?"

He said: "Lord, Peter would go back and raise that lady from the dead. But Lord, Peter's not here."

The Lord said to him: "What would I do?"

He said: "Lord, I know You'd go back there and raise that woman from the dead."

And the Lord said: "I'm in you. I'm in you. I'm in you."

So he ran back there and he said: "I command life in Jesus's name."

God breathed new life back in that woman, and she came off that floor totally healed by the power of God. When she went back to the doctor, he couldn't believe what he saw. She had been suffering from one of the worst heart conditions he'd ever seen, but now her heart was that of a baby.

What would Jesus do? Rise up big on the inside of you. That's what He would do. What did He do? He did it all. What does He want to do? He wants to do it all through you and me!

CHAPTER 6

THE BLOOD OF JESUS

But now in Christ Jesus ye who sometimes were far off are made nigh by the blood of Christ.

EPHESIANS 2:13

From the earliest times, blood has been a vital part of man's relationship with God, because life itself is in the blood. Blood had to be shed to pay for the sins men committed—the life of the blood to cover the death found in sin. Under the old covenant, the blood of bulls and goats was used to temporarily cover the sin of the people. As the people exercised their faith in the blood to cover their sin, God looked down through the blood and counted them righteous in His sight.

For the life of a creature is in the blood, and I have given it to you to make atonement for yourselves on the altar; it is the blood that makes atonement for one's life.

LEVITICUS 17:11

But God wanted a more permanent relationship with man than what the blood of bulls and goats could give. The sacrifices of animals only temporarily covered the sins of the people. God wanted to make a way for man's sin nature to be wiped out by His righteousness, by

His eternal life. Only the sinless, righteous, eternal blood of Jesus could do that.

God said: "I must send My Son and He will shed His eternal, sinless blood." This was not just the case of a *man dying*. Jesus was God and man combined—100 percent God, 100 percent man. He was God manifest in the flesh, coming to redeem us and pay the price for the sin of the world.

That's why the blood of Jesus is so precious to you and me today. When we talk about His blood, it's not that we're gross or bloodthirsty. This is totally different. It's the blood of Jesus that has given us life. It's His blood that has ransomed us. It's His blood that has set us free. It's His blood that has removed every sin and every guilt from our life. It's His blood that has made us new creatures in Christ Jesus. It's His blood that gives us access to the throne of God in Heaven. It's His blood that protects us. Hallelujah!

The blood of Jesus is so precious, because without it you and I would be lost. Without the blood of Jesus, we would be sacrificing animals with the high priest once a year. But we don't have to do that anymore. We have a high priest in the heavens, Jesus Christ, the Son of the Living God, and He has paid the price for the sin of the world. Like that old song says, "There's a fountain filled with blood drawn from Emmanuel's veins, and sinners plunged beneath that flood lose all their guilty stains." Today, tonight, tomorrow, and next week the blood is still flowing from Calvary. It has not dried up. It is eternally alive and it is precious. It's the blood that gives us identity. When the enemy sees you, he can't touch you because he sees the blood.

Let's look at what Jesus says about His blood. In Matthew 26:28, Jesus said: *"For this is my blood of the new testament, which is shed for many for the remission of sins."* The word "remission" is totally different from the word "atone." Atone means to cover. Under the old covenant, the sins of people were atoned for, or covered. The blood of the bulls and goats would merely cover the sin.

But remission means to wipe out and do away with so that it's not there. There's no record of it. There's no trace of it. You can't find it. It's gone. It's been done away with. In John 6:53-54, Jesus speaks of this remission in the Last Supper:

> Then Jesus said unto them, Verily, verily, I say unto you, Except ye eat the flesh of the Son of man, and drink his blood, ye have no life in you. Whoso eateth my flesh, and drinketh my blood, hath eternal life; and I will raise him up at the last day.

It's the blood of Jesus that gives us eternal life. If you're born-again, you're living in eternity right now. You are never going to die. You might die physically, but you're alive to God. You're going to live forever with Him. When you die physically, you're just going to step outside your body and go straight on to be with the Lord. John 6:55-56 goes on to say:

> For my flesh is meat indeed, and my blood is drink indeed. He that eateth my flesh, and drinketh my blood, dwelleth in me, and I in him.

That's why we can say, *"For in him we live, and move, and have our being"* (Acts 17:28). The blood has made us one with Him. Paul, describing that first communion in 1 Corinthians 11:25 says:

> After the same manner also he took the cup, when he had supped, saying, This cup is the new testament in my blood: this do ye, as oft as ye drink it, in remembrance of me.

In other words, every time we partake of communion, we remember what took place two thousand years ago at the cross of Calvary. We drink the wine and remember Jesus shed His blood for our sin. We eat the bread and remember that His body was broken for our healing.

When we go back to the Old Testament, we can see the whole plan of redemption portrayed in types and shadows, in patterns established with the children of Israel. Look at the Exodus, when the children of Israel left their bondage in Egypt. When we study the story, we see that they could not leave Egypt until they had the lamb in them and the blood over them. In the same way, you and I cannot leave Egypt—the life of sin—until we have the Lamb in us and the blood over us.

Let's read the story starting in Exodus 12:

> The Lord spake unto Moses and Aaron in the land of Egypt, saying, This month shall be unto you the beginning of months; It shall be the first month of the year to you. Speak ye unto all the congregation of Israel, saying, In the tenth day of this month they shall take to them every man a lamb, according to the house of their fathers, a lamb for an house: And if the household be too little for the lamb, let him and his neighbour next unto his house take it according to the number of the souls; every man according to his eating shall make your count for the lamb. Your lamb shall be without blemish, a male of the first year: ye shall take it out from the sheep, or from the goats: And ye shall keep it up until the fourteenth day of the same month: and the whole assembly of the congregation of Israel shall kill it in the evening. And they shall take of the blood, and strike it on the two side posts and on the upper doorpost of the houses, wherein they shall eat it. And they shall eat the flesh in that night, roast with fire, and unleavened bread; and with bitter herbs they shall eat it. Eat not of it raw, nor sodden at all with water, but roast with fire; his head with his legs, and with the purtenance thereof. And ye shall let nothing of it remain until the morning; and that which remaineth of it until the morning ye shall burn with fire. And thus shall ye eat it; with your loins girded, your shoes on your feet, and your staff in your hand; and yet shall eat it in haste: it is the Lord's passover.
>
> EXODUS 12:1-11

God told them that this was a meal that they had to eat, and then they needed to be ready to leave. "We're coming out of bondage," they said. "We're coming out of slavery! God is delivering us, but we can't leave Egypt till we have the lamb in us and the blood over us. So we first inspect the lamb to make sure it has no blemish. Then we kill the lamb, and with a branch of hyssop we put the blood on the doorposts and the lintels of the house. That way, when the angel of death passes over, it will not stop by and touch the firstborn. And then we're going to leave."

> For I will pass through the land of Egypt this night, and will smite all
> the firstborn in the land of Egypt, both man and beast; and against
> all the gods of Egypt I will execute judgment: I am the Lord.
>
> EXODUS 12:12

Can you imagine sitting in your house knowing the angel of death is coming by, but knowing because you've smeared blood on the doorposts and the lintels, he cannot touch you? You *are under the blood.* Then next door, you hear a scream, because they had no blood.

I believe the blood was so powerful that if an Egyptian family found out what was going on and just did what they saw the Hebrews doing, their firstborn was saved. Wherever the blood of the lamb was, there was safety and deliverance.

It's the same with salvation. God doesn't care if you're white, black, yellow, green, or turquoise. He doesn't care what denomination you are, what nationality you are, male or female, bond or free. He just looks for the blood. It's the blood of Jesus that cleanses us from every guilt and every stain. It's His blood that makes us whole and makes us one.

Now let's look at Hebrews 9:6-7:

> Now when these things were thus ordained, the priests went always
> into the first tabernacle, accomplishing the service of God. But into
> the second went the high priest alone once every year, not without
> blood, which he offered for himself, and for the errors of his people.

So every time the High Priest came around, there had to be blood, because it was by blood that he could gain access into the Holy of Holies, into the presence of God. It's the blood that gives us access to the very presence of God. If it weren't for the blood, when you got in the presence of God, you'd drop dead. It says here: "which he offered for himself." Notice, it didn't exclude the priest, and for the errors of the people. Let's continue with verse 8:

The Holy Ghost this signifying, that the way into the holiest of all was not yet made manifest, while as the first tabernacle was yet standing: Which was a figure for the time then present, in which were offered both gifts and sacrifices, that could not make him that did the service perfect, as pertaining to the conscience; Which stood only in meats and drinks, and divers washings, and carnal ordinances, imposed on them, until the time of reformation. But Christ being come an high priest of good things to come, by a greater and more perfect tabernacle, not made with hands, that is to say, not of this building; Neither by the blood of goats and calves, but by his own blood he entered in once into the holy place, having obtained eternal redemption for us. For if the blood of bulls and goats, and the ashes of an heifer sprinkling the unclean, sanctifieth to the purifying of the flesh: How much more shall the blood of Christ, who through the eternal Spirit offered himself without spot to God, purge your conscience from dead works to serve the living God? And for this cause he is the mediator of the new testament, that by means of death, for the redemption of the transgressions that were under the first testament, they which are called might receive the promise of eternal inheritance. For where a testament is, there must also of necessity be the death of the testator. For a testament is of force after men are dead: otherwise it is of no strength at all while the testator liveth. Whereupon neither the first testament was dedicated without blood. For when Moses had spoken every precept to all the people according to the law, he took the blood of calves and of goats, with water, and scarlet wool, and hyssop, and sprinkled both the book, and all the people, Saying, This is the blood of the testament which God hath enjoined unto you. Moreover he sprinkled with blood both the tabernacle, and all the vessels of the ministry. And almost all things are by the law purged with blood; and without shedding of blood is no remission. It was therefore necessary that the patterns of things in the heavens should be purified with these; but the heavenly things themselves with better sacrifices than these. For Christ is not entered into the holy places made with hands, which are the figures of the true; but into heaven itself, now to appear in the presence of God for us.

HEBREWS 9:8-24

On earth was this earthly tabernacle made with hands, and that earthly tabernacle was a duplicate of the heavenly tabernacle. But man could not go into that heavenly tabernacle. So whenever it was taking place on the earth, God looked at it as though it were being done in Heaven. But it wasn't sufficient. That's why Jesus had to come—He was the final sacrifice.

After Jesus said, "It is finished," and died on the cross, the veil of the earthly temple was torn in two, from top to bottom. The Holy Ghost came out of an earthly tabernacle that was made with the hands of men, never again to live therein, but to come and live in your heart and my heart.

When Jesus therefore had received the vinegar, he said, It is finished: and he bowed his head, and gave up the ghost.

JOHN 19:30

And, behold, the veil of the temple was rent in twain from the top to the bottom; and the earth did quake, and the rocks rent.

MATTHEW 27:51

And that's why we become temples of the Living God. For God has said: "I will dwell in them. I will walk in them. I will be their God. They will be My people." You are the temple of the living God, and the blood of Jesus washes you clean so He can come and live on the inside of you. Hallelujah!

And what agreement hath the temple of God with idols? for ye are the temple of the living God; as God hath said, I will dwell in them, and walk in them; and I will be their God, and they shall be my people.

2 CORINTHIANS 6:16

Now, look at that last verse: *"For Christ is not entered into the holy places made with hands, which are the figures of the true; but into heaven itself, now to appear in the presence of God for us."* When Jesus ascended, He went right into Heaven to the real temple, not the type and shadow on earth. He took His own blood and made sure that Heaven's court was satisfied, that the price for the sin of man was paid.

And it was paid for good.

> Nor yet that he should offer himself often, as the high priest entereth into the holy place every year with blood of others; For then must he often have suffered since the foundation of the world: but now once in the end of the world hath he appeared to put away sin by the sacrifice of himself.
>
> HEBREWS 9:25-26

It's done. There's no more sacrifice. And yet it seems the modern-day church is always trying to sacrifice something. I'm convinced that if some people could, they would sacrifice another bull or goat, because they don't know what was purchased at Calvary. They don't know that when Jesus said, "It is finished," He meant it.

> As it is appointed unto men once to die, but after this the judgment: So Christ was once offered to bear the sins of many; and unto them that look for him shall he appear the second time without sin unto salvation.
>
> HEBREWS 9:27-28

The blood of Jesus has the purchasing power to redeem a sinner from the jaws of hell. I don't care who they are or what they've done. The blood can set them free. We were purchased with that blood.

> Take heed therefore unto yourselves, and to all the flock, over the which the Holy Ghost hath made you overseers, to feed the church of God, which he hath purchased with his own blood.
>
> ACTS 20:28

If you're the Church of the Lord Jesus Christ, you do not belong to yourself anymore. You belong to Him. You have been purchased by His blood. I belong to Jesus. I've been purchased by His blood. I'm His personal property. Written on my heart is "Personal Property of the Lord Jesus Christ."

Jesus left His mighty throne in glory to come to earth to pay the price to buy me. He must have thought I was worth something, because He came to pay the price. He came Himself to pay the price. He didn't send anybody else. He came Himself.

And it's a signed deal! This is not something that still has to be negotiated. The deal has been done. The God-Man, Jesus Christ of Nazareth, the Son of the Living God, 100 percent God, 100 percent man, came down and on behalf of man and on behalf of God, cut the covenant in Himself to make sure that it couldn't go wrong on either side. It was done within Himself. Hallelujah!

Because of the blood of Jesus, we join the family of God and we're entitled to all that relationship implies.

In whom we have redemption through his blood, the forgiveness of sins, according to the riches of his grace.

EPHESIANS 1:7

In whom we have redemption through his blood, even the forgiveness of sins.

COLOSSIANS 1:14

And, having made peace through the blood of his cross, by him to reconcile all things unto himself; by him, I say, whether they be things in earth, or things in heaven.

COLOSSIANS 1:20

Through the blood we're justified. Through the blood we've been reconciled. My sins are forgiven and I'm part of the family of God.

And that's not all:

Much more then, being now justified by his blood, we shall be saved from wrath through him.

ROMANS 5:9

The day is coming when there will be a terrible judgment for all those who have rejected Jesus Christ—God's love and redemption extended to us—but not for you and me. For the believer, there will be the judgment seat of Christ which is going to be totally different. Every one of us will stand before Jesus to give an account of what we've done with our life, our calling, our ministry—and to give an account for every idle word spoken. And the Bible says our works will be tried as with fire. Some works will be wood, hay, and stubble...and burn up. Some will be gold, jewels, and precious stones and we'll carry them into eternity with us.

That's why I believe the Bible says that He's going to wipe away the tears from our eyes. Many people will get to Heaven and be ashamed that they never did more with what was purchased for them on the cross. Everything you're doing right now is going to count for eternity. Every act of kindness, every act of generosity, every time you help somebody and bring them to Jesus, you're laying up treasure in Heaven.

Don't take it lightly! Jesus came and gave His all. The least I can do is give my all because of what He did for me at Calvary. The least I can do is to be 100 percent committed to Him. The least I can do is live a holy life. The least I can do is live a sanctified life. The least I can do is renew my mind to the Word of God. The least I can do is put my flesh under. That's the least I can do!

The blood of Jesus not only cleanses me from sin and saves me from judgment, but it protects me from the enemy. When the enemy comes by me, he can't touch me, because he sees the blood. "Oh, he belongs to Jesus," the devil says. "I can't touch him. I have no authority over him. I can't put sickness and disease on him for long. I'll try, but I can't make it stick. He just keeps getting healed all the time."

People sometimes look at me and say, "Well, you're just a real bold individual." But you have to understand. I wasn't always that way. I was very shy. But I'm made bold because of the blood of Jesus. Hebrews 10:19-20 says:

> Having therefore, brethren, boldness to enter into the holiest by the blood of Jesus, By a new and living way, which be hath consecrated for us, through the veil, that is to say, his flesh.

I can be bold because of the blood. Not arrogant—bold. When you stand in front of somebody who is sick, you can be bold. You can lay your hands on them and know that the power of God is going to come into them and that sickness and disease are going to have to go. You can be bold when you speak to devils, and they're going leave.

Where does that boldness come from? People are trying to get bold by reading self-help books, but that's just confidence in human ability. People who are bold by the blood of Jesus don't trust in their own ability. They have no confidence in the flesh, but they have boldness in the blood, boldness in the name of Jesus, boldness in the Word of God. By the blood of Jesus, we can be bold.

Now, just because we can come boldly to the throne of grace to obtain mercy doesn't mean we can just sin, knowing that the blood will cover it. No! We've got to treat the blood with total respect. Hebrews 10:29 says:

> Of how much sorer punishment, suppose ye, shall he be thought worthy, who hath trodden underfoot the Son of God, and hath counted the blood of the covenant, wherewith he was sanctified, an unholy thing, and hath done despite unto the Spirit of grace?

That's why we don't play with sin. If you have a problem with sin in your life, deal with it. Put it out. If you don't put it out, it will take you out. It's not a game. The verse before that, Hebrews 10:26, says that if we sin willfully after we hear the truth, then we have no forgiveness. To sin willfully means to go ahead and practice sin, thinking it doesn't matter because we know that God will just forgive us one of these days. We can't live like heathens and then go back to the throne of grace after we're done.

You don't want to touch sin. It will kill you! It will destroy you. Keep it away from your thought life. Treat sin like your worst enemy, like you would a burglar coming into your house at night.

"Does that mean I need to live a holy life?" Yes! And you can, because if Jesus said you can live a holy life, then I believe you can live a holy life. And I'm not talking about being religious, pious, or "holier than thou." If Jesus said you could, you can.

"But can I do it?" Yes, you've got the power to live a holy life. You're not weak when it comes to temptation. That's a lie from hell. You're strong. You can do it. You've got faith in the blood of Jesus, and because you've got faith in the blood, you can do it; you can overcome.

"Well, then, how do I get this blood to work in my life?" You have to walk in the light. First John 1:7 says: *"But if we walk in the light, as he is in the light, we have fellowship one with another, and the blood of Jesus Christ his Son cleanseth us from all sin."* Just walk in the light. Everywhere you go, make sure you're walking in the light. If there's any darkness, don't put your foot in it. It's a pile of something that you don't want to get into! Walk in the light.

If we walk in the light as He is in the light, then we will have fellowship one with another. The first sign that somebody's backsliding is when they break fellowship with other Christians. That's why the Bible says not to forsake fellowship with other believers.

> Not forsaking the assembling of ourselves together, as the manner of some is; but exhorting one another: and so much the more, as ye see the day approaching.
>
> HEBREWS 10:25

On the other hand, when you get on fire for God, suddenly your unsaved friends won't want to be around you. What's happening is that you're now walking in the light and they want to walk in darkness. Your light is convicting them.

How do you activate the reality of the blood on a daily basis? You do it by testifying. Look at Revelation 12:11: *"And they overcame him by the blood of the Lamb, and by the word of their testimony; and they loved not their lives unto the death."* To make the blood a reality in your life, find somebody to tell your conversion to every day. Tell them about what Jesus did for you. If Jesus has really touched you, you cannot tell somebody else without getting excited. It takes you right back and you get all refreshed.

Activate the power of the blood daily in your life by telling the story. "Hallelujah! I was lost, but He found me," you can tell them. "I was blind, but now I can see. I was bound, but now I'm free. He washed me in His blood. He set me free. He cleansed me. He delivered me from all my guilt and all my shame. I've fallen in love with Jesus, and I just want to tell you about Him, how wonderful He is! Because of His blood, I'm His child and He loves me!"

CHAPTER 7

THE NAME OF JESUS

Now Peter and John went up together into the temple at the hour of prayer, being the ninth hour. And a certain man lame from his mother's womb was carried, whom they laid daily at the gate of the temple which is called Beautiful, to ask alms of them that entered into the temple; Who seeing Peter and John about to go into the temple asked an alms. And Peter, fastening his eyes upon him with John, said, Look on us. And he gave heed unto them, expecting to receive something of them. Then Peter said, Silver and gold have I none; but such as I have give I thee: In the name of Jesus Christ of Nazareth rise up and walk. And he took him by the right hand, and lifted him up: and immediately his feet and ankle bones received strength. And he leaping up stood, and walked, and entered with them into the temple, walking, and leaping, and praising God: And all the people saw him walking and praising God: And they knew that it was he which sat for alms at the Beautiful gate of the temple: and they were filled with wonder and amazement at that which had happened unto him. And as the lame man which was healed held Peter and John, all the people ran together unto them in the porch that is called Solomon's, greatly wondering. And when Peter saw it, he answered unto the people, Ye men of Israel, why marvel ye at this? or why look ye so earnestly on us, as though by our own power or holiness we had made this man to walk?

ACTS 3:1-12

Then Peter began to preach to the people about Jesus, in whose name he had just healed the lame man. Although about five thousand people got saved, the religious leaders arrested Peter and John.

And as they spake unto the people, the priests, and the captain of the temple, and the Sadducees, came upon them, Being grieved that they taught the people, and preached through Jesus the resurrection from the dead. And they laid hands on them, and put them in hold unto the next day: for it was now eventide. Howbeit many of them which heard the word believed; and the number of the men was about five thousand.

ACTS 4:1-4

They had only one question for them:

By what power, or by what name, have ye done this? Then Peter, filled with the Holy Ghost, said unto them, Ye rulers of the people, and elders of Israel...

Be it known, unto you all, and to all the people of Israel, that <u>by the name of Jesus Christ of Nazareth</u>, whom ye crucified, whom God raised from the dead, even by him doth this man stand here before you whole...

Neither is there salvation in any other: <u>for there is none other name under heaven given among men, whereby we must be saved.</u>

ACTS 4:7-8, 10, 12 (EMPHASIS MINE)

Then the men of the council got together and conferred among themselves:

Saying, What shall we do to these men? For that indeed a notable miracle hath been done by them is manifest to all them that dwell in Jerusalem; and we cannot deny it. But that it spread no further among the people, let us straitly threaten them, <u>that they speak henceforth to no man in this name.</u> And they called them, and commanded them not to speak at all nor teach in the name of Jesus. But Peter and John answered and said unto them, Whether it be right in the sight of God to hearken unto you more than unto God, judge ye. For we cannot but speak the things which we have seen and heard.

ACTS 4:16-20 (EMPHASIS MINE)

That name really stirred them up, didn't it? Now, look at verses 23 through 31:

And being let go, they went to their own company, and reported all that the chief priests and elders had said unto them. And when they heard that, they lifted up their voice to God with one accord, and said, Lord, thou art God, which hast made heaven, and earth, and the sea, and all that in them is: Who by the mouth of thy servant David hast said, Why did the heathen rage and the people imagine vain things? The kings of the earth stood up, and the rulers were gathered together against the Lord, and against his Christ. For of a truth against thy holy child Jesus, whom thou hast anointed, both Herod, and Pontius Pilate, with the Gentiles, and the people of Israel, were gathered together, For to do whatsoever thy hand and thy counsel determined before to be done. And now, Lord, behold their threatenings: and grant unto thy servants, that with all boldness they may speak thy word, By stretching forth thine hand to heal; and that signs and wonders may be done by the name of thy holy child Jesus. And when they had, prayed, the place was shaken where they were assembled together; and they were all filled with the Holy Ghost, and they spake the word of God with boldness.

The name of Jesus has been given to the Church as the Church's possession. Jesus gave us His name. A name is only as good as the person from whence it comes. How good a name is depends on what authority is backing up that name. When somebody knocks on your door and says, "I stand here by the authority of the police department," even though you don't know this particular policeman, you open up because you recognize the authority of the police. If you stand in the name of someone, then you'd better make certain they have what it takes to back you up. That's why the chief priests and elders asked Peter and John, "By what name have you done this?" They wanted to know whose power was backing the disciples up.

We come in the same name—Jesus—a name which is above every name. The name that, even at the mention of it, *"every knee should bow, of things in heaven, and things in earth, and things under the earth."* At the mention of that name, *"every tongue should confess that Jesus Christ is Lord."*

> That at the name of Jesus every knee should bow, of things in heaven, and things in earth, and things under the earth.
>
> PHILIPPIANS 2:10

> And that every tongue should confess that Jesus Christ is Lord, to the glory of God the Father.
>
> PHILIPPIANS 2:11

Have you ever wondered why there is only one name that is taken in vain? Only the name of one God is taken in vain: Jesus. You don't hear people scream in pain and say, "Oh, Buddha, I stubbed my toe," or "Oh, Mohammed, I jammed my finger." You don't see people hit their thumb with a hammer and say, "Oh, Confucius!" They always use the name of Jesus. Even the worst sinner uses the name of Jesus. Why? The devil knows that only Jesus's name has authority and power and he tries to get people to disrespect that name by using it as a curse. But he finds himself in big trouble when believers, washed in the blood, find out that he has no defenses against that name!

Jesus has given His name to you and me. It's our possession. It belongs to us. Hallelujah! We have authority over every evil thing in that name. In that name, sickness has to go. In that name, disease has to go. In that name, poverty has to go. In that name, oppression has to go. In that name, death has to go. When the believer speaks that name in faith, something's going to happen!

In John 16:23-24, Jesus says this about our use of His name:

> And in that day ye shall ask me nothing. Verily, verily, I say unto you, Whatsoever ye shall ask the Father in my name, he will give it you. Hitherto have ye asked nothing in my name: ask, and ye shall receive, that your joy may be full.

Jesus wants us to use His name so that our joy may be full. He also wants us to know the power of His name:

> And these signs shall follow them that believe; In my name shall they cast out devils; they shall speak with new tongues; They shall take up serpents; and if they drink any deadly thing, it shall not hurt them; they shall lay hands on the sick, and they shall recover.
>
> MARK 16:17-18

There are many people who believe in Jesus, but they don't believe in the power of His name, so they don't cast out devils or heal the sick. When you believe in His name, you can. I believe in that name, that name that's above every name, that name that's above cancer, that name that's above arthritis, that name that's above depression, that name that's above every sickness and disease. I believe that name is higher than any other name on the face of the earth, Jesus.

What authority stands behind that name? All of Heaven is behind that name. When we mention that name, Heaven stands at attention. When we mention that wonderful name, all Heaven stands up and says, "Did you call?" When we mention that name, the angels of God move to and fro saying, "He mentioned that name! She mentioned that name!"

There's a story that I heard many years ago about a lady whose beloved husband died, but she would not let him go. She stood by the bed and said: "I'll not let you go. In the name of Jesus, come back." And he was raised from the dead.

The man testified later that he went to Heaven and an angel came to him and said: "You have to go back. She's using that name. Although you'd love to stay, you'll have to go back. She's using that name."

That name carries authority.

And Jesus came and spake unto them, saying, All power is given unto me in heaven and in earth. Go ye therefore, and teach all nations, baptizing them in the name of the Father, and of the Son, and of the Holy Ghost: Teaching them to observe all things whatsoever I have commanded you: and, lo, I am with you always, even unto the end of the world. Amen.

MATTHEW 28:18-20

Jesus said: "I have been given all power and all authority. You go in My name, teach them in My name, and I will come to back up My name. So when you speak My name, I'm going to come. I will come and confirm My Word with signs following."

And they went forth, and preached every where, the Lord working with them, and confirming the word with signs following. Amen.

MARK 16:20

Now a person can acquire a name in three ways. In the world, people acquire names first of all by inheritance. Prince Charles inherited his name and title. There's no way that a commoner could be called a prince. You have to be born into the royal family.

Secondly, you could acquire a name by bestowal. It could be bestowed or conferred upon you. A university can confer a doctorate or the queen could knight you Sir or Dame Whoever. That name would be conferred upon you because of your achievements in a certain field.

A name can also be acquired by conquest. William the Conqueror or Emperor Napoleon got their names and their kingdoms by conquest in battle.

But Jesus got His name all three ways. He got His name first by inheritance.

> In the beginning was the Word, and the Word was with God, and the Word was God. And the Word was made flesh, and dwelt among us, (and we beheld his glory, the glory as of the only begotten of the Father,) full of grace and truth.
>
> JOHN 1:1,14

> God hath fulfilled the same unto us their children, in that he hath raised up Jesus again; as it is also written in the second psalm, Thou art my Son, this day have I begotten thee.
>
> ACTS 13:33

> God, who at sundry times and in divers manners spake in time past unto the fathers by the prophets, Hath in these last days spoken unto us by his Son, whom he bath appointed heir of all things, by whom also he made the worlds; Who being the brightness of his glory, and the express image of his person, and upholding all things by the word of his power, when he had by himself purged our sins, sat down on the right hand of the Majesty on high; Being made so much better than the angels, as he hath by inheritance obtained a more excellent name than they. For unto which of the angels said he at any time, Thou art my son, this day have I begotten thee? And again, I will be to him a Father, and he shall be to me a Son? And again, when he bringeth in the first begotten into the world, he saith, And let all the angels of God worship him.
>
> HEBREWS 1:1-6

The second way Jesus got His name was by bestowal:

> Wherefore God also hath highly exalted him, and given him a name which is above every name.
>
> PHILIPPIANS 2:9

In the *Amplified Bible, Classic Edition*, Philippians 2:9-11 says:

Therefore [because He stooped so low] God has highly exalted Him and has freely bestowed on Him the name that is above every name, That in (at) the name of Jesus every knee should (must) bow, in heaven and on earth and under the earth, And every tongue [frankly and openly] confess and acknowledge that Jesus Christ is Lord, to the glory of God the Father.

His name was bestowed because of His achievements, because Jesus paid the price on the cross and defeated sin, death, hell, and the grave, and then rose again. He is giving us that same power with which He overcame sin, and He said: "You go in My name." So when you and I stand in front of darkness and we say, "In the name of Jesus," darkness knows the power behind that name!

But you can't do this without knowing the Person behind the name. It's not going to work. In Acts 19:13-16, the seven sons of Sceva saw Paul casting out devils in the name of Jesus. They said: "Well, we'll just go and do the same thing in the name of Jesus Christ whom Paul preaches."

They used the name, but the demon said: "Well, Jesus I know. Paul I know, but who are you?" And the demon leaped on them, tore their clothes off, and they ran from the place naked.

Then certain of the vagabond Jews, exorcists, took upon them to call over them which had evil spirits the name of the Lord Jesus, saying, We adjure you by Jesus whom Paul preacheth. And there were seven sons of one Sceva, a Jew, and chief of the priests, which did so. And the evil spirit answered and said, Jesus I know, and Paul I know; but who are ye? And the man in whom the evil spirit was leaped on them, and overcame them, and prevailed against them, so that they fled out of that house naked and wounded.

ACTS 19:13-16

So not just anybody can use that name! It's only for the believer. It's only for the one who knows what that name represents. People come to me all the time and say, "Well, I used the name and nothing happened." It's got to become a living reality on the inside of you. I know when I speak that name of Jesus, something is going to happen, because I have faith in the authority bestowed upon that name.

First, Jesus got His name by inheritance; second, He got it by bestowal; and third, He got it by conquest.

Who hath delivered us from the power of darkness, and hath translated us into the kingdom of his dear Son.

COLOSSIANS 1:13

And having spoiled principalities and powers, he made a shew of them openly, triumphing over them in it.

COLOSSIANS 2:15

This same verse in the *Amplified Bible, Classic Edition* says:

[God] disarmed the principalities and the powers that were ranged against us and made a bold display and public example of them, in triumphing over them in Him and in it [the cross].

Through the cross, the devil's powers were rendered useless. Now if that name has done that, and that name has been given to you and me, do you understand what awesome power you and I have when we use the name of Jesus? It's not just a thing that we add on at the end of a prayer: "in the name of Jesus." It's something that is going to cause everything we pray about to come to pass.

"Whatsoever you ask the Father in My name," Jesus said, "I'm going to do it for you. If I don't have it, I'll make it for you. I'll make a way where there is no way. I'm the way, the truth, and the life. I'm Alpha and Omega, the beginning and the end, the first and the last, who was and is and is to come. When you speak My name, I'm going to come. I'll back you up in an impossible situation. When your back's against the wall and you don't know which way to turn, mention My name, and I'm going to be right there." When you fully understand the power in the name of Jesus, it will change the way you pray.

Now, as I said, a name is only as powerful as that which backs it up. I heard Richard Roberts say that when he was a young man, he wanted to rebel against his father. He wanted nothing to do with his dad's name, so he left and went to the University of Kansas. But no one knew him there, and he couldn't even open a bank account. Eventually he got so mad he said: "Listen, I'm Richard Roberts. My dad's Oral Roberts."

Suddenly, people started responding to him. "Oh, you're the son of Oral Roberts! Okay." He just mentioned his father's name and things happened. Even though he didn't want the name, in the end, it actually helped him.

Now people do that with the name of Jesus, too. They refuse to use the power in the name. How dumb can you get? When sickness and disease came knocking on your door today, did you use that name? No? Why not? When poverty tried to attach itself to you, did you use that name? No? Why not?

Do you understand that when you mention that name, all Heaven stands at attention and moves right in to back you up? Boom! Just like that! It's the key that unlocks the door to the blessing, and it's yours.

People might say, "Well, you're just using it as a formula."

But Jesus told us, "Use My name; go into all the world in My name."

"By whose authority do you come here?"

"I come here by the name of Jesus Christ of Nazareth, the Son of the Living God."

"By whose authority do you lay hands on these sick people?"

"By the authority of the name that's above every name, the name of Jesus."

When you realize the authority in the name of Jesus, you'll get bold.

When I left South Africa, people said: "There goes Rodney to America with nobody but God behind him." But I didn't need anyone or anything else. I came, and God blessed. Wherever we go in the world, whether by invitation or not, we go there in the name of Jesus and by His authority.

That name will give you supernatural, divine favor. That name will open the door for you into places where there is no door. That name will make a way where there is no way. That name will furnish a table in the wilderness. That name will make the crooked paths straight. That name will calm the worst storm in your life. That name will make things look like Heaven.

I'll tell you, you'll think twice before using that name carelessly again. Think twice before you just say, "Blah, blah, blah, in Jesus's name, amen." That name is powerful! And it belongs to you! It's your possession!

Jesus says: "I'm going to give you eternal life, and you will come to live in Heaven with Me, but while you're down here on earth, I'm going to give you My name."

I have His name! That's what Christian means: "Little anointed one, little Jesus."

Religious people get upset when you talk like this. "Well, who do you think you are?"

"I don't think I'm anything, but I know who *He* is."

I know *who* He is. He's given me His name. It's mine. It belongs to me and it belongs to you. It's yours at two o'clock in the morning. It's yours on Monday, Tuesday, Wednesday, Thursday, and Friday. That name is yours. You're His child. You just have to mention that name and a holy boldness comes upon you.

The late John Osteen was one of the boldest pastors I know. He was invited to a secular event with businessmen of different faiths. The coordinator of the dinner said: "Now listen, when you pray over the food, don't use the name of Jesus because you'll offend the people of other faiths."

Pastor Osteen didn't say anything until they called him up to pray. He said: "Father, in the name of Jesus, I thank You for this meal. I thank You for the name of Jesus, and for the food in Jesus's name. I pray that, in Jesus's name, You'll bless everybody here. Thank You Lord, in Jesus's name."

Another time, Pastor Osteen got on a hotel elevator and heard people on the elevator cussing up a storm, using the name of the Lord in vain, with the foulest language. So he boldly said: "Praise God! Oh, I love You, Jesus! I worship You. Oh, thank You, Jesus, You're so awesome. Lord, I just worship You. I give You praise. I give You honor."

They all looked at him. Finally, one said: "What are you doing?"

He said: "I'm just giving my God equal time."

Now some people get timid when it comes to using the name. They'll pray a prayer and then end it with, "for God's sake." Or, "Lord, bless this food for Jesus's sake." Well, Jesus is not eating the food, you are! "Lord, bless this food for Rodney's sake, in Jesus's name." Don't get to the end of the prayer and mumble, "in Jesus name." Don't be ashamed of the name—be bold!

I'm not ashamed of the name. I've been in places where somebody was cussing and using the name of Jesus. You know what I did? I said: "Oh, you know Him, too? Is He here? That's wonderful! He's my friend! You just mentioned my friend's name."

"What do you mean?"

"Well, you just mentioned Jesus. You know Him as well? You seem to know Him. You mention Him often."

The name of Jesus has authority in three worlds—in Heaven before God and all of the angels; in earth over men; and under the earth, over the devil and all the demons of hell. That name carries power. That name has authority.

When the enemy sees you coming, he says, "Get out of the way, He's using that name! She's using that name! We can't go to that house! They use that name in that house! We can't go near these people. They use that name. They know what that name stands for, and they know what that name means. Leave them alone. They're using that name!"

Whenever the enemy comes your way, don't even think about it. Just say, "I'm going to use that name, I'm going to pull that name out and it's loaded. It's ready to be fired. Satan, you're messing with a believer, and I'm going to use that name!"

Wherefore God also hath highly exalted him, and given him a name which is above every name: That at the name of Jesus every knee should bow, of things in heaven, and things in earth, and things under the earth; And that every tongue should confess that Jesus Christ is Lord, to the glory of God the Father.

PHILIPPIANS 2:9-11

CHAPTER 8

THE COMPASSION OF JESUS

He shall feed his flock like a shepherd: he shall gather the lambs with
his arm, and carry them in his bosom, and shall gently lead those
that are with young.

ISAIAH 40:11

Hollywood once tried to portray Jesus as a confused weak man who
was battling with His own identity. He didn't know who He was and
struggled with what He was called to do. But the Gospels show clearly
that Jesus knew exactly who He was. He was a person of very strong
character and great compassion—and He was no wimp. He knew He
came to the earth for a reason. He came to the earth with a purpose.

For this purpose the Son of God was manifested, that he might destroy
the works of the devil.

1 JOHN 3:8

Jesus came to destroy the works of the devil. Many try to make out
that Jesus really wasn't interested in mankind, that He was just interested in Himself and that He formed a following for His own benefit.
However, He came to pay the price for the sin of man and to give His
life for the world. He laid down His life so that you and I could live free

of the bondage of sin and overcome all the devil's attacks and schemes. He said: "I am come that you might have life, and that you might have it more abundantly."

> The thief cometh not, but for to steal, and to kill, and to destroy: I am come that they might have life, and that they might have it more abundantly.
>
> JOHN 10:10

In Acts 10:38, Peter preached about *"how God anointed Jesus of Nazareth with the Holy Ghost and with power: who went about doing good, and healing all that were oppressed of the devil; for God was with him."* The ministry of Jesus, the compassionate One, was to do good, to bless people, to touch people, and to change lives. Everywhere He went, He healed the sick and He cast out devils.

When we look at Jesus, we see not only was He able to do what He did, but because of His compassion, He was willing. If you ask many people in the world today, "Is God able?" they would say, "Yes, He's able." But they're not sure if He would be willing. Jesus is not only able, but He's willing. He wants to touch mankind more than mankind wants to be touched.

We've had people who have been bedridden whom God has raised up, and people bound by incurable disease whom God has healed. Why? Because Jesus's whole purpose and His whole desire is to touch and to change people's lives. His desire is not to offer you a home in Heaven, yet let you live in hell until you get there. The prayer that He taught the disciples was, *"Thy will be done in earth, as it is in heaven"* (Matthew 6:10). God's will is that you be touched, changed, set free, and delivered right here on earth.

Now in order to see how willing Jesus was, let's look at Him in operation. Matthew 8:1 says: *"When he was come down from the mountain, great multitudes followed him."*

Why do you think they followed Him? They followed Him because He had something special. You know, in the middle of summer, everybody wants to follow the ice cream truck. Now I am not calling Jesus an ice cream truck, but when people realize that you have what they need, they come and get it. Jesus had something people really needed and wanted. He had the words of life and His words brought about change in their lives. He could come into their lives and calm the storm.

Jesus never talked to people like the religious world does today. He never tried to put them down or condemn them. You've got to realize that Jesus loves people, and He loves sinners. He can't stand religion and He can't stand tradition. The people He was always bumping into and knocking heads with were the religious people of the day. They hated Him because He loved people and had the power to change lives. By His words and actions, He showed them to be the prideful hypocrites they were.

The people He fought with the most were the Pharisees, the Sadducees—the "wouldn't sees" and the "couldn't sees." He really had problems with them on the Sabbath. On the Sabbath, they came out ready to kill. I don't know if this happened, but I've just got a feeling that when Jesus woke up on Sabbath mornings, He rubbed His hands together and said: "Oh, boy! Sabbath day! Let's cause some trouble today! Let's find some sick people to heal, because you know it's gonna irritate those religious people."

Religious people also have a problem accepting the fact that God is always willing and desiring to heal people. One day, a leper came to Him, worshipping and saying, "Lord, if You will, You can make me clean" (Mark 1:40).

Did Jesus say: "I don't want to right now, be sick for another two years"? Did He say: "Nope, I've put this sickness on you to teach you a lesson"? Or did He say: "I don't want to heal you, I've put this sickness on you to bring you closer to Me"?

No! He said: "I will! I want to! Be clean." Jesus wanted to heal him, and He did heal him. Immediately, the man's leprosy was cleansed.

Well, the leper told everybody about how Jesus healed him, and His fame spread throughout the region. They began bringing the sick and the demon-possessed, and He set them free. Matthew 8:16-17 says:

When the even was come, they brought unto him many that were possessed with devils. And he cast out the spirits with his word, and healed all that were sick: That it might be fulfilled which was spoken by Esaias, the prophet, saying, Himself took our infirmities, and bare our sicknesses.

Let's compare the word "compassion" with the word "sympathy." Sometimes we think we have compassion, but we're actually having sympathy. They are two different things. Sympathy says, "I know how you feel," but compassion says, "I *feel* how you feel."

Jesus not only had *sympathy* for people, He went a step further. He had *compassion* for the people around Him. He *felt* how they felt. When He looked at people, He felt the burdens they had. He wept over the people of Jerusalem, even when He knew they would turn on Him and kill Him. Do we have that same compassion for the lost?

When the compassion of Jesus takes over the Church of the Lord Jesus Christ, we're not going to walk around with our noses up in the air, looking down at everybody, judging everybody. When we feel His compassion, we will be broken. We will begin to weep. I've driven through cities and found myself just beginning to weep over the lost. Do you weep over the lost?

One man of God told me that he was walking out of a hotel one day with another preacher, and a drunk was walking by them. The preacher he was with looked at the drunk, shook his head, and said: "That's just terrible, just sick."

The man of God turned to him and said: "That would be you and me without Jesus."

Religion looks at those who are lost, dying, and caught in the clutches of sin and turns up its nose with a "holier than thou" attitude. Religion wants to condemn. But Jesus never condemns. Jesus comes with compassion to forgive and heal and deliver.

But when he saw the multitudes, he was moved with compassion on them, because they fainted, and were scattered abroad, as sheep having no shepherd.

MATTHEW 9:36

Sympathy says, "I know how you feel," but sits and does not lift a hand to do a thing. Compassion says, "I feel exactly how you feel," and then compassion acts. Remember that: *Sympathy sits. Compassion acts.*

In Matthew 14:14, *"Jesus went forth, and saw a great multitude, and was moved with compassion toward them, and he healed their sick."* He didn't just say, "Oh, look at all these sick people. It's just terrible how things are in the world, but there's nothing you can do about it." No. He acted. He moved out. He began to heal the sick and cast out devils.

> Then Jesus called his disciples unto him, and said, I have compassion on the multitude, because they continue with me now three days, and have nothing to eat: and I will not send them away fasting, lest they faint in the way.
>
> MATTHEW 15:32

These people were with Him for three days, and they weren't staying at the Hilton. So what did Jesus do? Compassion acted. In His compassion, He took a little boy's lunch of a few loaves and fishes, blessed it, multiplied it, and fed the multitude. Look at Matthew 20:30-34:

> And, behold, two blind men sitting by the way side, when they heard that Jesus passed by, cried out, saying, Have mercy on us, O Lord, thou son of David. And the multitude rebuked them, because they should hold their peace: but they cried the more, saying, Have mercy on us, O Lord, thou son of David. And Jesus stood still, and called them, and said, What will ye that I should do unto you? They say unto him, Lord, that our eyes may be opened. So Jesus had compassion on them, and touched their eyes: and immediately their eyes received sight, and they followed him.

Now go to Luke 19:41-42:

> And when he come near, he beheld the city [Jerusalem], and wept over it, Saying, If thou hadst known, even thou, at least in this thy day, the things which belong unto thy peace! but now they are hid from thine eyes.

Jesus wept over Jerusalem. He wanted to bring the people close to Him, but they would not come, and He wept. When you see people who are bound by the chains of sin, the compassion of God rises up on the inside of you and breaks your heart, because you know Jesus wants to set them free.

We must extend the compassion Jesus has had for us to others. Since He's set us free, He can set others free. If He broke the chains off us, He can break the chains off others. We need to extend the same mercy to others that He extended towards us. We need to extend the same forgiveness to others that He extended towards us. Let us *never* get religious! Let us never look down on people.

How can we have the compassion that Jesus has? We can only have His compassion as we allow the Holy Spirit to do a work on the inside of us. So many people's hearts are hard and callous toward others. They're never moved by anything they see in the lives of other people. They're only moved when it directly touches them or their family. But Jesus knows exactly how people feel and what they're going through, and He is willing to do something about it.

> For we have not an high priest which cannot be touched with the feeling of our infirmities; but was in all points tempted like as we are, yet without sin.
>
> HEBREWS 4:15

There's nothing that you're going through that Jesus doesn't know about. Have you ever been in a situation or had a problem in your life, and you thought you were the only one in the whole universe to go through that problem? Well, you're not. Thousands upon thousands of people are facing the same situations that you're facing every day.

And who knows better than Jesus himself? Hebrews 4:16 goes on to say that we can come boldly to the throne of grace and we can obtain mercy and find grace to help in the time of need. Why? Because He suffered and He bore the curse for you and me. He knows the weight of sin and the condemnation, which He fought in the Garden of Gethsemane.

The Bible says that He sweat great drops of blood when He was striving against sin. His flesh was not willing to go through with the suffering that He knew He would endure over the next few days. He had to fight the temptation not to go through with it, and He prayed with His whole being as He strove to submit to the will of the Father.

> And being in an agony he prayed more earnestly: and his sweat was as it were great drops of blood falling down to the ground.
>
> LUKE 22:44

Jesus knows exactly what you're facing. He knows every temptation and every fault you're struggling with. He doesn't condemn you or judge you. He is moved with compassion towards you—to heal you, to touch you, to set you free, and to bring deliverance in your life.

And here's the bottom line: it's not like He has to do it in the future. It's already been done! Compassion acted two thousand years ago. All you have to do is to respond to it. You just have to say, "Lord, here I am. I surrender my life to You." Throw your hands up and just say, "Lord, I surrender." That's all it takes. Don't fight it!

When He looked at the woman caught in adultery, He said: "Where are your accusers?" She said: "I don't have any." He said: "Well, I don't condemn you either, so go and sin no more" (John 8:3-11). Just like that!

Peter, thinking he was going to impress Jesus with how spiritual he was, said: "Lord, if somebody wrongs us, how many times must we forgive them in a day? Seven times?" Peter thought Jesus would say, "Peter, calm down, seven's excessive. Three times will be enough, man!" But he underestimated the mercy and compassion that his Master brought. Jesus said: "Look, not seven times, *but seventy times seven!*"

> Then came Peter to him, and said, Lord, how oft shall my brother sin against me, and I forgive him? till seven times? Jesus saith unto him, I say not unto thee, Until seven times: but, Until seventy times seven.
>
> MATTHEW 18:21-22

Do you know how many times that is? Start out in the morning: "I forgive you, I forgive you, I forgive you, I forgive you, I forgive you, I forgive you, I forgive you, I forgive you, I forgive you, I forgive you, I forgive you, I forgive you, I forgive you, I forgive you, I forgive you, I forgive you some more."

Let's have some lunch. "I forgive you. I forgive you. I forgive you. I forgive you. I forgive you. I forgive you."

Time for supper. "I forgive you. I forgive you. I forgive you. I forgive you. I forgive you. Well, it's time to go to sleep. I think I still have a bunch of 'I forgive yous' in reserve." And then the next day you would start all over again!

If Jesus could give us one sentence to tell people of the world today, it would be, "Tell the world I love them and I'm not against them." Jesus would want to tell you, who are reading this book, that He loves you. He's not against you. He's for you. He loves you!

Before the Good Samaritan came and picked up the man who was lying bleeding and dying on the Jericho road, religion and tradition had passed by, and none of them did anything for him. They left him there. But the Good Samaritan came and, having compassion, picked him up, poured in the oil and the wine, and restored his soul.

But he, willing to justify himself, said unto Jesus, And who is my neighbour? And Jesus answering said, A certain man went down from Jerusalem to Jericho, and fell among thieves, which stripped him of his raiment, and wounded him, and departed, leaving him half dead. And by chance there came down a certain priest that way: and when he saw him, he passed by on the other side. And likewise a Levite, when he was at the place, came and looked on him, and passed by on the other side. But a certain Samaritan, as he journeyed, came where he was: and when he saw him, he had compassion on him, And went to him, and bound up his wounds, pouring in oil and wine, and set him on his own beast, and brought him to an inn, and took care of him. And on the morrow when he departed, he took out two pence, and gave them to the host, and said unto him, Take care of him; and whatsoever thou spendest more, when I come again, I will repay thee. Which now of these three, thinkest thou, was neighbour unto him that fell among the thieves? And he said, He that shewed mercy on him. Then said Jesus unto him, Go, and do thou likewise.

LUKE 10:29-37

That's what Jesus wants to do to hurting humanity. His compassion is here, extended towards you. If you're sick in your body, His compassion is extended towards you. If you have pain in your body, His compassion is extended towards you. Maybe you have a broken heart, you've been hurt, you've been bruised, and you've been lying by the highway of life. You've been beaten up by sin. If you've been beaten up by the Church or religious institutions, Jesus has compassion on you.

Jesus is extending His compassion to you right now, to touch the hearts of everyone—men and women, young and old. He is here to bind up the broken heart. He is here to set the captives free. He's come to deliver you from any form of addiction and bondage. Jesus has come to break the chains of sin and death and of hell.

The truth is, until we receive the compassion of Jesus for our own lives and allow Him to save, heal, and deliver us, we won't have a whole lot of compassion towards others. As we let the Holy Spirit move in our hearts and soften our hearts, our hearts will be moved with the compassion of Jesus towards others.

Heal the sick, cleanse the lepers, raise the dead, cast out devils: freely ye have received, freely give.

MATTHEW 10:8

Let Him touch you right now, and then go out and extend His compassion to others who are hurting.

CHAPTER 9

JESUS, THE JOY OF OUR SALVATION

In the end of the sabbath, as it began to dawn toward the first day of the week, came Mary Magdalene and the other Mary to see the sepulchre. And, behold, there was a great earthquake: for the angel of the Lord descended from heaven, and came and rolled back the stone from the door and sat upon it. His countenance was like lightning, and his raiment white as snow: And for fear of him the keepers did shake, and become as dead men. And the angel answered and said unto the woman, Fear not ye: for I know that ye seek Jesus, which was crucified. He is not here: for he is risen, as he said. Come, see the place where the Lord lay. And go quickly, and tell his disciples that he is risen from the dead; and, behold, he goeth before you into Galilee; there shall ye see him: lo, I have told you. And they departed quickly from the sepulchre with fear and great joy; and did run to bring his disciples word.

MATTHEW 28:1-8

When you read this scripture, you may think, *How can you have fear and great joy at the same time?* It's talking about a reverential awe and a fear of God, something that needs to come back in the body of Christ. If you were to see Jesus in all of His glory and all of His splendor, you'd just stand there, your mouth open, not knowing what to say. You would stand in awe of Him because He is so awesome.

When the two women came to the tomb, I imagine they walked slowly up to the sepulchre because their hearts were heavy. When your heart is heavy, you walk slowly, with your head and hands hanging down. They hadn't understood what He had told them. They hadn't understood that He would rise again. The closest friend they'd had for three-and-a-half years was dead, and they were walking up to His grave. They did not know what was about to take place. They had no clue. Had they known it, they would have run to the sepulchre.

But they left differently than they came. The Bible says that they departed quickly. They left with a glad heart and in reverential fear of the awesomeness of the power of God, because they had just witnessed something that nobody had ever seen before. They had just seen a stone being rolled away in an earthquake and the keepers of the tomb fall as dead men. And then the announcement was made: "He is not here."

"What do you mean, He is not here?"

"He's not here. He *was* here, but He's not here now. He does not occupy this space any longer. He is risen. He's not dead. He's alive. He's not sleeping. He's awake. He's risen. Come, let me show you the place where He lay. Now go quickly and tell His disciples. Tell them that He's risen from the dead. *He is risen from the dead!*

"I'm going to go tell Peter and John. I just have to tell somebody! *He's alive!*"

Can you imagine the sadness with which they came to the tomb and then the joy they had when they left? They were totally dumbstruck, completely dumbfounded. There's a saying in England— "gobsmacked,"—which literally means "smacked in the mouth." The Bible says they left with fear and great joy. Oh, hallelujah!

The *Amplified Bible, Classic Edition* says that they left the tomb hastily with fear and great joy and ran to tell the disciples. And what was their message? It was a joyous message. It was a Good News message. And that Gospel message is still being proclaimed. Everyone who comes to God comes through the power of the blood and the resurrection of Jesus Christ. They come into new life, into that same resurrection life made manifest on that resurrection morning. When that new life comes to dwell on the inside of us, we experience the same joy that they experienced on that day.

Even though we weren't there, we are now there by the Holy Ghost, because we are being quickened together in Christ. Two thousand years later that joy is still grabbing hold of us, and we stand in awe of the empty tomb. Then we run with joy to tell the world that He is alive and that He's risen. Hallelujah!

There are people who say: "We don't really have the same joy that they had because they were right there—and we were not." Listen, you were there in the Spirit. When you come to the cross and you surrender your life to Jesus, you realize that you were crucified with Him, that you died with Him, that you were buried with Him, and that you've been raised to a new life in Him.

> I am crucified with Christ: nevertheless I live; yet not I, but Christ liveth in me: and the life which I now live in the flesh I live by the faith of the Son of God, who loved me, and gave himself for me.
>
> GALATIANS 2:20

It gives us great joy that because He lives, I can live also. Because He Lives, death has no dominion over me. Sickness and disease have no dominion over me. Poverty has no dominion over me. Sin has no dominion over me because my life is hid with Christ in God. I can live today because He lives and He reigns. My heart rejoices and no man can take my joy from me (John 16:22)!

> Whom having not seen, ye love; in whom, though now ye see him not, yet believing, ye rejoice with joy unspeakable and full of glory.
>
> 1 PETER 1:8

The reason you and I can have that joy that's unspeakable and full of glory is because of that same resurrection life. That's what is happening in our Holy Ghost meetings—people are coming into contact with the power and the anointing of the Spirit of God. It's that resurrection life coming all over again. It's the same Spirit, who raised Jesus Christ from the dead, who dwells in you.

It's going to quicken your mortal body (Romans 8:11). Have you ever been quickened by the Holy Ghost?

Later on when Jesus walked with the disciples on the road to Emmaus, they didn't even know it was Him (Luke 24:13-33.) And when they discussed it among themselves later, they said: "Didn't our hearts burn within us when He spoke to us?"

Don't our hearts burn within us when He speaks to us? When you meet somebody who's been born-again, who's been washed in the blood of Jesus, who knows what took place at the cross of Calvary, doesn't your heart burn within you? When you look into their eyes and they begin to speak about the joy of their salvation, that same joyful realization of what took place two thousand years ago comes again. That's how the joy of the Good News is communicated.

Some people say, "Well, that joy business is just an emotional experience, and you shouldn't have an experience-based Gospel."

What a bunch of garbage! You mean going up to the tomb was not an experience? You mean when the stone was rolled away, it wasn't an experience? Go talk to the keepers of the tomb. They'll tell you what an experience they had. Only the people who have never had an experience with Jesus want to run down having an experience with Him.

When you seek God's presence as your vital need, He will become real to you, as real as any other person you have met. You meet Him in His Word. When you get a revelation of your salvation and the joy of it manifests in you, I guarantee that you will respond to it, because it is real. You can experience anything that is real. God's love can be manifested through your emotions and so can joy or any other fruit of the Spirit.

Several years ago we were having a conference in Jerusalem. Now, I'm probably one of the least religious people to ever go to the Holy Land, so I told the tour guides not to take me to any of the shrines or any of the churches. Well, that canceled out many of the places you can go!

I did agree to see the Garden Tomb though, one of two sites said to be the tomb of Jesus. The guide at the Garden Tomb was, in his rather religious way, telling us about the resurrection of the Lord Jesus Christ that took place there. He actually got a little excited and even laughed when he announced to everyone that Jesus is risen, the stone was rolled away, and that He is alive.

When we had a break, he looked over at me. He recognized me and said: "You're that preacher who goes around with that joy stuff," and started verbally attacking me ten feet from where the stone was rolled away!

I'm thinking, *Hello? Something's wrong with this picture.*

I said: "Excuse me, sir, did you know that when this stone was rolled away, the people around this tomb fell as dead men? Did you know that when they heard that He was risen, they were filled with joy—and they weren't just smiling. And besides that, you just got through telling me the story, and you even got a little excited for yourself that the stone was rolled away and that He is risen. Yet you attack me for traveling around the world with 'that joy stuff.'"

I can't help it if I get excited about what He did two thousand years ago! It's not just something off the pages of a history book; it's something that is real. He is alive, He is risen, and He's living in my heart. And I can't be quiet!

They can say that we are radical. They can say that we're overboard. But I will not be quiet, because He's alive and He lives on the inside of me. I've got something to shout about. I've got something to rejoice about. He is risen! The stone is rolled away! He's alive forevermore! Hallelujah!

Jesus, the joy of my salvation. It's not, "Jesus, the depression of my salvation." It's not, "Jesus, the sadness of my salvation."

If you watch the Easter services in churches all over the world on television, you'd think it was a mass funeral. They stand there, with a sad look on their faces, droning somberly, "And we are so thankful today that He died for us, that He arose again, and that He is Lord." Where's the joy?

The reality of the resurrection is more than just words. It's the joy of our salvation and it's emotional! I guarantee you, a month after the resurrection, those disciples were still excited about it. Somebody said: "Now, don't overdo it. We know that He rose from the dead, but don't get too excited about it. We've heard the story before, but let's be more mature about this thing now."

I want to tell you, this is not something that we "psych" ourselves into. This is not just a temporary emotional high. You can wake me up at two o'clock in the morning and I'll feel the same way. It has nothing to do with emotions gone awry. Jesus has touched me. He's changed me. And I just have to tell somebody!

Have you ever had some good news in the natural, and you couldn't wait to run and tell your friends? They don't know what news you've got and you say, "You won't believe this! You've got to see it! Remember how sad we were because He was dead? Well, He's not dead anymore, buddy! I just came from the tomb!"

Our critics say the Christian walk is not to be based on experience. But I want you to know that the whole of life is experience. When a woman gives birth to a baby, it's an experience. She can't say, "Well, I want to give birth to this baby but I don't want to have an experience. I don't want this birth to be based on experience."

Your whole life is experience. You ride a roller coaster and you have an experience. If you plug your finger into a light socket, you will have an experience. When you get married, you have an experience. Everyone should have the opportunity to experience a mother-in-law! It's an experience. Everything in life is an experience. You go eat at certain restaurants because you like the dining experience.

"What are you going to eat?"

"Ah, it doesn't matter, as long as I eat something. It doesn't really have to be an experience. This restaurant will do—the food's not that good, the decor's terrible, and the service is bad—but I don't really want an experience-based restaurant."

Why do you go back to a certain restaurant? Experience! You go back because the last time you went, you had a good experience.

Jesus is my joy. He's my experience of that joy. Jesus is my life. He's my experience of that life. Jesus is my peace. He's my experience of that peace.

People say: "I want to meet Jesus, but I don't really want to have an experience with Him. I don't want that joy. I don't want that walking and leaping and praising God. I don't want that stomping-on-the-riser stuff. They're just having an experience and I want none of that. I don't want that laughing-in-the-meeting stuff. I just want to listen to the message and have no experience."

Why? So you can leave the revival meeting and tell people that nothing happened? We can experience a roller coaster ride. We can experience a meal. We can experience the pleasure of friends and family. We can experience playing a sport. We can experience all those things. But then we come to church and say we don't want to experience joy because we don't want an experience-based Christianity?

Everything we believe should be based on the Word of God. Our experiences should be in line with the Word of God, but you cannot truly know Jesus without an experience with Him. *You have to have an experience with Him.*

When you have an experience with Jesus, it will result in a joy that is unspeakable and full of glory that will flow out of your innermost being. You will experience such joy that you won't be able to keep quiet about it. If you haven't experienced that, *then you've never met Him,* because Jesus is an experience! When you really experience Him, you will never be the same.

CHAPTER 10

JESUS, OUR RIGHTEOUSNESS

But seek (aim at and strive after) first of all His kingdom and His righteousness (His way of doing and being right), and then all these things taken together will be given you besides.

MATTHEW 6:33 AMPC

Therefore put on God's complete armor, that you may be able to resist and stand your ground on the evil day [of danger], and, having done all [the crisis demands], to stand [firmly in your place]. Stand therefore [hold your ground], having tightened the belt of truth around your loins and having put on the breastplate of integrity and of moral rectitude and right standing with God. And having shod your feet in preparation [to face the enemy with the firm-footed stability, the promptness, and the readiness produced by the good news] of the Gospel of peace. Lift up over all the [covering] shield of saving faith, upon which you can quench all the flaming missiles of the wicked [one]. And take the helmet of salvation and the sword that the Spirit wields, which is the Word of God.

EPHESIANS 6:13-17 AMPC

Do you know what Jesus did for you? One of the biggest problems in the Church is that many Christians don't know exactly what Jesus did for them at Calvary's cross two thousand years ago. They don't realize that Jesus came and took upon Himself the sin of the world that *so you could take upon yourself His righteousness.* Jesus *became* sin so that you and I could *become* righteous.

> For he hath made him to be sin for us, who knew no sin; that we might be made the righteousness of God in him.
>
> 2 CORINTHIANS 5:21

The Word of God tells us in Romans 8:1: *"There is therefore now no condemnation to them which are in Christ Jesus, who walk not after the flesh, but after the Spirit."* So if you're born-again and washed in the blood of Jesus, then there's no condemnation on you. And yet if you look in the Church world, you'll see that people are beating themselves and others up with guilty memories of what they did five, ten, fifteen, and twenty years ago. Some Christians go around with a guilt complex from this condemnation. I want you to know, the Bible says that there's no condemnation if you are in Christ Jesus.

When Jesus comes, He makes you righteous. He comes and points His scepter of righteousness at you and declares that you are righteous. That means that you can now stand in the presence of God without any sense of guilt, inferiority, or condemnation, because Jesus has paid for your sin and God has forgiven you. He's washed you in the blood of Jesus. The Bible says that He will take your sins from you as far as the east is from the west, and He will put them in the sea of forgetfulness.

Since your sins have been removed as far as the east is from the west and put in the sea of forgetfulness, what business do you have bringing them up again and again? In other words, you should not be talking about your past life. Stop talking about the days when you were in the world. They're dead and gone. You're a new person in Christ Jesus.

Sin goes with the sinner. Righteousness goes with the believer. Some people say, "Well, I'm just an old sinner saved by grace." Hold it! Which are you? Are you a sinner or are you saved by grace? Don't combine the two. You're trying to sound humble, but you don't realize you're being foolishly unscriptural. If I'm a child of God, how can I be a sinner?

Jesus came to deal with the sin problem by hanging on the cross for us, by becoming sin for us. *The Church needs to have a revelation of Jesus, our righteousness.*

For too long, the Church has focused on Heaven. "Well, when we get to Heaven there will be victory over sin. We'll be overcomers then. But while we're here, we're just little sinners saved by grace. We're so unworthy."

With that mind-set, we always come to God with guilt, with condemnation, with a feeling of unworthiness. People think that's being holy, but from that teaching comes the attitude that, this side of Heaven, all we can expect is failure, misery, disappointment, and weakness. "Oh, we're just going to struggle through life, and one day Jesus will come and He's going to get us out of this mess. Rodney, pray for me that I can make it another week in my walk with Gawwwd."

But Jesus, your righteousness, has come to you. He's already forgiven you. If you're out of fellowship, then get into fellowship. If there are sins in your life that you've been allowing to stay, then get rid of those. But once you're rid of them, don't keep trying to beat yourself up every week to get yourself back to that place where He's already taken you. He's already forgiven you; He's already made you righteous. You've got to walk in the reality of that.

Being constantly aware of your right-standing with God also helps you resist further sin. When the devil comes with condemnation and follows up with temptation, you say; "Sorry; you're knocking on the wrong door, baby. I'm free from that temptation because I'm no longer a slave to sin! I've been delivered! Sin will no longer have dominion over me, because I'm a child of the Living God. I've been washed in the blood of Jesus. I've been cleansed! He's taken out the stony heart and put in a heart of flesh. I have a new spirit within me! He has made me to be a new creature, I'm a new creature in Christ Jesus!"

Remember what we said about Paul in Chapter 5? Before the apostle Paul was saved, he worked to persecute, imprison, and kill Christians. But he is the one who wrote this to the church at Corinth:

> Therefore if any man be in Christ, he is a new creature: old things are passed away; behold, all things are become new.
>
> 2 CORINTHIANS 5:17

The apostle Paul realized this truth. That's why he told people all the time, "Receive us, we've wronged nobody," even though he had killed Christians for a living before he got saved. He understood that he had been made righteous through Jesus's blood.

> Receive us; we have wronged no man, we have corrupted no man, we have defrauded no man.
>
> 2 CORINTHIANS 7:2

When Jesus hung on the cross, He hung there in my sin. *"God made him who had no sin to be sin for us, so that in him we might become the righteousness of God"* (2 Corinthians 5:21 NIV). Jesus, He who knew no sin, was righteousness personified. He walked across the great divide and came and identified with you and me. He became sin so that we could become righteous.

Jesus took our place. He was our substitute. He became sin. He didn't have to do it, but He did it for you and me. We've been washed in His blood. We've been cleansed by His blood. We've been made whole. We've been set free. We are new creatures. That's why we can now come *boldly* to the throne of grace and obtain mercy and help in time of need. Why? Because He has made a way for us and He's made that way plain.

> Let us therefore come boldly unto the throne of grace, that we may obtain mercy, and find grace to help in time of need.
>
> HEBREWS 4:16

But what happens if we *do* sin? The Bible says if we do sin we have an advocate with the Father, Jesus Christ the righteous (1 John 2:1). That's why John said in 1 John 1:9: *"If we confess our sins, he is faithful and just to forgive us our sins, and to cleanse us from all unrighteousness."* The moment we sin and fall, we should ask Him to forgive us.

You might say, "Well, does that mean I have a license to sin?" No, you don't need a license. You'll sin without one. The verse 1 John 1:9 is not giving people a license to sin. It's giving a license to be righteous. When I love Him and see what He's done for me, I don't want to sin. If I even think about sinning, something rises up in me and says, "No, get that away from me." I don't want to do anything that's going to offend Jesus, that's going to grieve the Lord Jesus Christ, because I love Him so much.

Why do so many people just put up with their sin situation? Coming to church is hard for them when they come slinking in the door expecting to get beat up from the pulpit. They think: *I've been bad this week. Beat me. If the preacher can really beat me, then I'm going to feel condemned and I'm really going to feel sorry for what I did. I'll leave here feeling like something happened in my life.* Do you want to keep living through that whole thing again and again?

Adam knew God intimately. He walked and talked with God. But Adam, after he sinned, hid from God because he was afraid of Him.

Are you that way? If you've done something wrong, do you go to God and say, "Lord, I've done something wrong. Forgive me," or can you not worship like you really want to because you think He just might beat you?

God loves you and wants to forgive you. He's on your side. He's not against you. He wants to pull you to Himself, and say: "Come here, it's all right. There, there, it will be all right." That's what He wants to do. He wants to bless you.

You think He doesn't know what you're going through? He knows exactly what you're going through. Hebrews 4:15 says that Jesus was tempted in every way we are, but yet did not sin.

For we have not an high priest which cannot be touched with the feeling of our infirmities; but was in all points tempted like as we are, yet without sin.

HEBREWS 4:15

In other words, He was tempted every way we are, but He always *decided* not to sin. You have to constantly make decisions not to sin. Temptation comes, you look at it, and you decide. Listen, I leave many a restaurant with great victory because I resist the temptation of the seven-layer chocolate cake. And I feel so good!

Sin comes along, but you resist it. Sin will work in different areas in different people. Sin comes in many packages. Some sins are outward, where everybody can see. But some sins are inward, such as pride, unforgiveness, bitterness, jealousy, and all the hidden sins of the heart. But you make the choice. You have to have the same attitude with every choice you face. Each time you make a decision and say, "No, I won't partake of that because that's of the nature of death, and I'm of the nature of life. That's of darkness. I'm of light. And darkness and light don't mix."

When you realize that you're righteous, you can resist the devil and he will flee from you. "Hey," you say, "what are you doing around my house? You don't belong here. I'm the righteousness of God in Christ Jesus. I don't have anything to do with this sin thing."

Submit yourselves therefore to God. Resist the devil, and he will flee from you.

JAMES 4:7

Jude 24 tells us that He is able to keep us from falling. For too long Christians have gone around saying, "Well, I might fall this week. Rodney, pray for me that I don't fall." They act like mountain climbers who are going to climb a sheer 4,000-foot cliff and say, "Pray for me that I don't fall." You're on your way down already—I can already hear you screaming. Don't climb a mountain if you think that you're going to fall!

Many preachers are running, afraid they're going to fail. They're afraid they're going to fall. I had a preacher friend who was always saying that he didn't want his ministry to grow because he was afraid that if he got to a certain place, he might blow it and cause reproach on the body of Christ.

I said: "So you're really planning to do it, aren't you? You're planning to fall, aren't you? You've been talking about it for years." And the sad thing is that he went on, the ministry grew, and he fell. It was just like he planned it; he strategized his own fall.

But I'm not running the race like I'm going to fall. When you want to run a race, you don't stand at the starting line saying, "I don't want to start because I'm afraid I'll get a hundred yards down the road and fall."

If you run in the race and suddenly you fall, bless God, just get up, dust yourself off, and take off running again. You don't just lie down and cry, "Do you want to come join me at the First Church of the Fallen?"

"How you doing down there?"

"Oh, pray for me. I've fallen, Rodney. Pray for me."

"Well, *get up!* Get on your feet. What are you lying there in the mud for? Get up!"

"But what about all those other times I've fallen?"

There are no other times! You're a new creature in Christ. Jesus will never bring up your past. He will never bring up any failing that you've had. He will never even bring up your shortcomings. Religion will do that to you, but Jesus won't do that to you. He's not going to come and bring up your past faults and your failings because your sins are forgiven.

When we realize that we *are* righteous in Jesus Christ, we realize that we're not slaves to sin anymore. We don't have to dance to sin's tune. We've been set free. We've been delivered. We've been washed in the blood. We've been cleansed. We've been made righteous. Without Him we're a nothing, but thank God, we're in Him. If you can get this, you will walk in victory.

For in him we live, and move, and have our being; as certain also of your own poets have said, For we are also his offspring.

ACTS 17:28

And you, that were sometimes alienated and enemies in your mind by wicked works, yet now hath he reconciled In the body of his flesh through death, to present you holy and unblameable and unreproveable in his sight.

COLOSSIANS 1:21-22

Reconciliation has already been done for you in Christ. You stand complete in Him. Ephesians 5:27 says: *"That he might present it to himself a glorious church, not having spot, or wrinkle, or any such thing; but that it should be holy and without blemish."* You stand righteous and holy in Him!

Now I'm going to share something with you, and if this doesn't cause a reaction, you really need revival! Romans 5:17-19 explains how sin and death came through one man—Adam. Then it explains how sin and death were defeated through one man—Jesus—so that many— that's us—could be made righteous.

If by one man's offence death reigned by one; much more they which receive abundance of grace and of the gift of righteousness shall reign in life by one, Jesus Christ. Therefore as by the offence of one judgment came upon all men to condemnation; even so by the righteousness of one the free gift came upon all men unto justification of life. For as by one man's disobedience many were made sinners, so by the obedience of one shall many be made righteous.

ROMANS 5:17-19

Everybody wants to talk about the fall, about when Adam sinned and sin came into the world, but that's not the end of the story. The Bible says that there is a second Adam and His name is Jesus Christ of Nazareth, Son of the Living God. He sped across time and space, took on human flesh, was obedient even unto death on the cross, paid the price of sin on the cross of Calvary, and spent three days and three nights in the heart of the earth. Then He rose from the dead, and having spoiled principalities and powers, He made a show of them openly, triumphing over them in it.

And having spoiled principalities and powers, he made a shew of them openly, triumphing over them in it.

COLOSSIANS 2:15

Now here's where you and I come in. Jesus took with Him the keys of death and hell and the grave, and He said to us: "I've given you the keys of the kingdom. Whatever you bind on earth shall be bound in Heaven. Whatever you loose on earth shall be loosed in Heaven. Greater is He that is in you than he that is in the world. I've raised you up to sit with Me in heavenly places."

I am Alpha and Omega, the beginning and the ending, saith the Lord, which is, and which was, and which is to come, the Almighty.

REVELATION 1:8

And I will give unto thee the keys of the kingdom of heaven: and whatsoever thou shalt bind on earth shall be bound in heaven: and whatsoever thou shalt loose on earth shall be loosed in heaven.

MATTHEW 16:19

Ye are of God, little children, and have overcome them: because greater is he that is in you, than he that is in the world.

1 JOHN 4:4

And hath raised us up together, and made us sit together in heavenly places in Christ Jesus.

EPHESIANS 2:6

And it's not just in Heaven! Through Jesus, you reign as a king in this life, and if you reign as a king in this life, you have a kingdom, and you as king have dominion over it. Therefore, you have dominion over sin. You have authority over sin because you reign as a king in this life through Jesus Christ.

That's something to get excited about! I'm seated in the heavenly places with Christ Jesus. He's my righteousness. The Gospel comes to the beggar, to the tramp, to the leper, walks down into the ditch full of muck and mire, and pulls him out, washes him, puts a robe and a ring and shoes on him, and says, "This is my friend." That's what Jesus does.

Jesus is your righteousness. It doesn't matter what you've done. It's time to get rid of that old sin consciousness and those old sin rags that you've been draping yourself in, worshipping every day at the altar of sin. It's time to lay that aside, come over into righteousness, and realize what Jesus purchased for you at Calvary's cross. When guilt and condemnation come your way, you resist the enemy and say, "No! That person doesn't live here anymore! Jesus is my righteousness and I'm free! Jesus has set me free!"

CHAPTER 11

JESUS, OUR GREAT PHYSICIAN

The Spirit of the Lord is upon me, because he hath anointed me to preach the Gospel to the poor; he hath sent me to heal the brokenhearted, to preach deliverance to the captives, and recovering of sight to the blind, to set at liberty them that are bruised.

LUKE 4:18

I am the Lord that healeth thee.

EXODUS 15:26

No matter what the need, whether it was provision, forgiveness of sin, or healing of the body, Jesus always met it. And I want you to know that Jesus is the same today. He still heals as readily as He forgives sin. But often when folks accept Him as their Savior, they do not also accept Him as their Healer.

I remember when I first found out that Jesus was my Healer. When I was five years old, I noticed I had a lot of warts on my hands, so I went to my father and said: "Dad, I've got these warts."

He said: "Son, we can pray right now."

My dad prayed with me, and he cursed those warts. Within three or four days, every single one of them dried up and fell off my hands.

Can you imagine the impression that left on a five-year-old? I knew that Jesus healed as a solid fact. I'd seen it.

When I was about thirteen, my pastor and I got into a theological argument about healing. He was telling me that God sometimes put sickness and disease on you to teach you a lesson, and I was telling him, "Pastor, that's not true."

He got kind of angry.

I said, "It's not true, Pastor. My Bible says: *Every good gift and every perfect gift is from above, and cometh down from the Father of lights, with whom is no variableness, neither shadow of turning*" (James 1:17)! He got mad and stormed out of the house.

The next morning I woke up covered in spots—measles. I was shocked. My pastor came around the house to gloat over my sickness. I was sick now, and obviously God was gonna teach me a lesson. He walked to the door and said, "How are the sick and the diseased?"

I said, "Oh, I'm not sick and diseased."

"Yes, you are. You're covered in spots."

"No, Pastor," I said, "these spots are not here for me, they're here for you. The Bible says: *And for this cause God shall send them strong delusion, that they should believe a lie*" (2 Thessalonians 2:11). These spots are for you. I'm healed by the stripes that Jesus bore for me at the cross of Calvary two thousand years ago" (1 Peter 2:24)! Again, he got mad and left.

I went into my room, closed the door, took my Bible and spoke the Word of God out loud. I said, "Jesus, You're my Healer. I don't care what he says. I don't care if he thinks this is on me to teach me a lesson. You're my Healer." The next day the spots were gone. They had disappeared. When he came back that day and looked at me, he said: "What happened to the spots?"

I said, "I told you, they were just there for you."

You have to come to the place where you accept Him as your Healer. People here in America don't have to believe God for their healing because they know they've got the Blue Cross or the Red Cross or some other cross to run to—any "cross" except the cross of Calvary. But what happens if all the healthcare and health insurance fail and the doctors cannot help you?

"Well then, I'll have to start believing God." Is God your last resort? Too often we don't receive Jesus as our Healer all the time, and suddenly we come to a crisis and say, "Oh, I've got to believe God!" Well, if you can't exercise your faith over small illnesses, if you can't exercise your faith over a spider bite or the flu, then what are you going to do when they diagnose you with cancer? Then you're going to go to pieces. "I don't know what I'm gonna do!"

You have to exercise your faith, to build your faith in the fact that Jesus is your Healer. I'm not saying that you mustn't go to doctors or use medicine—there's nothing wrong with that. But they can't heal everything. You have to get it in your heart of hearts that Jesus is your Healer, because in the future, there could be some deadly incurable plague that sweeps through. What are you going to do? You better practice now. You better develop your faith in Jesus as your Healer now.

It's easier to believe God when you're healed and walking in divine health than to wait until you're in a mess and trying to believe God for your healing. You have to get up and tell your body to get in line every day. "Body, you're gonna get in line with the Word of God. Sickness and disease, you have to go. Jesus is my Healer!"

Once when my appendix was giving me tremendous pain, I told the Lord, "I need You to heal it now. I'm here on vacation, trying to rest. I don't have time to mess with this stupid thing, and I'm not going to go run to a doctor so he can stick a knife in me. You are my Doctor, You always have been my Doctor. You're my Healer and always have been. I need help! *I need it right now!*" I spoke God's Word over my body even as I lay there in pain on the bed.

When I woke up after two days of this, the pain was gone. I started weeping and said: "Yes, You always have been my Healer, haven't You?" Where do I go when I'm in trouble? Who do I turn to? Who do I run to? Jesus! Why? He's my Healer!

Far too many people base their faith on what happens to other people, and that's a big problem. "Well, I had an uncle once who believed God, and he died. And Aunt Minnie, she was believing God and she had a stroke. And Uncle Jack, he was believing God and got hit by a bus. So, you see, we shouldn't really believe God."

Listen, you can't go around basing your faith on what happened to Aunt Minnie and Uncle Jack. You've got to base your faith on Jesus. He's the author and the finisher of your faith, not someone else's experience! The Word of God is true! You have to line up with the Word of God. You can't go basing the validity of the Word of God on what happens to me or anyone else.

But we still imagine that there are limits on what God can do.

"Can He forgive sin?"

"Oh, yes."

"Can He forgive murder?"

"Yeah."

"So you're telling me that Jesus can forgive all manner of sin, but there are certain sicknesses that He cannot do anything about? And you'll just have to go see a doctor?"

Hold it. When we repent, He forgives all our sin. He washes us clean, and Jesus put sickness and sin in the same category.

And he entered into a ship, and passed over, and came into His own city. And behold, they brought to him a man sick of the palsy, lying on a bed: and Jesus seeing their faith said unto the sick of the palsy; Son, be of good cheer, thy sins are forgiven thee. And, behold, certain of the scribes said within themselves, This man blasphemeth. And Jesus knowing their thoughts said, Wherefore think ye evil in your hearts? For whether is easier, to say, Thy sins be forgiven thee; or to say, Arise, and walk? But that ye may know that the Son of Man hath power on earth to forgive sins (then saith he to the sick of the palsy,) Arise, take up thy bed and go unto thine house. And he arose, and departed to his house. But when the multitudes saw it, they marvelled, and glorified God, which had given such power unto men.

MATTHEW 9:1-8

Jesus is saying, "I can forgive your sin and I can heal your body. Your sins are forgiven, so take up your bed and walk." Have you ever noticed what Jesus would always say to people when He had healed them? He'd say: "Go and sin no more, lest a worse thing comes on you" (John 5:14, John 8:11).

Why did Jesus *forgive* the man of his sin and then tell him to take up his bed and walk? Why did Jesus repeatedly connect sin to sickness? Because the *root cause* of sickness and disease in the earth is *sin*. Sickness and disease were not a part of the Garden of Eden before Adam sinned. Sickness does not come from Heaven. It comes from the sin nature in man.

Now somebody is bound to say: "Are you trying to tell me that if I get sick then I'm full of sin?" *No!* I never said that. I'm just showing you that sickness has its root in sin, in the sin nature of man.

Of course, there are times when people do get sick because they're in sin. For example, if a person has a lot of unforgiveness and bitterness in their heart, it affects their body. If they have a violent temper and they're angry all the time, that's going to affect their body. The Bible says: *"A merry heart doeth good like a medicine: but a broken spirit drieth the bones"* (Proverbs 17:22). We've got people with broken spirits, and their bones are so dry you can hear them creak.

Because Jesus linked sickness and sin, it's easy for people to get upset, because they think we're saying that if somebody is sick they're in sin. I never said that. Again, I said sin and sickness go hand in hand, and sickness has its roots in sin. If you could get sin totally out of the way, you'd remove sickness completely. Sin and sickness are the foul offspring of the devil.

Jesus says: "I can do it all the same. It's not a problem to me. I'll forgive your sin and heal your body." In our services, we see people come down to the altar in the healing lines and start asking God to forgive them. The moment they repent of their sins, the healing power of God just floods their whole body.

To see the true origin of sickness, we need only look at the ministry of Jesus described in Acts 10:38:

How God anointed Jesus of Nazareth with the Holy Ghost and with power: who went about doing good, healing all that were oppressed of the devil; for God was with him.

Jesus went about healing all those who were oppressed of the devil. So that means sickness is the oppression of the devil. That's what the Bible said! Sickness is not a blessing from Heaven. Sickness is not God trying to teach us a lesson. What happens if you've been sick for forty years? Are you trying to tell me that you're too stupid to learn the lesson that God's trying to teach you? That's theology gone crazy!

Hebrews 13:8 says that Jesus Christ is the same yesterday, today, and forever. That means He hasn't changed! That means if He did it in Bible days, He's going to do it today! If He was a Healer in Matthew, Mark, Luke, and John, then He's a Healer today!

Then Jesus went thence, and departed into the coasts of Tyre and Sidon. And, behold, a woman of Canaan came out of the same coasts and cried unto him, saying, Have mercy on me, oh Lord, thou Son of David; my daughter is grievously vexed with a devil. But he answered her not a word. And his disciples came and besought him, saying, Send her away; for she crieth after us. But he answered and said, I am not sent but unto the lost sheep of the house of Israel. Then came she and worshipped him, saying, Lord, help me. But he answered and said, It is not meet to take the children's bread, and cast it to dogs. And she said, Truth, Lord: yet even the dogs eat of the crumbs which fall from their masters' table. Then Jesus answered and said unto her, O woman, great is thy faith: be it unto thee even as thou wilt. And her daughter was made whole from that very hour.

MATTHEW 15:21-28

Don't get distracted by Jesus comparing the Canaanites, who were long-time enemies of the Jews, to dogs. What you have to realize is that He said that healing is the children's bread! It's our birthright! It's not something that we have to beg for. Just as your children have the right to eat the food on your table, healing is your birthright from your heavenly Father! Healing belongs to us simply because we're in the family of God. We can come, sit down at the table of our Father, and we can eat the bread of healing.

Why did Jesus heal the sick? I'm going to give you five reasons why He healed the sick.

The first reason Jesus healed the sick was that it was promised in the Word of God. Jesus was fulfilling the Word of His Father.

> When the even was come, they brought unto him many that were possessed with devils: and he cast out the spirits with his word, and healed all that were sick: That it might be fulfilled which was spoken by Esaias the prophet, saving, Himself took our infirmities, and bare our sicknesses.
>
> MATTHEW 8:16-17

> Fear not; for thou shalt not be ashamed: neither be thou confounded; for thou shalt not be put to shame: for thou shalt forget the shame of thy youth, and shalt not remember the reproach of thy widowhood any more. For thy Maker is thine husband; the LORD of hosts is his name; and thy Redeemer the Holy One of Israel The God of the whole earth shall he be called.
>
> ISAIAH 54:4-5

Second, Jesus healed the sick in order to reveal His will. We saw this in Mark 1:40-42. He was willing!

> And there came a leper to him, beseeching him, and kneeling down to him, and saying unto him, If thou wilt, thou canst make me clean. And Jesus, moved with compassion, put forth his hand, and touched him, and saith unto him, I will; be thou clean. And as soon as be had spoken, immediately the leprosy departed from him, and he was cleansed.
>
> MARK 1:40-42

Jesus never turned down anyone who asked Him for healing—even the Syrophenician woman. Jesus delivered her daughter because of her persistent faith.

Third, He healed the sick to manifest the works of God.

Jesus answered, Neither bath this man sinned, nor his parents: but that the works of God should be made manifest.

JOHN 9:3

Fourth, Jesus healed the sick because of His compassion.

And Jesus went forth, and saw a great multitude, and was moved with compassion toward them, and he healed their sick.

MATTHEW 14:14

And, behold, two blind men sitting by the way side, when they heard that Jesus, passed by, cried out, saying, Have mercy on us, 0 Lord, thou son of David. And the multitude rebuked them, because they should hold their peace: but they cried the more, saying, Have mercy on us, 0 Lord, thou son of David. And Jesus stood still, and called them, and said, What will ye that I shall do unto you? They say unto him, Lord, that our eyes may be opened. So Jesus had compassion on them, and touched their eyes: and immediately their eyes received sight, and they followed him.

MATTHEW 20:30-34

Now when he came nigh to the gate of the city, behold, there was a dead man carried out, the only son of his mother, and she was a widow: and much people of the city was with her. And when the Lord saw her, he had compassion on her, and said unto her, Weep not. And he came and touched the bier: and they that bare him stood still. And he said, Young man, I say unto thee, Arise. And he that was dead sat up, and began to speak. And he delivered him to his mother.

LUKE 7:12-15

And Jesus went about all the cities and villages, teaching in their synagogues, and, preaching the Gospel of the kingdom, and healing every sickness and every disease among the people. But when he saw the multitudes, he was moved with compassion on them, because they fainted, and were scattered abroad, as sheep having no shepherd.

MATTHEW 9:35-36

And fifth, He healed people because of their faith. The centurion in Matthew 8:5-13 said: *"Lord, You don't have to go anywhere, just speak the Word and my servant will be healed."* Jesus marveled at the faith of this man who was not even an Israelite and declared that his servant was healed according to what he believed.

In Mark 5:25-34, the woman who had the issue of blood believed she would receive her healing if she could only touch Jesus's garment. Jesus did not notice her touching His garment until He felt the anointing flowing out of Him into her, drawn out by her faith. Jesus told her that it was her faith that had made her whole.

Is healing always the will of God?

And it came to pass, when he was in a certain city, behold a man full of leprosy: who seeing Jesus fell on his face, and besought him, saying, Lord, if thou wilt, thou canst make me clean. And he put forth his hand, and touched him, saying, I will: be thou clean. And immediately the leprosy departed from him.

LUKE 5:12-13

Many people in the religious world pray "Lord, if it be Thy will, heal Sister Bucketmouth. Lord, if it be Thy will, heal Brother Doodad." But we know from God's Word that healing is the will of God. We need to settle this issue in our hearts.

Yet some folks say, "If healing is God's will, why doesn't everybody get healed?" That's like saying, "Why doesn't everybody get saved?" Are we going to throw out salvation because not everybody gets saved? Even though people turn down salvation, it's not going to stop me from preaching salvation. Even though people might turn down healing, it's not going to stop me from preaching healing! Salvation and healing are set in the Gospel! They have been paid for and purchased by the blood of Jesus and by the stripes He bore at Calvary!

"I don't understand why some people receive their healing and some don't, Rodney." Well, there are a lot of things that we don't understand,

JESUS

and every case is different. There are reasons why you don't always see instantaneous miracles, but I'm not going to debate why one person is healed instantly and the next one isn't. That is an issue between them and God. I'm going to go for it like God *will* heal everybody every single time that we pray for them. If I didn't believe that, I would never pray for the sick. We have to remember that God's Word is true, regardless of our personal experience.

"Well, what happens if we pray and they die?" If they're born-again, they will go to heaven. Death for the child of God is not a problem. For the child of God, death is a blessing. The only ones who have a problem with death are the ones who are left behind. But if they are believers and the person who died is a believer, we do not mourn as those who have no hope. We know we will be together for eternity.

> But I would not have you to be ignorant, brethren, concerning them which are asleep, that ye sorrow not, even as others which have no hope.
>
> 1 THESSALONIANS 4:13

Is healing God's will? There are several phrases that I want you to note from the ministry of Jesus.

He healed all that were sick.

> When the even was come, they brought unto him many that were possessed with devils: and he cast out the spirits with his word, and healed all that were sick.
>
> MATTHEW 8:16

He healed them all.

> But when Jesus knew it, he withdrew himself from thence: and great multitudes followed him, and he healed them all.
>
> MATTHEW 12:15

He healed their sick.

> And Jesus went forth, and saw a great multitude, and was moved with compassion toward them, and he healed their sick.
>
> MATTHEW 14:14

As many as touched Him were made perfectly whole.

And besought him that they might only touch the hem of his garment: and as many as touched were made perfectly whole.

MATTHEW 14:36

Even though when Jesus went to Nazareth, He could do no *mighty* work because of their *unbelief,* He still healed some people. In other places He usually healed every single sick person in the place.

And Jesus went about all Galilee, teaching in their synagogues, and preaching the Gospel of the kingdom, and healing all manner of sickness and all manner of disease among the people. And his fame went throughout all Syria; and they brought unto him all sick people that were taken with divers diseases and torments, and those which were possessed with devils, and those that were lunatic, and those that had the palsy; and he healed them.

MATTHEW 4:23-24

When the even was come, they brought unto him many that were possessed with devils: and he cast out the spirits with his word, and he healed all that were sick.

MATTHEW 8:16

But when Jesus knew it, he withdrew himself from thence; and great multitudes followed him, and he healed them all.

MATTHEW 12:15

In Nazareth, Jesus healed a few sick people of minor ailments, but could do no mighty miracles because of their unbelief in other places, mentioned above. He healed and delivered *everyone* who came to Him. What was the difference? It was not Jesus—He is the same yesterday, today, and forever. The difference between miracles and no miracles was the faith—or unbelief—of the *people.* So which do you want to believe God for?

I believe for God to heal *everybody.* If I didn't believe that, I wouldn't preach. I believe that the day is coming soon when people will come into the presence of God crippled, broken, bruised, tattered and torn, and *every single one will be healed*. Every single sinner in the house will get saved. Every single backslider in the house will come back to God. And everyone who is possessed or tormented by demons will be gloriously set free.

Need more? Look at Matthew 14:14:

Jesus went forth, and saw a great multitude, and was moved with compassion towards them, and he healed their sick.

And how about Matthew 14:34-36?

And when they were gone over, they came into the land of Gennesaret. And when the men of that place had knowledge of him, they sent out into all that country round about, and brought unto him all that were diseased; And besought him that they might only touch the hem of his garment: and as many as touched him were made perfectly whole.

I didn't write this, Matthew did! Now look a little farther at Matthew 15:30-31:

And great multitudes came unto him, having with them those that were lame, blind, dumb, maimed, and many others, and cast them down at Jesus's feet; and he healed them: Insomuch that the multitude wondered, when they saw the dumb to speak, the maimed to be whole, the lame to walk, and the blind to see. and they glorified the God of Israel.

Now, proceed to Matthew 19:2:

And great multitudes followed him; and he healed them there.

Go to Matthew 21:14:

And the blind and the lame came to him in the temple; and he healed them.

Here's the bottom line for healing. You have to believe the truth of the Word of God and hide it in your heart. You must have your faith built in God and established in the Lord Jesus Christ as your Healer.

> Those who trust in the Lord are like Mount Zion, which cannot be shaken but endures forever. As the mountains surround Jerusalem, so the Lord surrounds his people both now and forevermore.
>
> PSALM 125:1-2 NIV

You've got to get it into your heart, "Jesus is my Healer." Even if those are the last words out of your mouth on your deathbed, it's better to go saying, "Jesus is my Healer," than just capitulating and going out filled with doubt and unbelief, saying, "Maybe He's not my Healer." You don't know that you won't be raised up from your so-called deathbed because you would not give up on God's promises.

"Okay," you say. "Jesus healed back then, and it's wonderful that He wants to heal today. It's also wonderful that He's the Great Physician, but how in the world does this relate to me?"

Friend, that's where you've got to grab hold of what I'm saying and realize that the Bible is not talking to anybody else. *God is talking to you.* His Word is for you. Are you born-again? Are you washed in the blood? Is Jesus your Lord and Savior? Then healing is yours. Healing belongs to you. Healing is the children's bread, and you are God's child. Healing belongs to you! It's *yours*. It's your birthright. It's not something you have to pay for. It's not something you have to beg for. *It's yours.* You have a new physician today—Jesus, M.D.

Maybe you have already been healed, but you wonder, "How can I walk in God's healing power all the time?" This is an easy one; start praying for the sick. When you pray for the sick, you activate God's healing power in your own life, and it becomes a living reality to you.

Make a point of finding somebody who's sick and lay hands on them. God's healing power, the same healing power that went through you to them, will start quickening your mortal body and become a living reality on the inside of you. I guarantee that if you make this a way of life, you will walk in the revelation that you are healed and Jesus is your Healer.

CHAPTER 12

JESUS, OUR PROTECTOR

He who dwells in the secret place of the Most High shall remain stable and fixed under the shadow of the Almighty [Whose power no foe can withstand]. I will say of the Lord, He is my Refuge and my Fortress, my God," on Him I lean and rely, and in Him I [confidently] trust! For [then] He will deliver you from the snare of the fowler and from the deadly pestilence. [Then] He will cover you with His pinions, and under His wings shall you trust and find refuge; His truth and His faithfulness are a shield and a buckler. You shall not be afraid of the terror of the night, nor of the arrow (the evil plots and slanders of the wicked) that flies by day, Nor of the pestilence that stalks in darkness, nor of the destruction and sudden death that surprise and lay waste at noonday. A thousand may fall at your side, and ten thousand at your right hand, but it shall not come near you. Only a spectator shall you be [yourself inaccessible in the secret place of the Most High] as you witness the reward of the wicked. Because you have made the Lord your refuge, and the Most High your dwelling place, There shall no evil befall you, not any plague or calamity come near your tent. For He will give His angels [especial] charge over you to accompany and defend and preserve you in all your ways [of obedience and service].

They shall bear you up on their hands, lest you dash your foot against a stone. You shall tread upon the lion and adder; the young lion and the serpent shall you trample underfoot. Because he has set his love upon Me, therefore will I deliver him; I will set him on high, because he knows and understands My name [has a personal knowledge of My mercy, love, and kindness — trusts and relies on Me, knowing I will never forsake him, no, never]. He shall call upon Me, and I will answer him; I will be with him in trouble, I will deliver him and honor him. With long life will I satisfy him and show him My salvation.

PSALM 91:1-16 AMPC

The Bible tells us that in the last days men's hearts will fail them for fear of the things that are going to come upon the earth. People are afraid of a lot of things. Some are afraid to get on an airplane. Some are afraid of the dark. Others are afraid of driving in the city. Fears grip the hearts of many of God's people for various reasons.

Men's hearts failing them for fear, and for looking after those things which are coming on the earth: for the powers of heaven shall be shaken.

LUKE 21:26

God, however, doesn't want His people fearful. God wants His people faithful. But you can't be faithful when you're fearful. We learned in an earlier chapter that the word "salvation" comes from the Greek word *sozo*, which means soundness, wholeness, healing, preservation, deliverance, provision, and *protection*. Jesus is not only our Savior, He's our protector. He's our all in all.

Jesus is your hiding place. He's your shelter in the time of storm. It doesn't matter where you are or what conditions of life surround you. You could be in the inner city in the middle of a drive-by shooting. You could be where bombs are going off or where planes are crashing. It doesn't matter—He's there to protect you and to shield you.

There's no more powerful description of God's protection than Psalm 91. As we just read in the *Amplified Bible, Classic Edition,* verse 1 says, Jesus, Our Protector: *"He who dwells in the secret place of the Most High shall remain stable and fixed under the shadow of the Almighty. [Whose power no foe can withstand]."* You must realize that God is all-powerful. There is no other power greater than Him. You need to focus on His power and His ability to protect you, rather than those things that cause fear to rise up in you.

Now if you don't have these truths firmly fixed and established in your heart, you will live in fear. You'll drive down the road at night, and you'll be afraid. You won't even be able to go out. When you get on an airplane, you'll be sitting there holding onto the seat, your knuckles white. Have you been afraid of something recently? You need a revelation of Psalm 91! Fear comes knocking on every door. It even has the nerve to call on me! But God wants you to get to the place where you've become stable and your heart is fixed on the fact that He is your protector and no foe can withstand Him.

There's no enemy big enough to prevail over Almighty God. So guess where I'm going to hide? Psalm 20:7 says: *"That some trust in chariots, and some trust in horses, but we will remember the name of our God."* Proverbs 18:10 says: *"The name of the Lord is a strong tower: the righteous runneth into it, and is safe."*

When this becomes a revelation to you, you're going to be believing differently and speaking differently. Psalm 91:2 in the *Amplified Bible, Classic Edition*, says: *"I will say of the Lord, He is my Refuge..."* When trouble comes, you will find out what a person believes, because it will come out of their mouth. When some people get into a crisis situation in an airliner, for instance, the first thing they say is, "Awwww, we're going to die!"

But when I get in an airplane, bless God, I don't care if there is a bomb on board. I know there will be ten angels holding that bomb, so it cannot go off until we've landed and deplaned. I believe that with all my heart. God is our protector. *"I will say of the Lord, He is my refuge, my fortress, my God, on Him I lean and rely and in Him I confidently trust."* This is our confidence; this is our hope. He will deliver us.

When you say that He is your refuge, your protector, that's when you stand still and you see the salvation and deliverance of God. You don't have to lie awake at night worrying about your family members. His hand is upon your family. He will protect them. He will protect their rising up and their lying down, their coming in and their going out.

You won't have to pray, "Lord, please give us blessing on this journey." I'm not saying you shouldn't; I'm saying you won't *have* to pray it when you say it. You'll just say, "He's my refuge and my fortress." You acknowledge Him because you know He's right there in the automobile with you. He's right there in the plane with you. He's right there when you get up. He's right there when you lie down. He's right there when you come in and go out. He's your refuge, your strong tower, your fortress, your shield, your protector, your bomb shelter.

In addition, *"He will deliver you from the snare of the fowler and from the deadly pestilence"* (v. 3). All around the world there's turmoil and wars and rumors of wars, men against men and nation against nation. But as believers, as those who are washed in the blood of the Lamb, with Jesus on our side, we'll just see it. It's not going to come near us, for He is there to protect us. And when the enemy comes against us, there's that wall of fire about us.

Remember the exodus? When the children of Israel left Egypt, God gave them a pillar of cloud by day and a pillar of fire by night. But when they got to the edge of the sea and Pharaoh started coming behind them, the fire of God went between the children of Israel and the enemy so they couldn't get near them. He's still our pillar of fire today!

Then it says in Psalm 91:4 (AMPC): *"He will cover you with His pinions, and under His wings shall you find trust and refuge; His truth and His faithfulness are a shield and a buckler."* This is not a tiny shield, it's a *giant* shield covering you. The enemy can't even find you. All he sees is God's shield.

That's why verse 5 says: *"You shall not be afraid of the terror of the night, nor of the arrow (the evil plots and slanders of the wicked) that flies by day."* Don't be afraid today. He's with you. I don't care if you've been threatened. Don't be afraid. Do not walk in fear, but lift up your head. Keep your eye on Him. He's your protector.

Neither should we be afraid of the *"pestilence that stalks in darkness"* (v. 6). Some people are afraid of every germ and all kinds of diseases. They can't even enjoy eating at a restaurant. I'm not afraid of disease or sickness, because He is my protector.

"A thousand may fall at your side, and ten thousand at your right hand, but it shall not come near you" (v. 7). In Rhodesia, during the long civil war before that country became Zimbabwe, a group of Rhodesian missionaries saw this scripture come true. A rebel military force had been killing white people on the farms all over the area, and this group of missionaries saw a large number of heavily armed soldiers coming toward them. They knew their lives were in grave danger. So these Rhodesian missionaries got down on their knees and began to pray, to call out to the name of the Lord as their protector.

Something phenomenal took place. When they looked out the window, they saw the rebel army soldiers fleeing in terror. Men armed with guns and hand grenades were fleeing, running as fast as they could. When they were captured later, they were asked why they ran.

They said: "Well, we thought that there were just a few people staying in the farm house. But as we came toward the house to capture it, we saw this whole army dressed in white surrounding the house, and we were so afraid that we took off running."

Those missionaries saw Psalm 91 come true. *"A thousand may fall at your side, and ten thousand at your right hand, but it shall not come near you"* (v. 7). It will not come near you, either!

You will only be a spectator to catastrophe. Why? Psalm 91:8 (AMPC) says: *"Only a spectator shall you be [yourself inaccessible in the secret place of the Most High] as you witness the reward of the wicked."* The enemy's trying to get you, but he can't find you. He's looking but you're caught up in that mist, that cloud, that fog of the glory of God.

That verse goes on to say: *"As you witness the reward of the wicked."* I'll tell you right now that things are going to escalate! There are going to be horrors in these final hours that we've never ever witnessed. The hurricanes, earthquakes, famines, and wars and rumors of wars are not going to get better. I want you to understand that. I'm not telling you that everything's going to get better and everything's to be wonderful. In the world, it's only going to get worse.

Nation will rise up against nation. We'll see diseases, the likes of which have never been heard before, as terrorist nations use chemical and biological warfare. They could drop a certain type of bomb right now on a city and kill everybody there without spoiling the cars, the houses, or anything else. That's the kind of thing that will be experienced in these last days.

And I want you to know, if you don't know how to trust God as your protector in these last days, I don't know how you and your family are going to make it. I don't want to frighten anybody, but you don't have to be a rocket scientist to see these things coming. However, if He's your shield and your protection, then that changes things a little bit, doesn't it! Bullets fired at point blank range are not going to hit their target because there's a giant angel standing with his finger stuck up the barrel. Don't believe it? Well then, get ready for the bullet. But I believe it.

For this to work in your life, you've got to take God's Word for it. You've got to accept it, believe it, and hide it in your heart. You've got to stand upon the Word of God. You've got to activate the Word of God in your life.

It's a cause and effect relationship that you can see in Psalm 91:9-10 (AMPC):

> Because you have made the Lord your refuge, and the Most High your dwelling place, There shall no evil befall you, nor any plague or calamity come near your tent.

These verses mean that you can sleep at night in total peace because He's there with you. We've heard testimonies from farmers who have been faithful to obey God, and when a freeze came, everybody else's farm froze up, but their farm didn't. Why? Because Jesus was their pro-tector. Do you know how many times I've heard testimonies of people, who love God with all their heart, who have a terrible car wreck and get out without one scratch on them? They should have been dead, but He was their protector.

Why will no evil nor any plague or calamity come near your tent? We've got angels looking after us, and I'm not talking about little babies with big diapers and a bow and arrow! I'm talking about ten- or twelve-foot angelic beings. Your enemies will be running around in total confusion when the angel of God encamps about you.

> For it is written, He will give His angels charge over you to guard and watch over you closely and carefully.
>
> LUKE 4:10 AMPC

> Are they not all ministering spirits, sent forth to minister for them who shall be heirs of salvation?
>
> HEBREWS 1:14

Angels are out there working on your behalf. They're all ministering spirits sent forth to minister to those of us who are heirs of salvation. If you're an heir of salvation, then the angels of God have been sent forth to minister for you and in your behalf. They are protecting you. They're working in your behalf. They're going ahead of you to make the crooked way straight. They're going ahead of you to give you the supernatural, divine favor of God.

> And when the servant of the man of God was risen early, and gone forth, behold, an host compassed the city both with horses and chariots. And his servant said unto him, Alas, my master! how shall we do? And he answered, Fear not: for they that be with us are more than they that be with them. And Elisha prayed, and said, LORD, I pray thee, open his eyes, that he may see. And the LORD opened the eyes of the young man; and he saw: and, behold, the mountain was full of horses and chariots of fire round about Elisha.
>
> 2 KINGS 6:15-17

It doesn't matter what or who comes against you to destroy you if you trust God's Word. A whole army of the enemy is no match for the army of angels that surrounds you to protect you! You cannot see them (unless God supernaturally opens your eyes), but they are there nonetheless.

> And there were four leprous men at the entering in of the gate: and they said one to another, Why sit we here until we die? If we say, We will enter into the city, then the famine is in the city, and we shall die there: and if we sit still here, we die also. Now therefore come, and let us fall unto the host of the Syrians: if they save us alive, we shall live; and if they kill us, we shall but die. And they rose up in the twilight, to go unto the camp of the Syrians." and when they were come to the uttermost part of the camp of Syria, behold, there was no man there. For the Lord had made the host of the Syrians to hear a noise of chariots, and a noise of horses, even the noise of a great host." and they said one to another, Lo, the king of Israel hath hired against us the kings of the Hittites, and the kings of the Egyptians, to come upon us. Wherefore they arose and fled in the twilight, and left their tents, and their horses, and their asses, even the camp as it was, and fled for their life.
>
> 2 KINGS 7:3-7

When God is on your side, armies will flee in terror before you. It doesn't make sense in the natural, but it is a reality. This is not going to happen for you if you do not believe God's Word. You must put your faith and trust in God's Word, and angels will work on your behalf.

Notice the last part of verse 11 in the *Amplified Bible, Classic Edition.* They will *"defend and preserve you in all your ways [of obedience and service]."* That's why you want to make sure that you're obeying Him and serving Him. The angels of the Lord are there, but they cannot defend you in your ways of disobedience. You can't be smoking crack and asking your angel to play lookout! Make sure that you're obeying God. Make sure that you're doing everything you know how to do to walk in the plan and the purpose of God for your life. When you obey God, the enemy cannot touch you, because the hand of God is upon your life.

This is crucial: *God's protection is in His presence.* You must stay in His presence in order to be under His protection. Sin removes you from His presence and His protection.

Now look to the next verses, Psalm 91:12-14 (AMPC):

> They shall bear you up on their hands, lest you dash your foot against a stone. You shall tread upon the lion and adder; the young lion and the serpent shall you trample underfoot. Because he has set his love upon Me, therefore, I will deliver him; I will set him on high, because he knows and understands My name [has a personal knowledge of My mercy, love, and kindness — trusts and relies on Me, knowing I will never forsake him, no, never].

God is with you constantly. He's with you in the dark hours, when the circumstances look bleak, when the storms rise up against you. When the wind's blowing and it looks like you're going down, He's there in the boat with you. "I'll never leave you nor forsake you," Jesus says.

> Let your conversation be without covetousness; and be content with such things as ye have: for he hath said, I will never leave thee, nor forsake thee.
>
> HEBREWS 13:5

Now, look at Psalm 91:15: *"He will call upon Me, and I will answer him; I will be with him in trouble, I will deliver him and honor him."* He's waiting for you to call on Him. Some people don't want to call on God because they're afraid to bother Him. They think that He's too busy. But you're not bothering Him. He wants you to bother Him! You have not because you ask not. Call unto Him!

> Ye lust, and have not: ye kill, and desire to have, and cannot obtain: ye fight and war, yet ye have not, because ye ask not.
>
> JAMES 4:2

Call unto me, and I will answer thee, and show thee great and mighty things, which thou knowest not.

JEREMIAH 33:3

And it shall come to pass, that before they call, I will answer; and while they are yet speaking, I will hear.

ISAIAH 65:24

I pray this word goes right into your heart and burns like a Holy Ghost firebrand on the inside of you!

Jesus is your shelter in the time of trouble. The Bible doesn't say you won't have any trouble, but God says: "I will be with you in trouble." He wants to remind you that while you're in trouble, He's there. Call upon Him. You could get into trouble and die, not knowing or else forgetting that He's right there with you. So call to Him. Cry out to Him.

If you find yourself in a problem and you call on the Lord and He doesn't deliver you, you come and tell me, and I'll quit the ministry and come and join you. That's a strong statement, but I want you to know that when you call out to Him with all of your heart, He's going to come. He didn't bring you this far to leave you. *"I will deliver him and honor him"* (v. 15). He not only wants to deliver you, He wants to honor you!

Look at the last verse: *"With long life I will satisfy him and show him My salvation."* They put preservatives in most of the that food we eat. In fact, I heard that a favorite snack of ours has a shelf life of twenty-seven years. If you want something to last long, you must preserve it. God says I will give you long life. That means He is going to preserve you.

"With long life, will I satisfy him and show him My salvation" (v. 16). There are people who have this passage of Scripture printed on a T-shirt, printed on a book mark, or printed on a wall hanging—yet they die young. They never experience the reality of this passage because they've never come to the place where they've said: "Yes, Jesus is my Savior, He's my Healer, He's my Deliverer, and He's also my Protector. He is my Shelter. He is my Rock. He's my Tower. He's my Wall of Fire."

They've never received it. They've never taken this word and made it personal and acted upon it and told it to their wife and told it to their children and told it to their loved ones. Have you?

God might be requiring you to do certain things that mean stepping out of your comfort zone, stepping out beyond the natural, carnal mind and into a place where you must confront your fear. That brings us to the life of Joshua, because if there was ever an individual who should have been afraid, it was Joshua.

Joshua was second in command to Moses, leading the children of Israel to the promised land. Then Moses died, and God told Joshua, "I want you to take his place." I don't know about you, but if that were me, my knees would be having close fellowship one with the other!

"Moses is dead, and I must take his place. God, are You sure?" Joshua was having the same argument with God that Moses had right at the beginning. When God called Moses, he was afraid that the Israelites wouldn't accept his authority, so he said: "Who must I say sent me?"

God said: "Tell them I AM sent you."

Now God was coming to Joshua to tell him, "I'm the same I AM with you as I AM with Moses." God is coming to us, by the power of His Word, saying, "I AM THAT I AM. I AM. As I was with Moses, as I was with Joshua, so I AM with you." It's not something that you've got to try to get. It's already yours. Just walk in it.

Now look at God's promise to Joshua in Joshua 1:5: *There shall not any man be able to stand before thee all the days of thy life: as I was with Moses, so I will be with thee: I will not fail thee, nor forsake thee.*" How can you be afraid of anybody when God is your Protector? No one's going to be able to stand against you, because God will not fail you.

Many times people say, "I know Jesus is my protector and I shouldn't be afraid, but you don't know my circumstances." No, you may know your circumstances, but you don't know God's promises like you say you do. If you really knew Jesus as your protector, you wouldn't go to pieces, working on your next nervous breakdown.

Can't you see Joshua getting braver and braver as God tells him:

There shall not any man be able to stand before thee all the days of thy life: as I was with Moses, so I will be with thee: I will not fail thee, nor forsake thee. Be strong and of a good courage: for unto this people shalt thou divide for an inheritance the land, which I sware unto their fathers to give them. Only be thou strong and very courageous, that thou mayest observe to do according to all the law, which Moses my servant commanded thee: turn not from it to the right hand or to the left, that thou mayest prosper whithersoever thou goest.

JOSHUA 1:5-7

It takes courage, but when you put your eyes on Jesus, keep them on Him and don't look to the left or to the right, you're going to be blessed in every area of your life—blessed coming in, blessed going out, blessed in the city, blessed in the field, blessed rising up, blessed lying down, blessed, blessed, blessed, blessed.

Joshua 1:8 says: *"This book of the law shall not depart out of thy mouth; but thou shalt meditate therein day and night."* This is the secret to success: meditating continually on God's Word, speaking it and thinking it constantly. Do that with Psalm 91: "I will say of the Lord, He's my refuge." Take these scriptures and carry them around with you and think about them.

Meditate on the Word of God. To meditate on the Word of God, you learn it and you talk about it with your family. "He's our strong tower. He's our refuge. He's our fortress." You're excited about it, so you talk about it.

When you meditate that way, and when you speak that way, the Bible says that you're going to make your way prosperous, and you're going to have good success. *"Be strong,"* He said: *"and of a good courage; be not afraid; neither be thou dismayed: for the Lord thy God is with thee whithersoever thou goest"* (v. 9). He is also with you!

Jesus is your Protector.

CHAPTER 13

JESUS, OUR PROVIDER

The thief comes only in order to steal and kill and destroy. I came that they might have and enjoy life, and have it in abundance (to the full, till it overflows). I am the Good Shepherd. The Good Shepherd risks and lays down His [own] life for the sheep.

JOHN 10:10-11 AMPC

God knows what you need. He knows everything about you. He knows when you're rising up and when you're lying down, when you're coming in and when you're going out. He knows your dreams and your desires. But most important, He wants to meet your needs. He wants to see the dreams and desires that He's placed in your heart fulfilled.

Jesus said that He came to give us abundant life, but most Christians are having just-getting-by life. How does that happen?

People in the Church accept Jesus as their Savior, and some in the Church accept Him as their Healer, but they often have a hard time accepting Him as their Provider. What's more, some of us accept Him as our Provider but we don't accept Him as our Provider *in every area of our lives*. When we not only accept Jesus as our Savior and Healer, but also our Provider, we're expecting His provision every day. We're believing Him to care for our every need.

Therefore I say unto you, Take no thought for your life, what ye shall eat, or what ye shall drink; nor yet for your body, what ye shall put on. Is not the life more than meat, and the body than raiment? Behold the fowls of the air: for they sow not, neither do they reap, nor gather into barns; yet your heavenly Father feedeth them. Are ye not much better than they? Which of you by taking thought can add one cubit unto his stature? And why take ye thought for raiment? Consider the lilies of the field, how they grow; they toil not, neither do they spin: And yet I say unto you, That even Solomon in all his glory was not arrayed like one of these. Wherefore, if God so clothe the grass of the field, which to day is, and tomorrow is cast into the oven, shall he not much more clothe you, O ye of little faith? Therefore take no thought, saying, What shall we eat? or, What shall we drink? or, Where withal shall we be clothed? (For after all these things do the Gentiles seek:) for your heavenly Father knoweth that ye have need of all these things. But seek ye first the kingdom of God, and his righteousness; and all these things shall be added unto you. Take therefore no thought for the morrow: for the morrow shall take thought for the things of itself; Sufficient unto the day is the evil thereof.

MATTHEW 6:25-34

According to Jesus, we should not even be thinking about our food, drink, and clothing, because our heavenly Father knows what we need and will take care of these things as we seek His kingdom and His righteousness. The problem is that most people—even Christians—spend most of their day worrying about small things that Jesus promised to take care of. We need to stop worrying and start expecting God's provision to be there for us as we serve Him.

When some people wake up in the morning, they're not expecting God's provision. They're expecting lack. They're not expecting God's favor; they're expecting to be attacked by ten o'clock! I don't live like that. I'm waking up looking for the blessing of Heaven. I'm looking for the provision of the Lord. The Bible says the blessing of the Lord makes one rich and He adds no sorrow with it (Proverbs 10:22).

God wants you to have abundant life—good measure, pressed down, shaken together, and running over (Luke 6:38). That's what you are to expect. What are you expecting from tomorrow? Good things. What are you expecting from this week? Good things. I'm not believing for bad things. I'm believing for good things. I'm believing for the provision of the Lord.

Sometimes, however, we slip and find ourselves worrying about the Lord's provision. This even happens to ministers. I remember a time when we were on the road, constantly, in crusades. I couldn't take a week off and believe that God was going to meet the needs of our ministry during my time off. I had a battle with that, and the Lord really had to speak to me about it, "You mean I can't meet the need if you take a holiday? Don't you work for Me?"

I said: "Yes, Lord, I work for You."

He said: "Well, can't you have a holiday on Me?"

I really had to come to a point of trusting God that even if I wasn't preaching, He still would provide for me. That's hard for a minister.

He's a Provider. His very presence, His very nature is that if He showed up at your house and there was no food, He would provide food. He said: *"I am the way, the truth, and the life"* (John 14:6). So when you're sitting there and you're saying to yourself, *There is no way*, you must realize that there *is* a way and His name is Jesus. He makes a way.

Somebody said, "I don't know what to do, I've got a brick wall behind me and I've got a brick wall in front of me." But Jesus will make a way. He'll open the door. If there's no door to open, He'll blow a hole in the wall!

In John, Chapter 2, we find that the very first miracle Jesus did was a miracle of provision. He provided for a need. Jesus, His mother Mary, and the disciples were at a wedding in Cana of Galilee. When the wine was all gone, Mary said to Jesus, "They have no more wine." Then she said to the servants. *"Whatever He says to you, do it."*

I believe that's the key to the provision of the Lord: *"Whatever He tells you to do, do it."* You may not know what to do, but the Word of the Lord will come to you—"Do this," or "Do that," and the door will open. God will make a way where there is no way, and the provision of the Lord will be there.

What was the result of this miracle? It wasn't just that the guests had something to drink that day. The purpose of Jesus's miracle is revealed in John 2:11 (AMPC):

> This, the first of His signs (miracles, wonderworks), Jesus performed in Cana of Galilee, and manifested His glory [by it He displayed His greatness and His power openly], and His disciples believed in Him [adhered to, trusted in, and relied on Him].

Because of His miracle of provision, His disciples believed in Him. When you have a need in your life and God, by His power, begins to supply your need, your whole life changes. Your trust in Him rises, so that you can believe Him for all kinds of things. "I saw Him do it last week," you say, "so I know He'll do it again today. I remember what He did ten years ago, so I know He's gonna do it again."

With that miracle, Jesus showed forth His glory and His goodness. I believe the reason He turned water into wine as His first miracle was because He wanted that to be a statement. Providing the wine is probably the least that He could have done.

First of all, Jesus came to save from sin and heal sick bodies. The last thing down the line would be to provide wine for a friend's wedding. But I believe He's trying to say, "I do the least thing I can do first, because I want to show you that there's nothing in your life that I can't take care of. If you accept Me as your Savior and your Healer, I'll also be your Provider, so that when you have a need, you know I will supply everything that you need."

In John 15:7, Jesus says: *"If ye abide in me, and my words abide in you, ye shall ask what ye will, and it shall be done unto you."* Whatever you need, ask, and He'll give it.

> After this, Jesus went to the farther side of the sea of Galilee — that is, the Sea of Tiberias, And a great crowd was following Him because

they had seen the signs (miracles) which He [continually] performed upon those who were sick. And Jesus walked up the mountainside and sat down there with His disciples. Now the Passover, the feast of the Jews, was approaching. Jesus looked up then, and seeing that a vast multitude was coming toward Him, He said to Philip, Where are we to buy bread, so that all these people may eat? But he said this to prove (test) him, for He well knew what He was about to do. Philip answered Him, Two hundred pennies' (forty dollars) worth of bread is not enough that everyone may receive even a little. Another of His disciples, Andrew, Simon Peter's brother, said to Him, There's a little boy here, who has [with him] five barley loaves, and two small fish; but what are they among so many people? Jesus said, Make all the people recline (sit down). Now the ground (a pasture) was covered with thick grass at the spot, so that the men threw themselves down, about 5,000 in number. Jesus took the loaves, and when He had given thanks, He distributed to the disciples and the disciples to the reclining people; so also [He did] with the fish, as much as they wanted. When they all had enough, He said to His disciples, Gather up now the fragments (the broken pieces that are left over), so that nothing may be lost and wasted. So accordingly they gathered them up, and they filled twelve [small hand] baskets with fragments left over by those who had eaten from the five barley loaves.

JOHN 6:1-13 AMPC

This is a very powerful miracle of provision. People are hungry so Jesus takes a little boy's lunch and then He multiplies it. Now it's one thing to hear that God provided food and drink in Bible times, but it happens now too. When my family was living in the Transkei region of South Africa, I heard of a miracle of provision among Baptist missionaries. About sixty people had gathered one night at the mission, and all they had was one chicken. But they prayed, and God multiplied their one chicken. All sixty ate chicken and were filled!

God's provision is not just for Bible times—it's for right now. It's for you and me. If we just believe God, He'll make a way where there is no way. God wants His people to live in a higher realm of the supernatural. It's time to move up and live in a higher realm of the provision of God in our lives. We've got to quit looking at our own resources. If we're looking at our salary as our source of supply, we're going to be devastated if our company closes down tomorrow.

This has got to become real in your daily life. It's easy to clap your hands and sing in church, "He's my Provider." But it's another thing to really trust in Him when you're in the middle of a problem. When you lose your job, suddenly you find out how much you really believe in the Lord's provision.

When you get into that position, you've got to truly believe that Jesus is a multiplier. You've got to believe that He doesn't look at how much you have, but takes what you have and multiplies it, stretches it, and makes it go further than it's ever gone before. You might look at your income as limited, but He will stretch it to do more than it's ever done before. When I look at what God does through this ministry with the income we receive, I'm amazed. Our income is not even a tenth of what some of the larger ministries in America receive, yet what God's doing through this ministry is so tremendous! God can stretch it. He can make it go further than ever before!

Of course, we realize that God blesses us also because we're good stewards of our resources, we tithe, and give offerings to honor Him. When we honor Him, He blesses us. My wife, Adonica, and I have seen that when we have limited resources available and God tells us to give, we give. We still end up doing everything we wanted to do with the limited resources—even minus what we've given—because God stretches it and multiplies it. Faithful tithers have long seen that the 90 percent they retain after tithing goes much farther than if they'd kept 100 percent.

God not only provides food, drink, and clothing, He provides open doors. He provides supernatural favor to meet our every need. I want to show you several more miracles of provision.

When they arrived in Capernaum, the collectors of the half shekel [the temple tax] went up to Peter and said, Does not your Teacher pay the half shekel? He answered, Yes. And when he came home, Jesus spoke to him [about it] first, saying, What do you think, Simon ? From whom do earthly rulers collect duties or tribute — from their own sons or from others not of their own family? And when Peter said, From other people not of their own family, Jesus said, Then the sons are exempt. However, in order not to give offense and to cause them to stumble [that is, to cause them to judge unfavorably and unjustly] go down to the sea and throw in a hook. Take the first fish that comes up, and when you open its mouth you will find there a shekel. Take it and give it to them to pay the temple tax for Me and for yourself.

MATTHEW 17:24-27 AMPC

Now Peter's a fisherman, and in all of Peter's years of fishing, He's never caught a fish with a coin in its mouth. But he never needed it until now. It's a relief to know that Jesus knows where the fish are and that He wants to take care of your needs!

When they were getting near to Jerusalem, to Bethphage and Bethany at the Mount of Olives, He sent ahead two of His disciples And instructed them, Go into the village in front of you, and as soon as you enter it, you will find a colt tied, which has never been ridden by anyone; unfasten it and bring it [here] If anyone asks you, Why are you doing this? answer, The Lord needs it, and He will send it back here presently. So they went away and found a colt tied at the door out in the [winding] open street, and they loosed it. And some who were standing there said to them, What are you doing, untying the colt? And they replied as Jesus had directed them, and they allowed them to go. And they brought the colt to Jesus and threw their outer garments upon it, and He sat on it.

MARK 11:1-7 AMPC

Jesus needed a vehicle. If this happened today, He'd say: "Now go to the dealership down the road, and you'll see a car on the lot. Just get in it and bring it over here. If they ask what you're doing with the car, just say: "My Master has need of it. We'll bring it back." There was a need, and God provided for that need.

When they needed the upper room, the same thing happened. In Mark 14:12-16, the apostles said they needed a place to get together for the Passover meal. Jesus told them to look for a man with a big pot and to follow him home. "Go in there," Jesus said, "and tell them that we need their guest room. You'll find everything laid out for you."

God provides, no matter how impossible it looks. He furnishes a table in the wilderness. He makes the crooked paths straight. He'll provide for you. All He wants you to do is to trust Him.

Will you trust Him? Maybe you want to go to Bible school, but you're worried about your tuition. Would you trust Him? If you can't believe God for your tuition, how are you ever going to believe God when it comes to funding your ministry or missions operation?

A lot of people have said, "Well, you know, it's great that you preach this message of provision and all that, but Jesus didn't have anything and Jesus even said it Himself: "Foxes have holes, birds have nests, but the Son of man hath not where to lay His head."

Jesus didn't have a home because He didn't need one. What He did need, He got. You don't really need anything when you're all you need. When you walk on water just as a hobby, do you think you're going to lose one night's sleep about a need?

Jesus knows what you have need of, though. He knows you have a family. He knows you need to work and earn money to provide for your family. He knows! That's why He tells you to seek first the kingdom of God and His righteousness and all these things will be added—not subtracted—unto you. He knows what you have need of!

For years, my family didn't need a home either. We just traveled, lived in hotels, and kept our stuff in storage. For years, we'd wanted to get a home, but we'd stopped talking about it, because every time we asked the Lord if we could get a home, He said: "No." I said, "Lord, I'd love to give my wife and kids a house. I don't want the kids growing up in a hotel room."

When the revival broke out in central Florida in 1993, the Lord spoke to me and said: "It's time for you to get a home, Son. Go and get some property and build a house for your family." So we soon found the piece of property and started building the house.

One day, as I was walking out on the foundation, I just lifted up my hands, with tears rolling down my cheeks, and said: "Lord, thank You so much for this house for my family." As I said that, the Lord spoke to me audibly and said: "Son, you've built My house for the last fourteen years. Now I'm going to build your house."

I said, "Lord, do You really mean that? You're going to build my house?"

He said: "Yes, you watch it; I'm building your house. I'll make a way for you."

Jesus knew my desire. It's such a pleasure just to come home, to have a place called "home."

When we moved into the house, I got my wife and the kids together and said, "This home is just a blessing from God, and if God tells us to give it away, we will." You see, everything we have belongs to Him— we're just stewards, managers, of what He blesses us with. As stewards, we need to do whatever He tells us to do with everything we have. So if He ever needs my house, He has it without a question.

Jesus can provide a home and transportation. We know that He can provide you with a job. We know that He can provide you with food. What else do you need? What are your needs today? Jesus meets them all.

The [uncompromisingly] righteous shall flourish like the palm tree [be long-lived, stately, upright, useful, and fruitful]; they shall grow like a cedar in Lebanon [majestic, stable, durable, and incorruptible]. Planted in the house of the Lord, they shall flourish in the courts of our God. [Growing in grace] they shall still bring forth fruit in old age; they shall be full of sap [of spiritual vitality] and [rich in the] verdure [of trust, love, and contentment]. [They are living memorials] to show that the Lord is upright and faithful to His promises; He is my Rock, and there is no unrighteousness in Him.

PSALM 92:12-15 AMPC

Some people are so worried about dying early, but God's Word says the uncompromisingly righteous will be long-lived, stately, upright, useful, and fruitful. The *King James Version* says that they shall be *"fat and flourishing."* The *Amplified Bible, Classic Edition* says: *"they shall be full of sap."* Are you full of sap? Are you full of spiritual vitality? Are you rich in trust, love, and contentment?

We are living memorials! Our lives show the world that the Lord is upright and faithful to His promises. He is our rock. There's no unrighteousness in Him and our lives exhibit this truth to a lost and dying world.

Psalm 23:1 AMPC says: *"The Lord is my Shepherd [to feed, guide, and shield me], I shall not lack."* To feed, guide, and shield me is everything I need. I shall not lack! I wake up in the morning with an air of expectancy—looking for the favor of God, looking for the blessing of God.

Have you come to that place where you just trust the Lord? Trust Him! You've got nothing to lose, so trust Him. He's there to help you. He's there to make the way for you. He's your Provider. He loves you. He'll walk into your house and multiply food. He knows how to pay the bills, and He knows how to pay tax money. He knows about transportation needs, and He knows about accommodation needs. And most of all, He can make a way where there is no way!

> And you shall return and obey the voice of the Lord and do all His commandments which I command you today. And the Lord your God will make you abundantly prosperous in every work of your hand, in the fruit of your body, of your cattle, of your land, for good; for the Lord will again delight in prospering you, as He took delight in your fathers.
>
> DEUTERONOMY 30:8-9 AMPC

Your heavenly Father will make you *abundantly prosperous*, for He *delights* in prospering you because you obey His commandments. God loves to bless His obedient children.

Are you His child? Do you submit to His will and His Word? Then

God will bless you and enjoy every moment of it. You don't have to run after blessing. Run after Jesus; and blessing and provision will run after you.

CHAPTER 14

JESUS, THE BAPTIZER IN THE HOLY SPIRIT

Jesus answered and said unto her, Whosoever drinketh of this water shall thirst again. But whosoever drinketh of the water that I shall give him shall never thirst; but the water that I shall give him shall be in him a well of water springing up into everlasting life.

JOHN 4:13-14

In the last day, that great day of the feast, Jesus stood and cried, saying, If any man thirst, let him come unto me, and drink. He that believeth on me, as the scripture bath said, out of his belly shall flow rivers of living water (But this spake be of the Spirit, which they that believe on him should receive: for the Holy Ghost was not yet given; because that Jesus was not yet glorified.)

JOHN 7:37-39

In John 4:14, Jesus speaks about a well of water springing up into everlasting life. But in John 7:38, He says: *"out of your belly shall flow rivers of living water."*

He's talking about two different things taking place in the life of every believer. Number one, there is a well of water springing up into everlasting life. Number two, there is a river coming out of their belly.

You could call salvation a *well anointing*. And what a well it is! The Bible says: *"Therefore with joy shall ye draw water out of the wells of salvation"* (Isaiah 12:3). Joy is the bucket that goes down and pulls up the water of life from the well of your salvation. Your salvation should be a source of life and joy, not a dry and heavy burden.

The water of the Spirit can also gush out like a mighty river. There are people who believe that there's just one experience—when you get saved, you are automatically baptized with the Holy Spirit at the same time. But that's not true. Otherwise, Jesus wouldn't have spoken about both the well and the river. You can get baptized in the Holy Spirit at the same time as you get saved, but they are two separate and distinct experiences.

John the Baptist, Jesus's cousin, was a forerunner to the ministry of the Lord Jesus Christ, and he announced what Jesus's ministry would be about.

> I indeed baptize you with water unto repentance: but he that cometh after me is mightier than I, whose shoes I am not worthy to bear: he shall baptize you with the Holy Ghost, and with fire.
>
> MATTHEW 3:11

John proclaimed how the ministry of Jesus would differ from his own. John was saying—and I mean no offense—"I'm a Baptist, but there's coming a Pentecostal after me and He will baptize you with the Holy Ghost and fire." This One is coming after him, he says in Matthew 3:12: *"Whose fan is in his hand, and he will thoroughly purge his floor, and gather his wheat into the garner; but he will burn up the chaff with unquenchable fire."*

What does fire do? Fire purges. Fire purifies. If you want to refine gold, you've got to put it through the fire, and it will come out pure. As the molten gold liquifies, the impurities float to the top, where they can be scooped away. And that's what the Holy Ghost comes to do in our life. He comes to purify us by melting our hearts and scooping off the sin and impurities.

Now let's look at the words of Jesus once again in John 14. He's preparing His disciples for the time when He is going to leave. He says that He's going to go away, but He's not going to leave them alone. He's going to send the Holy Ghost, the Comforter. He's going to send the *Paraclete* (the "One called alongside to help"), the Teacher, the Advocate, the Intercessor, to help every believer.

Jesus prayed to the Father to send the Holy Ghost. The Bible says that the Father sent the Son, and then the Son sent the Spirit. The Father sent the Son and the Son sent the Spirit, but the Spirit never came until the Son left. Jesus goes on to say:

> And I will pray the Father, and be shall give you another Comforter, that he may abide with you forever; Even the Spirit of truth; whom the world cannot receive, because it seeth him not, neither knoweth him: but ye know him: for he dwelleth with you, and shall be in you. I will not leave you comfortless." I will come to you. But the Comforter, which is the Holy Ghost, whom the Father will send in my name, he will teach you all things, and bring all things to your remembrance, whatsoever I have said unto you.
>
> JOHN 14:16-18, 26

No wonder we need the Holy Spirit! We need Him every day of our lives, every waking moment. He will teach us and bring all things to our remembrance—whatever Jesus has said unto us.

> But when the Comforter is come, whom I will send unto you from the Father, even the Spirit of truth, which proceedeth from the Father, he shall testify of me.
>
> JOHN 15:26

The Holy Spirit will bear witness and will testify about Jesus. We have testimonies coming in from remote parts of the world—China, the mountains of Tibet and Nepal, India, and even Saudi Arabia. People there have watched videotapes of our revival services, and even though some of them couldn't speak a word of English, the power of the Holy Spirit put them on the floor.

Their testimony is that while they were on the floor, Jesus appeared to them and said: "When you get up, ask these missionaries to tell you about Me, because I love you." These people, who had never heard the Gospel, went to the missionaries and said, "Could you tell us about Jesus?"

The missionaries said, "What do you mean, tell you about Jesus? Who told you about Him?"

They said, "Well, we were lying on the floor just a while ago and a man in a white robe stood before us and told us that He loved us, and that when we got up off the floor, we should come and ask you about Him."

The Holy Spirit will testify about Jesus just as Jesus was testifying about the coming of the Holy Ghost because He knew we needed the Holy Spirit. He knew that we needed to know Him intimately and that we needed to have a personal relationship with the Holy Spirit. He wanted us not just to be saved and have the well on the inside, but He wanted us also to have the overflowing river coming out of us, because He wanted us to be witnesses unto Him everywhere we go.

Now, let me show you this. There are a lot of people who have been filled with the Spirit of God but have never had the release of the Spirit in their life. Why? Because they never yielded to the Spirit of God in the area of speaking in other tongues. I've seen people who just shook until their false teeth rattled when the power of God came on them, yet they never had the release of their prayer language. From time to time the anointing of God would come on them so strongly, they didn't know what to do with themselves, but nobody was there to teach them how to yield to the Spirit of God.

> Nevertheless I tell you the truth; It is expedient for you that I go away: for if I do not go away, the Comforter will not come unto you; but if I depart, I will send him unto you.
>
> JOHN 16:7

Can you imagine Peter, James, and John standing there, listening to Jesus say: "It's better for you that I go away?" Their minds must have struggled to grasp what He meant by that.

"We don't want You to go away. Stay around some more."

"But," He says, "it's better for you that I go away. If I don't go away, the Comforter will not come unto you. If I depart, I will send Him to you."

> And when he is come, he will reprove the world of sin, and of righteousness, and of judgment. Of sin, because they believe not on me; Of righteousness, because I go to my Father, and ye see me no more; Of judgment, because the prince of this world is judged. I have yet many things to say unto you, but you cannot bear them now.
>
> JOHN 16:8-12

What did Jesus mean by that? They not only wouldn't be able to bear it, but they wouldn't be able to understand it just then. Why? Because the Holy Spirit is the one who gives you understanding and insight into the Word of God. That's why we have people in the earth who read the same Bible as we do and can't see what it's saying. They read the same Bible and can't even see it. They don't believe healing is for today, don't believe God wants to bless them, and can't see the powerful reality of the Gospel.

> Howbeit when be, the Spirit of truth, is come, he will guide you into all truth.
>
> JOHN 16:13A

Jesus said that the Holy Spirit will guide us. Let's take the underground Church in China, which has been undergoing persecution for decades, as an example. Millions of Christians in China can't announce where their services will be the next week because the secret police might hear. Do you know how those people go to church? By the Holy Ghost. They have to pray and get the mind of God. The Holy Spirit tells them where their next meeting is, and they show up on Sunday in the right place.

The people come into this little room and they pack in there with no comfy pews, no music, none of what we'd call praise and worship. They just sing with tears rolling down their cheeks as they worship.

But in America, we can definitely have church without the Holy Ghost! There are churches strewn all over the nation without the Holy Ghost. They don't need Him to move, because man has perfected the art of gathering people together. Just as Disney has perfected the art of moving masses of people through an amusement park, the Church has perfected the art of gathering people and just tickling their ears. That's the whole idea for many churches: "We want 'em to come back, so get 'em in and out. As long as they're putting their money in, we're happy."

We don't want you just to get in and out. We want you *in* and we want you *staying in* and we want you full of the Holy Ghost and full of the fire of God!

I've heard many stories of people who are truly led by the Holy Spirit. When I was in Norway, I heard about two brothers whose father had pioneered a church in a remote region of China at the turn of the century. The two brothers decided to go back to China to find the church their father had pioneered. They could still speak Chinese, as they had learned it while growing up in China. The Communists had changed the name of the town, but they finally got into the region and found someone to take them there. They arrived in the town at eleven o'clock at night.

As they got out of the car, a man walked towards them. He said, "Hello, I'm the pastor here. We've been waiting for you." There were several hundred Chinese Christians gathered at a house. The Norwegian men asked if somebody told them they were coming.

The Chinese said, "Oh, yes. Three nights ago, the Word of the Lord came forth prophetically declaring, 'The sons of the one who brought you the Good News will be here. Be ready for them. They will arrive at eleven o'clock.'"

Our brothers and sisters in China know far more about living in the realm of the Spirit of God than we do here. We're led by natural things and circumstances, but these people are led by the Holy Ghost. The church in China is growing at an incredible rate. More than forty thousand people are being saved into the church in China every single day. These people know how to hear the voice of God.

We totally underestimate the power of the Holy Ghost. Jesus knew these things when He walked the earth. How did *He* function all the time? By the Holy Ghost. He was led by the Spirit. He said: *"The Son can do nothing of himself, but what he seeth the Father do"* (John 5:19). He was watching the Holy Spirit morning, noon, and night, everywhere He went. He would follow the promptings and the leadings of the Spirit of God—nothing more, nothing less.

That's the cry of my heart: for the body of Christ to become more sensitive to the Spirit of God. We must be more sensitive to His promptings and leadings. The Church in America has gotten so comfortable that they don't need to hear the voice of God. They don't need to listen to the promptings and leadings of the Spirit of God.

That's why we must strip away all of the things that would hold us back. We must strip away all the things that would block our ears and our hearts from being sensitive to the Spirit of grace. Stop looking for your comfort. Stop staying in your comfort zone. Press in and get to the point where you only do what the Holy Spirit wants you to do and go where He wants you to go.

You know that if the Holy Spirit tells you to do something, He will make a way for you. We just don't believe God enough. After the former Soviet Union opened up to the Gospel, American missionaries prophesied over a local pastor. The Holy Spirit said: "God's going to start using you in an unusual way." They left, and when they came back a year later and asked about his ministry, he said: "Well, I have three churches, but they're very far apart. They're eight hundred miles to a thousand miles apart. I preach at each every Sunday."

They said: "What are you talking about? How could you?"

He said: "Well, you know you prophesied that God would use me in an unusual way? He does. Each Sunday I preach at the one place, and I walk out and then I just suddenly find myself at the next place. Then I preach to them and then I walk out and I find myself instantly at the next church. And then I go home."

We badly underestimate the power of the Holy Ghost. Jesus felt that we would need the Holy Spirit to lead us, to guide us, to teach us, to empower us, to enable us, to grace us, to anoint us, and to point us. That's why He sent the Holy Spirit. If Jesus felt we needed the Holy Ghost, then we need the Holy Ghost—not just in a meeting when we get touched, but when we walk out the door—and tomorrow and the next day and the next day and the next day!

I'm concerned about the Church in the western world. I'm concerned about America and our whole attitude toward the Spirit of God. The Holy Spirit has been relegated to a mere minor manifestation—somebody giving a tongue or an interpretation, a word of wisdom, or a word of knowledge—but He's far beyond that. He's more than that. He's greater than that. I'm talking about the Spirit of God indwelling you, rising up and then coming out of you like a mighty river, a mighty river of God!

God's wanting His people to learn to lean on the Holy Spirit and to trust the Holy Spirit. We've got to trust that God's going to make a way, so that even if you don't know where you're going two, three, four, or five days from now, the Holy Spirit already knows. He's already moving situations together. He's already bringing things together, preparing the way for you, going ahead of you, making the crooked paths straight.

The Bible says that He will show you things to come. Jesus says: *"He shall glorify Me, for He shall receive of Mine and shew it unto you"* (John 16:14).

> And, being assembled together with them, commanded them that they should not depart from Jerusalem, but wait for the promise of the Father, which, saith he, ye have heard of me. For John truly baptized with water; but ye shall be baptized with the Holy Ghost not many days hence. But ye shall receive power, after that the Holy Ghost is come upon you: and you shall be witnesses unto me both in Jerusalem, and in all Judea, and in Samaria and unto the uttermost part of the earth.
>
> ACTS 1:4-5, 8

Well, then that's exactly what happened in Acts, chapter 2:

When the day of Pentecost was fully come, they were all with one accord in one place. And suddenly there came a sound from heaven as of a rushing mighty wind, and it filled all the house where they were sitting. And there appeared unto them cloven tongues like as of fire, and it sat upon each of them. And they were all filled with the Holy Ghost, and began to speak with other tongues, as the Spirit gave them utterance. And there were dwelling at Jerusalem Jews, devout men, out of every nation under heaven. Now when this was noised abroad, the multitude came together, and were confounded, because that every man heard them speak in his own language. And they were all amazed and marvelled, saying one to another, Behold, are not all these which speak Galilaeans? And how hear we every man in our own tongue, wherein we were born? Parthians, and Medes, and Elamites, and the dwellers in Mesopotamia, and in Judea and Cappadocia, and Pontus, and Asia, Phrygia, and Pamphylia, in Egypt, and in the parts of Libya about Cyrene, and strangers of Rome, Jews and proselytes, Cretes and Arabians, we do hear them speak in our tongues the wonderful works of God. And they were all amazed, and were in doubt, saying one to another, What meaneth this? Others mocking said, These men are full of new wine. But Peter, standing up with the eleven, lifted up his voice, and said unto them, Ye men of Judea, and all ye that dwell at Jerusalem, be this known unto you, and hearken to my words: For these are not drunken, as ye suppose, seeing it is but the third hour of the day. But this is that which was spoken by the prophet Joel; And it shall come to pass in the last days, saith God, I will pour out of my Spirit upon all flesh: and your sons and your daughters shall prophesy, and your young men shall see visions, and your old men shall dream dreams: And on my servants and on my handmaidens I will pour out in those days of my Spirit; and they shall prophesy.

ACTS 2:1-18

Now let's go to Acts 2:38-39:

> Then Peter said unto them, Repent, and be baptized every one of
> you in the name of Jesus Christ for the remission of sins, and ye shall
> receive the gift of the Holy Ghost. For the promise is unto you, and
> to your children, and to all that are afar off, even as many as the Lord
> our God shall call.

Some people say that the gift of the Holy Spirit passed away, that
it was only for that time. But this scripture says: *"The promise is unto
you, and to your children, and to all that are afar off, even as many as the
Lord our God shall call."*

Is God still calling people now? If God's still calling people now,
then the promise of the Holy Ghost is for you and your children, even
those who are afar off, as many as the Lord shall call. And that means
you and me. There is an experience subsequent to salvation, and it's
known as the baptism in the Holy Ghost and fire.

> Now when the apostles which were at Jerusalem heard that Samaria
> had received the word of God, they sent unto them Peter and John:
> Who, when they were come down, prayed for them, that they might
> receive the Holy Ghost: (For as yet he was fallen upon none of them:
> only they were baptized in the name of the Lord Jesus.) Then they
> laid their hands on them, and they received the Holy Ghost.
>
> ACTS 8:14-17

They were saved, but they had not received the Holy Ghost. Peter
and John had to go down there and lay hands upon them. Then they
got the Holy Ghost.

Are you convinced of the necessity of allowing Jesus to baptize
you in the Holy Spirit? If not, I can prove it to you again. Go to Acts
9, where Saul of Tarsus got saved on the road to Damascus. Look in
Acts 9:17:

> And Ananias went his way, and entered into the house; and putting his
> hands on him said, Brother Saul, the Lord, even Jesus, that appeared

unto thee in the way as thou camest, hath sent me, that thou mightest receive thy sight, and be filled with the Holy Ghost.

Saul is born-again, but He's not yet full of the Holy Ghost. God sent Ananias to come and lay hands upon Saul so that he could get the gift of the Holy Ghost.

Go to Acts 10:44. Peter is at the house of Cornelius, a Gentile, and He's preaching. The Bible says:

While Peter yet spake these words, the Holy Ghost fell on all them which heard the word. And they of the circumcision which believed were astonished, as many as came with Peter, because that on the Gentiles also was poured out the gift of the Holy Ghost. For they heard them speak with tongues, and magnify God. Then answered Peter, Can any man forbid water, that these should not be baptized, which have received the Holy Ghost as well as we?

ACTS 10:44-47

Again, we have people who get saved, but then they got something more—the gift of the Holy Ghost.

Now, one last passage of Scripture to see the necessity of the baptism of the Holy Spirit. Go with me to Acts 19:1-6:

And it came to pass, that, while Apollos was at Corinth, Paul having passed through the upper coasts came to Ephesus: and finding certain disciples, He said unto them, Have ye received the Holy Ghost since ye believed? And they said unto him, We have not so much as heard whether there be any Holy Ghost. And he said unto them, Unto what then were ye baptized? They said, Unto John's baptism. Then said Paul, John verily baptized with the baptism of repentance, saying unto the people, that they should believe on him which should come after him, that is, on Christ Jesus. When they heard this, they were baptized in the name of the Lord Jesus. And when Paul laid his hands upon them, the Holy Ghost came on them; and they spake with tongues, and prophesied.

They were already disciples. Then Paul baptized them in water because they were only baptized under John's baptism. He laid hands upon them, the Holy Spirit came upon them, and they spoke with tongues and prophesied.

Jesus is the baptizer in the Holy Ghost. If He felt that it was important, then it's important for every single one of us to be baptized in the Holy Ghost. And when we receive the Holy Spirit, we'll notice that our lives will be millions of times more powerful than ever before. Hallelujah!

The power of the Holy Spirit is power to overcome sin. Power to reject temptation will come upon you when you get baptized in the Holy Ghost. If you are trying to live a holy life, but you can't because your flesh, your carnal nature, always gets the better of you, then you need to get full of the Holy Ghost, and you won't yield to temptation like you used to. The Spirit of God will rise up big and strong on the inside of you and empower you to resist and overcome temptations!

If you haven't allowed Jesus to baptize you in the Holy Ghost, let Him do it right now! Don't live another second without all of God's power working in your life.

CHAPTER 15

JESUS, THE TRADITION BREAKER

And it came to pass on the second sabbath after the first, that he went through the corn fields; and his disciples plucked the ears of corn, and did eat, rubbing them in their hands. And certain of the Pharisees said unto them, Why do ye that which is not lawful to do on the sabbath days? And Jesus answering them said, Have ye not read so much as this, what David did, when himself was an hungered, and they which were with him; How he went into the house of God, and did take and eat the shewbread, and gave also to them that were with him; which it is not lawful to eat but for the priests alone? And he said unto them, That the Son of man is Lord also of the sabbath.

LUKE 6:1-5

Sabbath days were the days that the Pharisees sought to scrutinize Jesus, so they could catch Him doing or saying something in violation of the Law and the Prophets. Matthew, Mark, Luke, and John reported what Jesus did on the Sabbaths and how the Pharisees reacted with all kinds of accusations and curses. He seemed to relish the opportunity to show them that every Sabbath was for man and healing people was exactly what the Sabbath was all about.

On one Sabbath, Jesus taught in the synagogue. That was acceptable to the Pharisees, but there was a man in the congregation whose
right hand was withered. The scribes and Pharisees watched Jesus to
see whether He would heal him on the Sabbath day. If He did, they
could find an accusation against Him. To their way of thinking, healing
would be considered work, and it was against the Law to work on the
Sabbath. Can you believe that some religious people actually got their
kicks by following Jesus to see if He broke tradition?

> And it came to pass also on another sabbath, that he entered into the
> synagogue and taught: and there was a man whose right hand was
> withered. And the scribes and Pharisees watched him, whether he
> would heal on the sabbath day; that they might find an accusation
> against him. But he knew their thoughts, and said to the man which
> had the withered hand, Rise up, and stand forth in the midst. And
> he arose and stood forth. Then said Jesus unto them, I will ask you
> one thing; Is it lawful on the sabbath days to do good, or to do evil?
> to save life, or to destroy it? And looking round about upon them all,
> he said unto the man, Stretch forth thy hand. And he did so: and his
> hand was restored whole as the other. And they were filled with mad-
> ness; and communed one with another what they might do to Jesus.
>
> LUKE 6:6-11

"How dare you heal on the Sabbath day," the Pharisees said. They
had every other day of the week to heal the man and could not and
would not do so, but Jesus comes and heals on the Sabbath day, and
they want to nail Him for it.

Now, when you look at Jesus's ministry closely, you'll see one thing
that sticks out. Everywhere He went, He went head to head with religion
and tradition. And the closer we get to Jesus, the more we're going to
come head to head with religion and tradition. When that happens,
we have a tendency to back off, to find the path of least resistance. We
don't want to rock the boat. Well, most of us don't!

I go into churches and the pastors say they want me to have a revival,

JESUS, THE TRADITION BREAKER

but they also say, "Rodney, please don't rock the boat. It's taken us fourteen years to build this dinghy. Don't rock it."

And I have to tell them: "Oh, I didn't come to rock the boat. I came to turn the stupid thing over!"

These Pharisees were not concerned about setting people free. They didn't care to see people delivered, coming out of darkness into light. Their job, they felt, was to protect the Law to the very letter—every jot, every tittle, every line of the Law. Unfortunately, they had warped and perverted God's Law to the point where "the Law" meant all the rules and traditions *they* had devised—their self-serving, religious interpretations of the Law.

The Bible tells us in Hebrews 4:15 that Jesus was without sin and Luke 24:44 tells us that Jesus fulfilled the *whole* law while He walked on the earth. But when the Pharisees saw Jesus and the disciples picking grain on the Sabbath, the Pharisees considered that to be work. Religious people extend the "letter" of the law and have no understanding of the "spirit" of the law."

> For we have not an high priest which cannot be touched with the feeling of our infirmities; but was in all points tempted like as we are, yet without sin. that Jesus was without sin.
>
> HEBREWS 4:15

> And he said unto them, These are the words which I spake unto you, while I was yet with you, that all things must be fulfilled, which were written in the law of Moses, and in the prophets, and in the psalms, concerning me.
>
> LUKE 24:44

Religion and tradition will kill you, like a python that wraps its coils around you and slowly squeezes the life out of you until there is nothing left. Religion and tradition will rob you of your joy. They will rob you of your freedom. They will rob you of the joy of your salvation. You once may have been on fire for God, but it has slowly waned. There is nothing left but a shell.

Look at Christians who have been pulled into a religious attitude ten or fifteen years after salvation. They've been abused and bullied through the system of religious tradition and then discarded like empty shells along the highway of life. That's not why Jesus came! Jesus came to set us free. Jesus came to give us life, to give us life more abundantly.

Religion and the traditions of men will kill you, because religion and traditions are not interested in you, they're only interested in promoting themselves. When we started our church, people in other churches got upset and said, "We're going to lose some people to that church, and then we're going to lose their tithe." I suddenly realized that too many pastors are not interested in people, they're just interested in their money. Something's wrong somewhere.

More tradition: "You have to have a Sunday night service."

I said, "Why?"

"Well, if you don't have a Sunday night service, the people are going to go to other churches."

I said, "So?"

"Well, if they go to other churches, they might leave you."

I said, "Are we supposed to have a service just to keep people in our church? That's not the purpose of this place. The purpose of this place is to get people free."

The experts say you can't have services over ninety minutes long if you expect your church to grow large. In other words, if we cut it down to forty-five-minute services, we'll have a huge church. But at what price? A huge church full of lukewarm believers? Some churches have perfected a twenty-two-minute Sunday morning service, from the first hymn to the benediction including the offering. Why don't you just open up a drive-through window and call it McChurch—"You want Communion with that?"

The pastor of a great church in Shreveport, Louisiana, told me they've always been under pressure to have a short Sunday morning service—an hour and a half. Quickly get people in, quickly get people out. He thought, *Lord, if only we could have longer Sunday morning services, where we could be free, not be pressured, and just worship You.*

The pastor told me, "You won't believe what we did. We dumped our Sunday night service. In our traditional mindset, we always had to have the Sunday morning service quick, so we could get the people to come back that night. So we dumped our Sunday night service, extended Sunday morning, and started a Saturday night service."

Now their Saturday nights are as full as Sunday morning. Why? Because He's breaking tradition. If you want Jesus to show up, you have to break tradition.

Am I against *all* tradition? No. There are good traditions and bad traditions. There are good traditions based on the Word of God, and those we want to keep. Second Thessalonians 2:15 says: *"Therefore, brethren, stand fast, and hold the traditions which you have been taught, whether by word, or our epistle."* Hold to the good traditions in God's Word, such as the laying on of hands, casting out devils, speaking in tongues, and worshipping and praising God. These are all good traditions which are in the Word and were practiced by the early Church. But we don't want to do them just because of tradition. We want to do them with substance, with our whole heart.

> Now we command you, brethren, in the name of our Lord Jesus Christ, that ye withdraw yourself from every brother that walketh disorderly, and not after the tradition which he received of us.
>
> 2 THESSALONIANS 3:6

There's good tradition and then there's bad tradition. What are bad traditions? The traditions of men.

> Beware lest any man spoil you through philosophy and vain deceit, after the tradition of men, after the rudiments of the world, and not after Christ.
>
> COLOSSIANS 2:8

Psalm 1:1 says: *"Blessed is the man that walketh not in the counsel of the ungodly, nor standeth in the way of sinners, nor sitteth in the seat of the scornful.* " That verse shows that there's a progression that happens to those who follow after the traditions of men. You first start to walk in the counsel of the ungodly. After a while, you end up standing in the way of sinners. Pretty soon, you're sitting in the seat of the scornful, the mockers. Nobody goes straight to the seat of mockers. They first start walking in the counsel of the ungodly.

Be careful who you listen to. That's why you shouldn't allow your television to teach your children the standards they should adopt in their lives. Hollywood fathers all look and act like idiots. The children on television are the ones with all the answers, and they show no respect for their fathers. If I had ever spoken to my dad the way the kids talk to their fathers on television, I would have been the first kid in orbit!

But those are the traditions of man, and in most homes, they are just accepted. Then we wonder why we have trouble with our children later in their lives. We allow the world's traditions into our homes, and those worldly traditions work to destroy the Christian home.

But the closer you get to Jesus, and the more time you spend in the Gospels, the more you will find something rising up on the inside of you that is contrary to what people say. When people say, "It cannot be done this way," you will say, "It *can* be done this way because all things are possible with God."

> Forasmuch as ye know that ye were not redeemed with corruptible things, as silver and gold, from your vain conversation [manner of life] received by tradition from your fathers.
>
> 1 PETER 1:18

Jesus redeemed us from tradition. We were redeemed from the useless, vain way of living inherited from our forefathers. The fight that you're going to have is not just in your flesh or in your mind. The fight you're going to have walking the Spirit-filled life is against religious tradition. Tradition will try to stop the flow of the anointing of the Spirit of God.

You have to make a decision. Every time you feel like you're getting religious and traditional, go spend some time with Jesus in the Gospels. I like hanging around Him.

> Neither give heed to fables and endless genealogies, which minister questions, rather than godly edifying which is in faith: so do.
>
> 1 TIMOTHY 1:4

Religion and tradition minister questions and arguments, but God's Word and the Holy Spirit always bring the answers.

> But refuse profane and old wives fables, and exercise thyself rather unto godliness.
>
> 1 TIMOTHY 4:7

Refuse these old wives' tales. The Church in America is bound by old wives' tales. In other words, people live in a fantasy world, detached from reality. For instance, you have people blaming the devil for disasters in their lives that were actually caused by their own stupidity and disobedience. They try to cast devils out of rebellious children when what they need to do is straighten up themselves. They need to set a good example, give the child a whole lot of love and understanding—and probably a good spanking—and they will be on their way to straightening things out. Now, let's look at the traditions of the elders versus the commandments of God.

> Then came to Jesus scribes and Pharisees, which were of Jerusalem, saying, Why do thy disciples transgress the tradition of the elders? for they wash not their hands when they eat bread. But he answered and said unto them, Why do ye also transgress the commandment of God by your tradition?
>
> MATTHEW 15:1-3

It's one or the other. You can't have the traditions of the elders and the commandments of God. The two are diametrically opposed. The two will fight each other. You can't have a nice, dignified, staid, traditional religious church and the power of God at the same time. "All right, folks, this morning we have a diluted version of God and His power, and after the service, if you seek God in a deeper way, you can go in the back room where we have Him hidden away where He won't offend people."

In Matthew 15:8, Jesus quoted the prophet Isaiah's words from the heart of God: *"This people draweth nigh unto me with their mouth, and honoureth me with their lips; but their heart is far from me."*

In how many churches all over the world today do they draw near the Lord with their mouths, but keep their hearts far from Him? They're looking at their watches saying, "I wish the preacher would shut up. I need to get home. I've got a goose in the oven." But their goose was cooked a long time ago!

The Scripture goes on to say: *"But in vain they do worship me, teaching for doctrines the commandments of men"* (Matthew 15:9).

For too long, we've had the teachings of men taught in the Church as doctrines.

People say, "Well, this is the way it should be."

But I say, "Who said? Show me in the Bible." (They can never show you in the Bible.)

"Well, um, this is the, ah, history of the, ah, ah, well, we've kind of always done it, ah, this way, ah, haven't we?" Tradition.

We don't do things the normal way in our church. When we have a water baptism, we line them up and have them lift their hands and pray, then the power of God knocks them under the water. And you know what I've come to realize? That is normal. God is normal, and all this tradition is abnormal. So when they say, "Can't you do anything the normal way?" we say, "We *are* normal. This *is* normal."

TRADITION IS ABNORMAL. RELIGION IS ABNORMAL.

For the Pharisees, and all the Jews, except they wash their hands oft, eat not, holding the tradition of the elders.

MARK 7:3

In other words, these poor guys are washing their hands every five minutes. Now, there's nothing wrong with washing your hands. When I come out of a crusade and I've laid hands on everybody's head, the first thing I do is wash my hands. But the Pharisees can't eat because they haven't ceremonially washed their hands. There were so many rules and regulations about the washing of their cups, pots, brazen vessels, and tables. Everything had to be so clean on the outside, but they were rotten on the inside. They were like a rosy apple that has a big worm inside.

The Pharisees asked Jesus, "Why don't Your disciples walk according to the traditions of the elders? They eat bread with unwashed hands." Jesus said to them:

> Well hath Esaias prophesied of you hypocrites, as it is written, This people honoureth me with their lips, but their heart is far from me. Howbeit in vain do they worship me, teaching for doctrines the commandments of men. For laying aside the commandments of God, ye hold the tradition of men, as the washing of pots and cups: and many other such like things ye do. And he said unto them, Full well ye reject the commandment of God, that ye may keep your own tradition.
>
> MARK 7:6-9

To religious tradition, it doesn't matter what God says. They will lay those commandments aside to hold the traditions of men.

Look at Matthew 15:6, the second part of the verse: *"Thus have ye made the commandment of God of none effect by your tradition."* In other words, the Word of God is there, but it's been made powerless. The Word of God is there, but you're not going to get the benefit from it because your tradition has neutralized it.

If the devil cannot stop the Word of God from being preached, he will try to strip it of its power by introducing the tradition of man into it. Beware of the tradition of man—it refuses to acknowledge the power of God!

God cannot move within the framework of religious tradition. He's looking for a people who are hungry, who are thirsty, who are saying:

"Oh God, move! God, I'm tired of the status quo! Lord, I'm hungry for You. God, just come and touch me!" Then He touches them, and the church explodes.

In many cases, a few years go by and these exploding churches become religious and traditional themselves. They develop the status quo and don't want to rock the boat. God can't move anymore. Then He has to bring people from the outside again, raise people up from nothing, because He's always looking for a people who will run with the Spirit of God. You cannot please God while you try to please and satisfy people!

If Jesus was a tradition-buster, don't you want to be a tradition-buster? Well, the only thing that will burn tradition out of you is the fire of the Holy Ghost. When the fire of God comes, it's going to burn religion and tradition out of your life. You'll never be the same again.

The Lord wants to touch people first of all by His Word. The Word comes like a hammer and breaks the rock of tradition into pieces. And then He wants to come by His Spirit and begin a work deep down inside of your heart. The Spirit will bring about a change and put the fire of revival deep down inside of you, a fire that will burn through every fiber of your being.

For a tradition-buster, revival's not a meeting you have. Revival is a way of life. You live it, you eat it, you sleep it, you walk it, you talk it, you drink it, you pray it. Everything is revival. You have revival when you go home. There's revival in your car driving down the road. *It is not a meeting. It is a way of life.*

I'm not talking about just doing something crazy on the outside. I'm talking about a whole attitude of heart. We've watched people come into crusades on a Tuesday night who look like death warmed over. But by Friday night, they're exuberantly worshipping God! There's a light in their eyes. The glory's on their face. Tradition is broken!

But you can't leave it up to a preacher or a service. You've got to do it every day. You've got to shake yourself loose from tradition every day. I know what God had to do in my own life to break me free from religious tradition. I was raised in a godly home, and I thank God for my mother and father, but we were part of a traditional church, and if it weren't for the grace of God, I'd be somewhere in the traditional church playing some traditional religious game. But I'm so grateful that Jesus came and set me free.

Let Him set you free too!

CHAPTER 16

THE HEALING AND MIRACLE MINISTRY OF JESUS

Jesus returned in the power of the Spirit into Galilee: and there went out a fame of him through all the region round about. And he taught in the synagogues, being glorified of all. And he came to Nazareth, where he had been brought up: and, as his custom was, he went in the synagogue on the sabbath day, and stood up for to read. And there was delivered unto him the book of the prophet Esaias. And when he had opened the book, he found the place where it was written, The Spirit of the Lord is upon me, because he hath anointed me, (empowered me, enabled me, graced me) to preach the Gospel to the poor; he hath sent me to heal the brokenhearted, to preach deliverance to the captives, and recovering of sight to the blind, to set at liberty them that are bruised, To preach the acceptable year of the Lord.

LUKE 4:14-19

But so much the more went there a fame abroad of him: and great multitudes came together to hear, and to be healed of their infirmities. And he withdrew himself into the wilderness, and prayed. And it came to pass on a certain day, as he was teaching, that there were

Pharisees and doctors of the law sitting by, which were come out of every town of Galilee, and Judea, and Jerusalem: and the power of the Lord was present to heal them.

LUKE 5:15-17

As we've studied the Gospels of Matthew, Mark, Luke, and John, no matter what miracle Jesus was performing—whether it was a miracle of provision, whether He was casting devils out of somebody, whether He was healing them, or forgiving their sin—it was all the same for Him. Whether Jesus said: "Your sins are forgiven you. Take up your bed and walk," or "Fill the water-pots to the brim," it was all the same to Him, because He was operating by His heavenly Father's anointing, by the power of the Holy Spirit.

He hasn't changed yet, even two millennia later. The same anointing that brings healing and miracles is the same anointing that brings joy, freedom, liberty, and deliverance to *your* situation.

We simply need to be ready to apply the lessons that we've learned from our study of Jesus's life. When you apply faith to what you're believing God for, you'll have miracles. You'll have miracles of provision if you'll release your faith in that area. You'll have creative miracles if you'll release your faith in that area. You'll get healing miracles if you release your faith in that area—it's all covered under the same anointing.

The anointing that raises the dead is the same anointing that heals a person of cancer. God shows up in the person of the Lord Jesus Christ and miracles start happening. Signs and wonders start happening and the impossible begins to take place. All it takes is people with the anointing who just believe and say, "Lord, I trust You, I believe You, I'm looking for a miracle."

If you need tax money, He'll tell you where the fish is. If you run out of wine at a wedding, He'll tell you what to do to get wine. Nothing is impossible with Him. We have to build our faith in His Word and the touch of the Lord Jesus Christ—not only that He performed miracles in Bible days, but He still does today. He's the same yesterday, today and forever (Hebrews 13:8). We just have to activate the promises of God, because what God promises, He will perform (Romans 4:21).

> For the word of God is quick, and powerful, and sharper than any twoedged sword, piercing even to the dividing asunder of soul and spirit, and of the joints and marrow, and is a discerner of the thoughts and intents of the heart.
>
> HEBREWS 4:12

Just one word from Jesus and the cripples will walk. Just one word from Jesus and the blind will see. Just one word from Jesus and the deaf will hear again. Just one word from Jesus and the dead will be raised. If we have a problem with results, the problem is not with Jesus. The problem is with our ability to trust Him and to believe His Word.

Down through the years, God has anointed different people to flow in healing and miracles and signs and wonders. We still need people who will believe God, who will stretch their faith and say, "I believe that Jesus is alive, and I believe that He can perform miracles, signs, and wonders."

Although we've already studied it in depth, let's glance again at the very first miracle that Jesus did, one of provision in John 2:1-11. As you recall, there was a marriage in Cana of Galilee and Jesus, His mother, and His disciples were there. When their host ran out of wine, Mary said to Jesus: "They have no wine." And then she turned to the servants and told them to get ready to do whatever Jesus told them to do. If we want to get into the position where miracles and healing start flowing, we must get into the place where we do whatever Jesus tells us to do.

> And the third day there was a marriage in Cana of Galilee; and the mother of Jesus was there: And both Jesus was called, and his disciples, to the marriage. And when they wanted wine, the mother of Jesus saith unto him, They have no wine. Jesus saith unto her, Woman, what have I to do with thee? mine hour is not yet come. His mother saith unto the servants, Whatsoever he saith unto you, do it. And there were set there six waterpots of stone, after the manner of the

purifying of the Jews, containing two or three firkins apiece. Jesus saith unto them, Fill the waterpots with water. And they filled them up to the brim. And he saith unto them, Draw out now, and bear unto the governor of the feast. And they bare it. When the ruler of the feast had tasted the water that was made wine, and knew not whence it was: (but the servants which drew the water knew;) the governor of the feast called the bridegroom, And saith unto him, Every man at the beginning doth set forth good wine; and when men have well drunk, then that which is worse: but thou hast kept the good wine until now. This beginning of miracles did Jesus in Cana of Galilee, and manifested forth his glory; and his disciples believed on him.

JOHN 2:1-11

In a church we pioneered in Africa, a gentleman who suffered from a heart condition and high blood pressure was there for healing. Under the anointing of the Holy Spirit, I just pointed to him and said, "Run." He took off running right across the front of the church, across the back, then back up to the front, and just fell out under the power of God. He got up totally healed.

Why did I say to run? God told me to tell him to run. When I spoke to the man later, he said: "I just felt like I needed to run, and then you said to run, and it was like confirmation to me." *Whatever He says unto you, do it.*

One Sunday, I went to the hospital to see a man who'd just had a car wreck. He was in a neck brace and in a lot of pain from a severe injury. As I began to pray, the power of God went into him. He said: "When you prayed, I felt this warmth go right up through my body and into my neck."

I said: "What do you feel like you want to do?"

He said: "I'd like to get up."

I said: "Take that brace off right now."

The man looked at me and his eyes got big. He grabbed the brace, pulled it off, moved his head around, then jumped out of bed and started running around the hospital ward, totally healed by the power of God. Then they took me from ward to ward, just praying for everybody. I don't know how many people were released from that place that night!

The message of the cross and the resurrection is a message of goodness. The Gospel is a message of miracles, signs, and wonders. When you preach it and proclaim it, there will be people who will be saved, healed, and delivered. Everywhere Jesus went, He not only preached and taught, but He demonstrated the power of God. Jesus did not preach just to hear the sound of His own voice. He preached His message to obtain an end result, to see the works of God manifested in the lives of men. That's what we should be doing.

But for you to live what Jesus said, these truths must be rooted and established in your heart once and for all. The enemy will come to challenge all of these truths, because he knows if he can shake you off of them, your walk will be wobbly. If you don't know what you believe, you will be double-minded and unstable in all your ways. But once the truth of God's Word is established in your heart, the devil cannot move you away from God's best.

These truths are like an oak tree when it is planted in the ground. The first time you hear the Word, it is like an acorn. The Word is the seed, planted in your heart. But as you reinforce the seed, water it, and fertilize it, it continues to grow and mature. As the tree grows up, the roots run broad and deep underneath. The enemy knows that, so once you become firmly fixed and established in the Word of God concerning the fact that He's your Savior, He's your Healer, He's your Provider— then that's it. You are like a mighty oak who cannot be uprooted, no matter how strong the wind.

I want to challenge you to establish the truth once and for all in your heart, because I really believe in these last days, you're going to need deep roots. As things go haywire, different kinds of disasters will force you to rely fully on God for your healing, your provision, or your deliverance. What do you do when doctors can't help you anymore? What do you do when your bank can't help you anymore? If a crisis arose, many people would go to pieces because they don't believe the Word of God.

To see the power in the words spoken by Jesus, let's go to the second miracle that He did:

> So Jesus came again unto Cana of Galilee, where he made the water wine. And there was a certain nobleman, whose son was sick at Capernaum. When he heard that Jesus was come out of Judea into Galilee, he went unto him, and besought him that he would come down, and heal his son: for he was at the point of death. Then said Jesus unto him, Except ye see signs and wonders ye will not believe. The nobleman saith unto him, Sir, come down ere my child die. Jesus saith unto him, Go thy way; thy son liveth. And the man believed the word that Jesus had spoken unto him, and he went his way. And as he was now going down, his servants met him and told him, saying, Thy son liveth. Then inquired he of them the hour when he began to amend. And they said unto him, Yesterday at the seventh hour the fever left him. So the father knew that it was at the same hour, in the which Jesus said unto him, Thy son liveth: and himself believed, and his whole house.
>
> JOHN 4:46-53

A nobleman, whose son was at the point of death, heard that Jesus was headed his way. So, he came to Jesus and told Him what he needed. Rather than coming to touch the boy as the father had requested, Jesus just spoke the Word and said: "Your son lives." The father *accepted Jesus's word in faith,* then turned around and headed home. On the way home, his servants met him and said, "Hey, your boy's fine."

He said, "What time did it happen?"

They said, "The seventh hour." Then he realized it was the exact same time that Jesus had spoken the Word and he had believed.

This miracle shows us something powerful. This father didn't need to see a sign or watch Jesus touch his son. He simply took Jesus at His word. It's the same now. Just one word from Jesus will make it right. Just one word from Jesus will calm the storm. Just one word from Jesus will set the captives free. Just one word from Jesus will cause the blind to see. Just one word from Jesus will cause the deaf to hear. Just one word from Jesus will cause the lame to walk. *Just one word from Jesus!*

That's why, before I even pray for people, I get quiet. I wait in my spirit to see what the Lord would say. I know that one word from Jesus spoken over those circumstances will change everything. Sometimes they're healed instantly. Sometimes the Lord says: "Within the next thirty days." Some will see a total turnaround and a transformation within the next ninety days. With other people, the Lord will say, "In the next twelve months, there will come a change."

We've seen that happen with couples who have been trying to have children without success. Couples all over the world have brought their babies to us to show us the fruit of our prayers. We laid hands on them to be fruitful and multiply and replenish the earth—and they did! Some people had been trying to have a baby for sixteen years without success, but God gave them the desire of their heart after we prayed. Some of these couples gave birth barely nine months later!

At all times, we have to believe the words of Jesus, even and especially when they don't make sense at all in the natural. Luke 5:1-5 describes Simon Peter's reaction to Jesus's words:

> And it came to pass, that, as the people pressed upon him to hear the word of God, he stood by the lake of Gennesaret, And saw two ships standing by the lake; but the fishermen were gone out of them, and were washing their nets. And he entered one of the ships, which was Simon's, and prayed him that he would thrust out a little from the land. And he sat down, and taught the people out of the ship. Now when he had left speaking, he said unto Simon, Launch out into the deep, and let down your nets for a draught. And Simon answering said unto him, Master, we have toiled all the night and have taken nothing; nevertheless at thy word I will let down the net.
>
> LUKE 5:1-5

Simon Peter was a career fisherman and Jesus wasn't, but Peter showed us the kind of faith we need when he said: "Nevertheless at thy word I will let down the net." Many times, a miracle will come when the natural circumstances look totally bleak. The word of the Lord may come and be totally opposite to the circumstances. The doctors may have told you that you're going to die and, in the natural, that's the way it looks. But when Jesus comes, He will speak a word that will override your circumstances.

Why? Because He can make a way where there is no way. Nothing's impossible with Him, and He illustrated that point with Simon Peter. Peter said: "Nevertheless at thy word I will let down the net." And he did.

> And when they had this done, they inclosed a great multitude of fishes: and their net brake. And they beckoned unto their partners, which were in the other ship, that they should come and help them. And they came, and filled both ships, so that they began to sink. When Simon Peter saw it, he fell down at Jesus's knees, saying, Depart from me; for I am a sinful man, O Lord. For he was astonished, and all that were with him, at the draught of the fishes which they had taken: And so was also James, and John, the sons of Zebedee, which were partners with Simon. And Jesus said unto Simon, "Fear not; from henceforth thou shall catch men. And when they had brought their ships to land, they forsook all, and followed Him.
>
> LUKE 5:6-11

After Peter, James, and John saw what happened, they dropped their nets and walked away from their boats to follow Jesus. Who wants to just keep fishing after seeing Jesus do an incredible miracle? When people see what miracles occur in their lives as they act on God's Word, they'll make life-changing decisions too.

As you go forth with faith in His Word and in His miracle-working power, God will use you in a place where there's lack and work a miracle of provision through you. Some friends of ours, a pastor and his wife, needed to cook several hundred turkeys to feed the needy one Thanksgiving. A family in the church who owned a restaurant volunteered to cook the turkeys. They cooked the turkeys morning, noon, and night.

While they were cooking, the restaurant owners mentioned to the pastor and his wife that their business was really struggling, but they didn't want to accept anything for cooking the turkeys. They just wanted to do it to help the homeless and those who were in need for Thanksgiving. Well, later the pastor and his wife went back there for lunch, and they had to wait outside because the place was so packed. They asked the owners, "What happened to your business?"

They said, "Well, we don't understand what happened, but from the moment we started cooking your turkeys, business just took off." When you act on the Word of God, things change in your life. Not only that, when you walk with Jesus and act on His words, your own words take on new power.

> And there was in their synagogue a man with an unclean spirit; and he cried out, Saying, Let us alone; what have we to do with thee, thou Jesus of Nazareth? art thou come to destroy us? I know thee who thou art, the Holy One of God. And Jesus rebuked him, saying, Hold thy peace, and come out of him. And when the unclean spirit had torn him, and cried with a loud voice, he came out of him. And they were all amazed, insomuch that they questioned among themselves, saying, What thing is this? What new doctrine is this, for with authority commandeth he even the unclean spirits, and they do obey him.
>
> MARK 1:23-27

Jesus walked in the anointing, so His words carried authority. When He walked in the place, the devils in the person began to cry out. When light comes, darkness has to flee. And so when you are walking in the power and anointing of the Spirit of God and you walk into a place where people are bound by devils, they'll begin to cry out.

These devils knew who Jesus was and started blabbing. Jesus said, in effect: "Shut up and come out." Those nearby were amazed. What thing is this? When we walk in God's Word and the power of His Spirit, we can speak with that authority too.

When we were in Bangor, Maine, there was a gentleman who would cause a disturbance at every revival meeting in town. He'd come in and start cussing, and preachers would go over and start binding and rebuking. They'd spend an hour or two focusing on him without results, and he'd just wreck the whole service.

When I walked out to preach one night, he was sitting up front, staring at me. So I felt led to just pick on him. When I preached, I looked right in his eyes. My words were provoking words, and after I'd preached forty-five minutes or so, I leaned over and put my hand on his head. When I did, he stuck his hand right up in my face and made a very rude sign and started spewing profanities at me. I immediately burst out laughing because I was shocked.

As I had my hand on his head, I just said, "Shut up!" and he collapsed in the seat and didn't move. The wind went right out of his sails. He just collapsed in the seat.

You've just got to get ready. You never know what's going to happen. But when you know your authority, it doesn't matter. Whether it's a devil or just a rebellious individual, you can take authority over them. However, you have to know what you're dealing with, because devils obey the name of Jesus, but the flesh doesn't necessarily do so.

Another time, back in 1990, I was ministering and there was a man who was glaring daggers at me. As another minister was walking up the aisle, he lost his balance and put his hand on the man's shoulder. I heard the man say to him, "I'm going to kill you," and he started following him to the back of the church.

It was right at the end of the service, so I went to the back and the guy stood there and said to me, "I've killed eight people. I'm going to kill you." Now I'd just come out of the meeting and I was under a heavy anointing of the power of God, so I just burst out laughing. He said, "You don't understand. I'm going to." And he went on with a whole string of profanity.

I looked at him straight in the eye and said: "You can't kill me, I'm already dead. Anytime you want to try, go ahead and start. But I love you, man."

"Don't you come with that stuff," he said.

I said, "Man, I love you. Jesus loves you. You can't kill me." He said, "I'll be back tomorrow. I'll know if you're a man of God or not."

He disappeared out the back door and I started praying. I mean I *really* prayed. I said, "God, we've got twenty-four hours. We need a miracle. I need You to visit this guy in the night, send an angel, do whatever it takes. The guy's a psychopath. He's going to blow me away. He told me he would know if I was a man of God or not, and God, You know I am a man of God, but if ever I need confirmation, I need it tonight. If he comes back tomorrow and blows me away, then everybody will believe I'm not a man of God."

The next night there he was, sitting and glaring at me. I thought, *This is my final service on planet Earth. So, since it's my last night on the earth, I'm just going to preach right in his face. I mean just preach!* "Jesus loves you and He wants to save you, sir." I was preaching for my life!

Then I gave the altar call. The first person to move was this man. He came running down the aisle, fell on his knees, tears rolling down his cheeks, crying out to God, "Save me, save me." And then he fell to the floor and, for about twenty minutes, he just lay there and quoted whole chapters of the Bible.

It turned out that he had been called by God to be a minister when he backslid. He'd joined the military, become a mercenary, and had killed many people. He was tormented by the devil.

After the service, I asked him what changed his mind.

He said, "Well, I know you're a man of God."

I said, "How do you know?"

He said, "Last night I tried to run my truck into a wall, but I couldn't do it. So I went home, loaded a gun, and tried to shoot myself, but I wasn't able to do that either. Eventually, I just started trembling and shaking. I knew that you'd been praying for me."

The Lord saved this man, filled him with the Holy Ghost, and I believe that he's in the ministry. Today, he's serving God. As powerful as the spoken Word is, it's not the only way Jesus applied the power of God. There's a miracle that gets mentioned in Matthew, Mark, and Luke, where Jesus heals Peter's mother-in-law. Read it in Matthew 8:14-15:

> And when Jesus was come into Peter's house, he saw his wife's mother laid, and sick of a fever. And he touched her hand, and the fever left her: and she arose, and ministered unto them.

We've been talking about speaking the Word and receiving a miracle, but here we see something different. Jesus just touched her hand and the fever left her. Here Jesus never even said one word—all He did was touch her, and the fever left.

So many times people make a big production of healing. They pray a big, long prayer like, "Ohhhhhh, God, as we're gathered in this place, Lord, we thank Thee that Thou seest Sister Jones, Lord, and how that she has a need. And God we just pray that Thou wouldst reach down and touch her, Lord." And they go on and on. But in the Gospels, you never find Jesus actually praying for anybody when he ministered to them. He spoke the Word, and they were healed. He touched people, and they were healed.

Right now, Jesus has spoken His Word to you: "Be healed!" Right now, Jesus has His nail-scarred hand on your body, on your broken heart. Be made whole!

Right now, Jesus wants to meet your needs, open doors of opportunity, and give you the blessings of Heaven. All you need to do is believe His Word, and His healing miracle ministry will flow into your life.

THE HEALINGS AND MIRACLES OF JESUS

1. Converts water into wine

And the third day there was a marriage in Cana of Galilee; and the mother of Jesus was there: And both Jesus was called, and his disciples, to the marriage. And when they wanted wine, the mother of Jesus saith unto him, They have no wine. Jesus saith unto her,

Woman, what have I to do with thee? mine hour is not yet come. His mother saith unto the servants, Whatsoever he saith unto you, do it. And there were set there six waterpots of stone, after the manner of the purifying of the Jews, containing two or three firkins apiece. Jesus saith unto them, Fill the waterpots with water. And they filled them up to the brim. And he saith unto them, Draw out now, and bear unto the governor of the feast. And they bare it. When the ruler of the feast had tasted the water that was made wine, and knew not whence it was: (but the servants which drew the water knew;) the governor of the feast called the bridegroom, And saith unto him, Every man at the beginning doth set forth good wine; and when men have well drunk, then that which is worse: but thou hast kept the good wine until now. This beginning of miracles did Jesus in Cana of Galilee, and manifested forth his glory; and his disciples believed on him.

JOHN 2:1-11

2.   Heals the nobleman's son

So Jesus came again into Cana of Galilee, where he made the water wine. And there was a certain nobleman, whose son was sick at Capernaum. When he heard that Jesus was come out of Judaea into Galilee, he went unto him, and besought him that he would come down, and heal his son: for he was at the point of death. Then said Jesus unto him, Except ye see signs and wonders, ye will not believe. The nobleman saith unto him, Sir, come down ere my child die. Jesus saith unto him, Go thy way; thy son liveth. And the man believed the word that Jesus had spoken unto him, and he went his way. And as he was now going down, his servants met him, and told him, saying, Thy son liveth. Then enquired he of them the hour when he began to amend. And they said unto him, Yesterday at the seventh hour the fever left him. So the father knew that it was at the same hour, in the which Jesus said unto him, Thy son liveth:

and himself believed, and his whole house. This is again the second miracle that Jesus did, when he was come out of Judaea into Galilee.

JOHN 4:46-54

3. Heals the demoniac

And there was in their synagogue a man with an unclean spirit; and he cried out, Saying, Let us alone; what have we to do with thee, thou Jesus of Nazareth? art thou come to destroy us? I know thee who thou art, the Holy One of God. And Jesus rebuked him, saying, Hold thy peace, and come out of him. And when the unclean spirit had torn him, and cried with a loud voice, he came out of him.

MARK 1:23-26

And in the synagogue there was a man, which had a spirit of an unclean devil, and cried out with a loud voice, Saying, Let us alone; what have we to do with thee, thou Jesus of Nazareth? art thou come to destroy us? I know thee who thou art; the Holy One of God. And Jesus rebuked him, saying, Hold thy peace, and come out of him. And when the devil had thrown him in the midst, he came out of him, and hurt him not. And they were all amazed, and spake among themselves, saying, What a word is this! for with authority and power he commandeth the unclean spirits, and they come out.

LUKE 4:33-36

4. Heals Peter's mother-in-law

And when Jesus was come into Peter's house, he saw his wife's mother laid, and sick of a fever. And he touched her hand, and the fever left her: and she arose, and ministered unto them.

MATTHEW 8:14-15

And forthwith, when they were come out of the synagogue, they entered into the house of Simon and Andrew, with James and John.

But Simon's wife's mother lay sick of a fever, and anon they tell him of her. And he came and took her by the hand, and lifted her up; and immediately the fever left her, and she ministered unto them.

MARK 1:29-31

And he arose out of the synagogue, and entered into Simon's house. And Simon's wife's mother was taken with a great fever; and they besought him for her. And he stood over her, and rebuked the fever; and it left her: and immediately she arose and ministered unto them.

LUKE 4:38-39

5.   Cleanses the leper

When he was come down from the mountain, great multitudes followed him. And, behold, there came a leper and worshipped him, saying, Lord, if thou wilt, thou canst make me clean. And Jesus put forth his hand, and touched him, saying, I will; be thou clean. And immediately his leprosy was cleansed. And Jesus saith unto him, See thou tell no man; but go thy way, shew thyself to the priest, and offer the gift that Moses commanded, for a testimony unto them.

MATTHEW 8:1-4

And there came a leper to him, beseeching him, and kneeling down to him, and saying unto him, If thou wilt, thou canst make me clean. And Jesus, moved with compassion, put forth his hand, and touched him, and saith unto him, I will; be thou clean. And as soon as he had spoken, immediately the leprosy departed from him, and he was cleansed. And he straitly charged him, and forthwith sent him away; And saith unto him, See thou say nothing to any man: but go thy way, shew thyself to the priest, and offer for thy cleansing those things which Moses commanded, for a testimony unto them.

MARK 1:40-44

And it came to pass, when he was in a certain city, behold a man full of leprosy: who seeing Jesus fell on his face, and besought him, saying, Lord, if thou wilt, thou canst make me clean. And he put forth his hand, and touched him, saying, I will: be thou clean. And immediately the leprosy departed from him. And he charged him to tell no man: but go, and shew thyself to the priest, and offer for thy cleansing, according as Moses commanded, for a testimony unto them.

LUKE 5:12-14

6. Heals the paralyzed man

And he entered into a ship, and passed over, and came into his own city. And, behold, they brought to him a man sick of the palsy, lying on a bed: and Jesus seeing their faith said unto the sick of the palsy; Son, be of good cheer; thy sins be forgiven thee. And, behold, certain of the scribes said within themselves, This man blasphemeth. And Jesus knowing their thoughts said, Wherefore think ye evil in your hearts? For whether is easier, to say, Thy sins be forgiven thee; or to say, Arise, and walk? But that ye may know that the Son of man hath power on earth to forgive sins, (then saith he to the sick of the palsy,) Arise, take up thy bed, and go unto thine house. And he arose, and departed to his house. But when the multitudes saw it, they marvelled, and glorified God, which had given such power unto men.

MATTHEW 9:1-8

And again he entered into Capernaum after some days; and it was noised that he was in the house. And straightway many were gathered together, insomuch that there was no room to receive them, no, not so much as about the door: and he preached the word unto them. And they come unto him, bringing one sick of the palsy, which was borne of four. And when they could not come nigh unto him for the press, they uncovered the roof where he was: and when they had broken it up, they let down the bed wherein the sick of the palsy lay. When Jesus saw their faith, he said unto the sick of the palsy, Son, thy sins be forgiven thee. But there was certain of the scribes sitting there, and reasoning in their hearts, Why doth this man thus speak blasphemies? who can forgive sins but God only? And immediately when Jesus perceived in his spirit that they so reasoned within themselves, he said unto them, Why reason ye these things in your hearts? Whether is it easier to say to the sick of the palsy, Thy sins be forgiven thee; or to say, Arise, and take up thy bed, and walk? But that ye may know that the Son of man hath power on earth to forgive sins, (he saith to the sick of the palsy,) I say unto thee, Arise, and take up thy bed, and go thy way into thine house. And immediately he arose, took up the bed, and went forth before them all; insomuch that they were all amazed, and glorified God, saying, We never saw it on this fashion.

MARK 2:1-12

And it came to pass on a certain day, as he was teaching, that there were Pharisees and doctors of the law sitting by, which were come out of every town of Galilee, and Judaea, and Jerusalem: and the power of the Lord was present to heal them. And, behold, men brought in a bed a man which was taken with a palsy: and they sought means to bring him in, and to lay him before him. And when they could not find by what way they might bring him in because of the multitude, they went upon the housetop, and let him down through the tiling with his couch into the midst before Jesus. And when he saw their faith, he said unto him, Man, thy sins are forgiven thee. And the scribes and the Pharisees began to reason, saying, Who is this which speaketh blasphemies? Who can forgive sins, but God alone? But when Jesus perceived their thoughts, he answering said unto them, What reason ye in your hearts? Whether is easier, to say, Thy sins be forgiven thee; or to say, Rise up and walk? But that ye may know that the Son of man hath power upon earth to forgive sins, (he said unto the sick of the palsy,) I say unto thee, Arise, and take up thy couch, and go into thine house. And immediately he rose up before them, and took up that whereon he lay, and departed to his own house, glorifying God. And they were all amazed, and they glorified God, and were filled with fear, saying, We have seen strange things to day.

LUKE 5:17-26

7. Heals the impotent man

After this there was a feast of the Jews; and Jesus went up to Jerusalem. Now there is at Jerusalem by the sheep market a pool, which is called in the Hebrew tongue Bethesda, having five porches. In these lay a great multitude of impotent folk, of blind, halt, withered, waiting for the moving of the water. For an angel went down at a certain season into the pool, and troubled the water: whosoever then first after the troubling of the water stepped in was made whole of whatsoever disease he had. And a certain man was there, which had an infirmity thirty and eight years. When Jesus saw him lie, and knew that he had been now a long time in that case, he saith unto him, Wilt thou be made whole? The impotent man answered him, Sir, I have no man, when the water is troubled, to put me into the pool: but while I am coming, another steppeth down before me. Jesus saith unto him, Rise, take up thy bed, and walk. And immediately the man was made whole, and took up his bed, and walked: and on the same day was the sabbath. The Jews therefore said unto him that was cured, It is the sabbath day: it is not lawful for thee to carry thy bed. He answered them, He that made me whole, the same said unto me, Take up thy bed, and walk. Then asked they him, What man is that which said unto thee, Take up thy bed, and walk? And he that was healed wist not who it was: for Jesus had conveyed himself away, a multitude being in that place. Afterward Jesus findeth him in the temple, and said unto him, Behold, thou art made whole: sin no more, lest a worse thing come unto thee. The man departed, and told the Jews that it was Jesus, which had made him whole. And therefore did the Jews persecute Jesus, and sought to slay him, because he had done these things on the sabbath day.

JOHN 5:1-16

8.   Restores the withered hand

And when he was departed thence, he went into their synagogue: And, behold, there was a man which had his hand withered. And they asked him, saying, Is it lawful to heal on the sabbath days? that they might accuse him. And he said unto them, What man shall there be among you, that shall have one sheep, and if it fall into a pit on the sabbath day, will he not lay hold on it, and lift it out? How much then is a man better than a sheep? Wherefore it is lawful to do well on the sabbath days. Then saith he to the man, Stretch forth thine hand. And he stretched it forth; and it was restored whole, like as the other.

MATTHEW 12:9-13

And he entered again into the synagogue; and there was a man there which had a withered hand. And they watched him, whether he would heal him on the sabbath day; that they might accuse him. And he saith unto the man which had the withered hand, Stand forth. And he saith unto them, Is it lawful to do good on the sabbath days, or to do evil? to save life, or to kill? But they held their peace. And when he had looked round about on them with anger, being grieved for the hardness of their hearts, he saith unto the man, Stretch forth thine hand. And he stretched it out: and his hand was restored whole as the other.

MARK 3:1-5

And it came to pass also on another sabbath, that he entered into the synagogue and taught: and there was a man whose right hand was withered. And the scribes and Pharisees watched him, whether he would heal on the sabbath day; that they might find an accusation against him. But he knew their thoughts, and said to the man which had the withered hand, Rise up, and stand forth in the midst. And he arose and stood forth. Then said Jesus unto them, I will ask you one thing; Is it lawful on the sabbath days to do good, or to do evil? to save life, or to destroy it? And looking round about upon them all, he said unto the man, Stretch forth thy hand. And he did so: and his hand was restored whole as the other. And they were filled with madness; and communed one with another what they might do to Jesus.

LUKE 6:6-11

9. Restores the centurion's servant

And when Jesus was entered into Capernaum, there came unto him a centurion, beseeching him, And saying, Lord, my servant lieth at home sick of the palsy, grievously tormented. And Jesus saith unto him, I will come and heal him. The centurion answered and said, Lord, I am not worthy that thou shouldest come under my roof: but speak the word only, and my servant shall be healed. For I am a man under authority, having soldiers under me: and I say to this man, Go, and he goeth; and to another, Come, and he cometh; and to my servant, Do this, and he doeth it. When Jesus heard it, he marvelled, and said to them that followed, Verily I say unto you, I have not found so great faith, no, not in Israel. And I say unto you, That many shall come from the east and west, and shall sit down with Abraham, and Isaac, and Jacob, in the kingdom of heaven. But the children of the kingdom shall be cast out into outer darkness: there shall be weeping and gnashing of teeth. And Jesus said unto the centurion, Go thy way; and as thou hast believed, so be it done unto thee. And his servant was healed in the selfsame hour.

MATTHEW 8:5-13

Now when he had ended all his sayings in the audience of the people, he entered into Capernaum. And a certain centurion's servant, who was dear unto him, was sick, and ready to die. And when he heard of Jesus, he sent unto him the elders of the Jews, beseeching him that he would come and heal his servant. And when they came to Jesus, they besought him instantly, saying, That he was worthy for whom he should do this: For he loveth our nation, and he hath built us a synagogue. Then Jesus went with them. And when he was now not far from the house, the centurion sent friends to him, saying unto him, Lord, trouble not thyself: for I am not worthy that thou shouldest enter under my roof: Wherefore neither thought I myself worthy to come unto thee: but say in a word, and my servant shall be healed. For I also am a man set under authority, having under me soldiers, and I say unto one, Go, and he goeth; and to another, Come, and he cometh; and to my servant, Do this, and he doeth it. When Jesus heard these things, he marvelled at him, and turned him about, and said unto the people that followed him, I say unto you, I have not found so great faith, no, not in Israel. And they that were sent, returning to the house, found the servant whole that had been sick.

LUKE 7:1-10

10. Raises the widow's son to life at the village of Nain

And it came to pass the day after, that he went into a city called Nain; and many of his disciples went with him, and much people. Now when he came nigh to the gate of the city, behold, there was a dead man carried out, the only son of his mother, and she was a widow: and much people of the city was with her. And when the Lord saw her, he had compassion on her, and said unto her, Weep not. And he came and touched the bier: and they that bare him stood still. And he said, Young man, I say unto thee, Arise. And he that was dead sat up, and began to speak. And he delivered him to his mother. And there came a fear on all: and they glorified God, saying, That a great prophet is risen up among us; and, That God hath visited his people.

LUKE 7:11-16

11. Heals a demoniac

Then was brought unto him one possessed with a devil, blind, and dumb: and he healed him, insomuch that the blind and dumb both spake and saw. And all the people were amazed, and said, Is not this the son of David? But when the Pharisees heard it, they said, This fellow doth not cast out devils, but by Beelzebub the prince of the devils. And Jesus knew their thoughts, and said unto them, Every kingdom divided against itself is brought to desolation; and every city or house divided against itself shall not stand: And if Satan cast out Satan, he is divided against himself; how shall then his kingdom stand? And if I by Beelzebub cast out devils, by whom do your children cast them out? therefore they shall be your judges. But if I cast out devils by the Spirit of God, then the kingdom of God is come unto you. Or else how can one enter into a strong man's house, and spoil his goods, except he first bind the strong man? and then he will spoil his house. He that is not with me is against me; and he that gathereth not with me scattereth abroad. Wherefore I say unto you, All manner of sin and blasphemy shall be forgiven unto men: but the blasphemy against the Holy Ghost shall not be forgiven unto men. And whosoever speaketh a word against the Son of man, it shall be forgiven him: but whosoever speaketh against the Holy Ghost, it shall not be forgiven him, neither in this world, neither in the world to come. Either make the tree good, and his fruit good;

or else make the tree corrupt, and his fruit corrupt: for the tree is known by his fruit.

MATTHEW 12:22-33

And unclean spirits, when they saw him, fell down before him, and cried, saying, Thou art the Son of God.

MARK 3:11

And he was casting out a devil, and it was dumb. And it came to pass, when the devil was gone out, the dumb spake; and the people wondered. But some of them said, He casteth out devils through Beelzebub the chief of the devils.

LUKE 11:14-15

12. Stills the storm

And when he was entered into a ship, his disciples followed him. And, behold, there arose a great tempest in the sea, insomuch that the ship was covered with the waves: but he was asleep. And his disciples came to him, and awoke him, saying, Lord, save us: we perish. And he saith unto them, Why are ye fearful, O ye of little faith? Then he arose, and rebuked the winds and the sea; and there was a great calm. But the men marvelled, saying, What manner of man is this, that even the winds and the sea obey him!

MATTHEW 8:23-27

And when they were come into the ship, the wind ceased.

MATTHEW 14:32

And the same day, when the even was come, he saith unto them, Let us pass over unto the other side. And when they had sent away the multitude, they took him even as he was in the ship. And there were also with him other little ships. And there arose a great storm of wind, and the waves beat into the ship, so that it was now full. And he was in the hinder part of the ship, asleep on a pillow: and they awake him, and say unto him, Master, carest thou not that we perish? And he arose, and rebuked the wind, and said unto the sea, Peace, be still. And the wind ceased, and there was a great calm. And he said unto them, Why are ye so fearful? how is it that ye have no faith? And they feared exceedingly, and said one to another, What manner of man is this, that even the wind and the sea obey him?

MARK 4:35-41

Now it came to pass on a certain day, that he went into a ship with his disciples: and he said unto them, Let us go over unto the other side of the lake. And they launched forth. But as they sailed he fell asleep: and there came down a storm of wind on the lake; and they were filled with water, and were in jeopardy. And they came to him, and awoke him, saying, Master, master, we perish. Then he arose, and rebuked the wind and the raging of the water: and they ceased, and there was a calm. And he said unto them, Where is your faith? And they being afraid wondered, saying one to another, What manner of man is this! for he commandeth even the winds and water, and they obey him.

LUKE 8:22-25

13. Casts demons out of the man from Gadara

And when he was come to the other side into the country of the Gergesenes, there met him two possessed with devils, coming out of the tombs, exceeding fierce, so that no man might pass by that way. And, behold, they cried out, saying, What have we to do with thee, Jesus, thou Son of God? art thou come hither to torment us before the time? And there was a good way off from them an herd of many swine feeding. So the devils besought him, saying, If thou cast us out, suffer us to go away into the herd of swine. And he said unto them, Go. And when they were come out, they went into the herd of swine: and, behold, the whole herd of swine ran violently down a steep place into the sea, and perished in the waters. And they that kept them fled, and went their ways into the city, and told every thing, and what was befallen to the possessed of the devils. And, behold, the whole city came out to meet Jesus: and when they saw him, they besought him that he would depart out of their coasts.

MATTHEW 8:28-34

And they came over unto the other side of the sea, into the country of the Gadarenes. And when he was come out of the ship, immediately there met him out of the tombs a man with an unclean spirit, Who had his dwelling among the tombs; and no man could bind him, no, not with chains: Because that he had been often bound with fetters and chains, and the chains had been plucked asunder by him, and the fetters broken in pieces: neither could any man tame him. And always, night and day, he was in the mountains, and in the tombs, crying, and cutting himself with stones. But when he saw Jesus afar off, he ran and worshipped him, And cried with a loud voice, and said, What have I to do with thee, Jesus, thou Son of the most high God? I adjure thee by God, that thou torment me not. For he said unto him, Come out of the man, thou unclean spirit. And he asked him, What is thy name? And he answered, saying, My name is Legion: for we are many. And he besought him much that he would not send them away out of the country. Now there was there nigh unto the mountains a great herd of swine feeding. And all the devils besought him, saying, Send us into the swine, that we may enter into them. And forthwith Jesus gave them leave. And the unclean spirits went out, and entered into the swine: and the herd ran violently down a steep place into the sea, (they were about two thousand;) and were choked in the sea. And they that fed the swine fled, and told it in the city, and in the country. And they went out to see what it was that was done. And they come to Jesus, and see him that was possessed with the devil, and had the legion, sitting, and clothed, and in his right mind: and they were afraid. And they that saw it told them how it befell to him that was possessed with the devil, and also concerning the swine. And they began to pray him to depart out of their coasts. And when he was come into the ship, he that had been possessed with the devil prayed him that he might be with him. Howbeit Jesus suffered him not, but saith unto him, Go home to thy friends, and tell them how great things the Lord hath done for thee, and hath had compassion on thee. And he departed, and began to publish in Decapolis how great things Jesus had done for him: and all men did marvel.

MARK 5:1-20

And they arrived at the country of the Gadarenes, which is over against Galilee. And when he went forth to land, there met him out of the city a certain man, which had devils long time, and ware no clothes, neither abode in any house, but in the tombs. When he saw Jesus, he cried out, and fell down before him, and with a loud voice said, What have I to do with thee, Jesus, thou Son of God most high? I beseech thee, torment me not. (For he had commanded the unclean spirit to come out of the man. For oftentimes it had caught him: and he was kept bound with chains and in fetters; and he brake the bands, and was driven of the devil into the wilderness.) And Jesus asked him, saying, What is thy name? And he said, Legion: because many devils were entered into him. And they besought him that he would not command them to go out into the deep. And there was there an herd of many swine feeding on the mountain: and they besought him that he would suffer them to enter into them. And he suffered them. Then went the devils out of the man, and entered into the swine: and the herd ran violently down a steep place into the lake, and were choked. When they that fed them saw what was done, they fled, and went and told it in the city and in the country. Then they went out to see what was done;

and came to Jesus, and found the man, out of whom the devils were departed, sitting at the feet of Jesus, clothed, and in his right mind: and they were afraid. They also which saw it told them by what means he that was possessed of the devils was healed. Then the whole multitude of the country of the Gadarenes round about besought him to depart from them; for they were taken with great fear: and he went up into the ship, and returned back again. Now the man out of whom the devils were departed besought him that he might be with him: but Jesus sent him away, saying, Return to thine own house, and shew how great things God hath done unto thee. And he went his way, and published throughout the whole city how great things Jesus had done unto him.

LUKE 8:26-39

14. Raises the daughter of Jairus from the dead

While he spake these things unto them, behold, there came a certain ruler, and worshipped him, saying, My daughter is even now dead: but come and lay thy hand upon her, and she shall live. And Jesus arose, and followed him, and so did his disciples. And when Jesus came into the ruler's house, and saw the minstrels and the people making a noise, He said unto them, Give place: for the maid is not dead, but sleepeth. And they laughed him to scorn. But when the people were put forth, he went in, and took her by the hand, and the maid arose. And the fame hereof went abroad into all that land.

MATTHEW 9:18-19, 23-26

And, behold, there cometh one of the rulers of the synagogue, Jairus by name; and when he saw him, he fell at his feet, And besought him greatly, saying, My little daughter lieth at the point of death: I pray thee, come and lay thy hands on her, that she may be healed; and she shall live. And Jesus went with him; and much people followed him, and thronged him. While he yet spake, there came from the ruler of the synagogue's house certain which said, Thy daughter is dead: why troublest thou the Master any further? As soon as Jesus heard the word that was spoken, he saith unto the ruler of the synagogue, Be not afraid, only believe. And he suffered no man to follow him, save Peter, and James, and John the brother of James. And he cometh to the house of the ruler of the synagogue, and seeth the tumult, and them that wept and wailed greatly. And when he was come in, he saith unto them, Why make ye this ado, and weep? the damsel is not dead, but sleepeth. And they laughed him to scorn. But when he had put them all out, he taketh the father and the mother of the damsel, and them that were with him, and entereth in where the damsel was lying. And he took the damsel by the hand, and said unto her, Talitha cumi; which is, being interpreted, Damsel, I say unto thee, arise. And straightway the damsel arose, and walked; for she was of the age of twelve years. And they were astonished with a great astonishment. And he charged them straitly that no man should know it; and commanded that something should be given her to eat.

MARK 5:22-24, 35-43

And, behold, there came a man named Jairus, and he was a ruler of the synagogue: and he fell down at Jesus's feet, and besought him that he would come into his house: For he had one only daughter, about twelve years of age, and she lay a dying. But as he went the people thronged him. While he yet spake, there cometh one from the ruler of the synagogue's house, saying to him, Thy daughter is dead; trouble not the Master. But when Jesus heard it, he answered him, saying, Fear not: believe only, and she shall be made whole. And when he came into the house, he suffered no man to go in, save Peter, and James, and John, and the father and the mother of the maiden. And all wept, and bewailed her: but he said, Weep not; she is not dead, but sleepeth. And they laughed him to scorn, knowing that she was dead. And he put them all out, and took her by the hand, and called, saying, Maid, arise. And her spirit came again, and

she arose straightway: and he commanded to give her meat. And
her parents were astonished: but he charged them that they should
tell no man what was done.

LUKE 8:41-42, 49-56

15. Heals the woman with the issue of blood

And, behold, a woman, which was diseased with an issue of blood
twelve years, came behind him, and touched the hem of his garment:
For she said within herself, If I may but touch his garment, I shall
be whole. But Jesus turned him about, and when he saw her, he said,
Daughter, be of good comfort; thy faith hath made thee whole. And
the woman was made whole from that hour.

MATTHEW 9:20-22

And a certain woman, which had an issue of blood twelve years,
And had suffered many things of many physicians, and had spent
all that she had, and was nothing bettered, but rather grew worse,
When she had heard of Jesus, came in the press behind, and touched
his garment. For she said, If I may touch but his clothes, I shall be
whole. And straightway the fountain of her blood was dried up;
and she felt in her body that she was healed of that plague. And
Jesus, immediately knowing in himself that virtue had gone out
of him, turned him about in the press, and said, Who touched my
clothes? And his disciples said unto him, Thou seest the multitude
thronging thee, and sayest thou, Who touched me? And he looked
round about to see her that had done this thing. But the woman
fearing and trembling, knowing what was done in her, came and
fell down before him, and told him all the truth. And he said unto
her, Daughter, thy faith hath made thee whole; go in peace, and be
whole of thy plague.

MARK 5:25-34

And a woman having an issue of blood twelve years, which had spent all her living upon physicians, neither could be healed of any, Came behind him, and touched the border of his garment: and immediately her issue of blood stanched. And Jesus said, Who touched me? When all denied, Peter and they that were with him said, Master, the multitude throng thee and press thee, and sayest thou, Who touched me? And Jesus said, Somebody hath touched me: for I perceive that virtue is gone out of me. And when the woman saw that she was not hid, she came trembling, and falling down before him, she declared unto him before all the people for what cause she had touched him, and how she was healed immediately. And he said unto her, Daughter, be of good comfort: thy faith hath made thee whole; go in peace.

LUKE 8:43-48

16. Restores the sight of two blind men

And when Jesus departed thence, two blind men followed him, crying, and saying, Thou son of David, have mercy on us. And when he was come into the house, the blind men came to him: and Jesus saith unto them, Believe ye that I am able to do this? They said unto him, Yea, Lord. Then touched he their eyes, saying, According to your faith be it unto you. And their eyes were opened; and Jesus straitly charged them, saying, See that no man know it. But they, when they were departed, spread abroad his fame in all that country.

MATTHEW 9:27-31

17. Heals a demoniac

As they went out, behold, they brought to him a dumb man possessed with a devil. And when the devil was cast out, the dumb spake: and the multitudes marvelled, saying, It was never so seen in Israel.

MATTHEW 9:32-33

18. Walks upon the sea of Galilee

And straightway Jesus constrained his disciples to get into a ship, and to go before him unto the other side, while he sent the multitudes away. And when he had sent the multitudes away, he went up into a mountain apart to pray: and when the evening was come, he was there alone. But the ship was now in the midst of the sea, tossed with waves: for the wind was contrary. And in the fourth watch of the night Jesus went unto them, walking on the sea. And when the disciples saw him walking on the sea, they were troubled, saying, It is a spirit; and they cried out for fear. But straightway Jesus spake unto them, saying, Be of good cheer; it is I; be not afraid. And Peter answered him and said, Lord, if it be thou, bid me come unto thee on the water. And he said, Come. And when Peter was come down out of the ship, he walked on the water, to go to Jesus. But when he saw the wind boisterous, he was afraid; and beginning to sink, he cried, saying, Lord, save me. And immediately Jesus stretched forth his hand, and caught him, and said unto him, O thou of little faith, wherefore didst thou doubt? And when they were come into the ship, the wind ceased. Then they that were in the ship came and worshipped him, saying, Of a truth thou art the Son of God.

MATTHEW 14:22-33

And straightway he constrained his disciples to get into the ship, and to go to the other side before unto Bethsaida, while he sent away the people. And when he had sent them away, he departed into a mountain to pray. And when even was come, the ship was in the midst of the sea, and he alone on the land. And he saw them toiling in rowing; for the wind was contrary unto them: and about the fourth watch of the night he cometh unto them, walking upon the sea, and would have passed by them. But when they saw him walking upon the sea, they supposed it had been a spirit, and cried out: For they all saw him, and were troubled. And immediately he talked with them, and saith unto them, Be of good cheer: it is I; be not afraid. And he went up unto them into the ship; and the wind ceased: and they were sore amazed in themselves beyond measure, and wondered.

MARK 6:45-51

And when even was now come, his disciples went down unto the sea, And entered into a ship, and went over the sea toward Capernaum. And it was now dark, and Jesus was not come to them. And the sea arose by reason of a great wind that blew. So when they had rowed about five and twenty or thirty furlongs, they see Jesus walking on the sea, and drawing nigh unto the ship: and they were afraid. But he saith unto them, It is I; be not afraid. Then they willingly received him into the ship: and immediately the ship was at the land whither they went.

JOHN 6:16-21

19. Heals the daughter of the Syrophenician woman

Then Jesus went thence, and departed into the coasts of Tyre and Sidon. And, behold, a woman of Canaan came out of the same coasts, and cried unto him, saying, Have mercy on me, O Lord, thou son of David; my daughter is grievously vexed with a devil. But he answered her not a word. And his disciples came and besought him, saying, Send her away; for she crieth after us. But he answered and said, I am not sent but unto the lost sheep of the house of Israel. Then came she and worshipped him, saying, Lord, help me. But he answered and said, It is not meet to take the children's bread, and to cast it to dogs. And she said, Truth, Lord: yet the dogs eat of the crumbs which fall from their masters' table. Then Jesus answered and said unto her, O woman, great is thy faith: be it unto thee even as thou wilt. And her daughter was made whole from that very hour.

MATTHEW 15:21-28

And from thence he arose, and went into the borders of Tyre and Sidon, and entered into an house, and would have no man know it: but he could not be hid. For a certain woman, whose young daughter had an unclean spirit, heard of him, and came and fell at his feet: The woman was a Greek, a Syrophenician by nation; and she besought him that he would cast forth the devil out of her daughter. But Jesus said unto her, Let the children first be filled: for it is not meet to take the children's bread, and to cast it unto the dogs. And she answered and said unto him, Yes, Lord: yet the dogs under the table eat of the children's crumbs. And he said unto her, For this saying go thy way; the devil is gone out of thy daughter. And when she was come to her house, she found the devil gone out, and her daughter laid upon the bed.

MARK 7:24-30

20. Feeds more than four-thousand people

Then Jesus called his disciples unto him, and said, I have compassion on the multitude, because they continue with me now three days, and have nothing to eat: and I will not send them away fasting, lest they faint in the way. And his disciples say unto him, Whence should we have so much bread in the wilderness, as to fill so great a multitude? And Jesus saith unto them, How many loaves have ye? And they said, Seven, and a few little fishes. And he commanded the multitude to sit down on the ground. And he took the seven loaves and the fishes, and gave thanks, and brake them, and gave to his disciples, and the disciples to the multitude. And they did all eat, and were filled: and they took up of the broken meat that was left seven baskets full. And they that did eat were four thousand men, beside women and children. And he sent away the multitude, and took ship, and came into the coasts of Magdala.

MATTHEW 15:32-39

In those days the multitude being very great, and having nothing to eat, Jesus called his disciples unto him, and saith unto them, I have compassion on the multitude, because they have now been with me three days, and have nothing to eat: And if I send them away fasting to their own houses, they will faint by the way: for divers of them came from far. And his disciples answered him, From whence can a man satisfy these men with bread here in the wilderness? And he asked them, How many loaves have ye? And they said, Seven. And he commanded the people to sit down on the ground: and he took the seven loaves, and gave thanks, and brake, and gave to his disciples to set before them; and they did set them before the people. And they had a few small fishes: and he blessed, and commanded to set them also before them. So they did eat, and were filled: and they took up of the broken meat that was left seven baskets. And they that had eaten were about four thousand: and he sent them away.

MARK 8:1-9

21. Restores hearing to the deaf-mute man

And again, departing from the coasts of Tyre and Sidon, he came unto the sea of Galilee, through the midst of the coasts of Decapolis. And they bring unto him one that was deaf, and had an impediment in his speech; and they beseech him to put his hand upon him. And he took him aside from the multitude, and put his fingers into his ears, and he spit, and touched his tongue; And looking up to heaven, he sighed, and saith unto him, Ephphatha, that is, Be opened. And straightway his ears were opened, and the string of his tongue was loosed, and he spake plain. And he charged them that they should tell no man: but the more he charged them, so much the more a great deal they published it; And were beyond measure astonished, saying, He hath done all things well: he maketh both the deaf to hear, and the dumb to speak.

MARK 7:31-37

22. Restores sight to a blind man

And he cometh to Bethsaida; and they bring a blind man unto him, and besought him to touch him. And he took the blind man by the hand, and led him out of the town; and when he had spit on his eyes, and put his hands upon him, he asked him if he saw ought. And he looked up, and said, I see men as trees, walking. After that he put his hands again upon his eyes, and made him look up: and he was restored, and saw every man clearly. And he sent him away to his house, saying, Neither go into the town, nor tell it to any in the town.

MARK 8:22-26

23. Heals the epileptic boy

And when they were come to the multitude, there came to him a certain man, kneeling down to him, and saying, Lord, have mercy on my son: for he is lunatick, and sore vexed: for ofttimes he falleth into the fire, and oft into the water. And I brought him to thy disciples, and they could not cure him. Then Jesus answered and said, O faithless and perverse generation, how long shall I be with you? how long shall I suffer you? bring him hither to me. And Jesus rebuked the devil; and he departed out of him: and the child was cured from that very hour. Then came the disciples to Jesus apart, and said, Why could not we cast him out? And Jesus said unto them, Because of your unbelief: for verily I say unto you, If ye have faith as a grain of mustard seed, ye shall say unto this mountain, Remove hence to yonder place; and it shall remove; and nothing shall be impossible unto you. Howbeit this kind goeth not out but by prayer and fasting.

MATTHEW 17:14-21

And when he came to his disciples, he saw a great multitude about them, and the scribes questioning with them. And straightway all the people, when they beheld him, were greatly amazed, and running to him saluted him. And he asked the scribes, What question ye with them? And one of the multitude answered and said, Master, I have brought unto thee my son, which hath a dumb spirit; And wheresoever he taketh him, he teareth him: and he foameth, and gnasheth with his teeth, and pineth away: and I spake to thy disciples that they should cast him out; and they could not. He answereth him, and saith, O faithless generation, how long shall I be with you? how long shall I suffer you? bring him unto me. And they brought him unto him: and when he saw him, straightway the spirit tare him; and he fell on the ground, and wallowed foaming. And he asked his father, How long is it ago since this came unto him? And he said, Of a child. And ofttimes it hath cast him into the fire, and into the waters, to destroy him: but if thou canst do any thing, have compassion on us, and help us. Jesus said unto him, If thou canst believe, all things are possible to him that believeth. And straightway the father of the child cried out, and said with tears, Lord, I believe; help thou mine unbelief. When Jesus saw that the people came running together, he rebuked the foul spirit, saying unto him, Thou dumb and deaf spirit, I charge thee, come out of him, and enter no more into him. And the spirit cried, and rent him sore, and came out of him: and he was as one dead; insomuch that many said, He is dead. But Jesus took him by the hand, and lifted him up; and he arose. And when he was come into the house, his disciples asked him privately, Why could not we cast him out? And he said unto them, This kind can come forth by nothing, but by prayer and fasting.

MARK 9:14-29

And it came to pass, that on the next day, when they were come down from the hill, much people met him. And, behold, a man of the company cried out, saying, Master, I beseech thee, look upon my son: for he is mine only child. And, lo, a spirit taketh him, and he suddenly crieth out; and it teareth him that he foameth again, and bruising him hardly departeth from him. And I besought thy disciples to cast him out; and they could not. And Jesus answering said, O faithless and perverse generation, how long shall I be with you, and suffer you? Bring thy son hither. And as he was yet a coming, the devil threw him down, and tare him. And Jesus rebuked the unclean spirit, and healed the child, and delivered him again to his father. And they were all amazed at the mighty power of God. But while they wondered every one at all things which Jesus did, he said unto his disciples.

LUKE 9:37-43

24. Obtains tax money from a fish's mouth

And when they were come to Capernaum, they that received tribute money came to Peter, and said, Doth not your master pay tribute? He saith, Yes. And when he was come into the house, Jesus prevented him, saying, What thinkest thou, Simon? of whom do the kings of the earth take custom or tribute? of their own children, or of strangers? Peter saith unto him, Of strangers. Jesus saith unto him, Then are the children free. Notwithstanding, lest we should offend them, go thou to the sea, and cast an hook, and take up the fish that first cometh up; and when thou hast opened his mouth, thou shalt find a piece of money: that take, and give unto them for me and thee.

MATTHEW 17:24-27

25. Heals ten lepers—only one of them returns to thank Jesus

And it came to pass, as he went to Jerusalem, that he passed through the midst of Samaria and Galilee. And as he entered into a certain village, there met him ten men that were lepers, which stood afar off: And they lifted up their voices, and said, Jesus, Master, have mercy on us. And when he saw them, he said unto them, Go shew yourselves unto the priests. And it came to pass, that, as they went, they were cleansed. And one of them, when he saw that he was healed, turned back, and with a loud voice glorified God, And fell down on his face at his feet, giving him thanks: and he was a Samaritan. And Jesus answering said, Were there not ten cleansed? but where are the nine? There are not found that returned to give glory to God, save this stranger. And he said unto him, Arise, go thy way: thy faith hath made thee whole.

LUKE 17:11-19

26. Restores sight to a man born blind

And as Jesus passed by, he saw a man which was blind from his birth. And his disciples asked him, saying, Master, who did sin, this man, or his parents, that he was born blind? Jesus answered, Neither hath this man sinned, nor his parents: but that the works of God should be made manifest in him. I must work the works of him that sent me, while it is day: the night cometh, when no man can work. As long as I am in the world, I am the light of the world. When he had thus spoken, he spat on the ground, and made clay of the spittle, and he anointed the eyes of the blind man with the clay, And said unto him, Go, wash in the pool of Siloam, (which is by interpretation, Sent.) He went his way therefore, and washed, and came seeing. The neighbours therefore, and they which before had seen him that he was blind, said, Is not this he that sat and begged? Some said, This is he: others said, He is like him: but he said, I am he. Therefore said they unto him, How were thine eyes opened? He answered and said, A man that is called Jesus made clay, and anointed mine eyes, and said unto me, Go to the pool of Siloam, and wash: and I went and washed, and I received sight. Then said they unto him, Where is he? He said, I know not. They brought to the Pharisees him that aforetime was blind. And it was the sabbath day when Jesus made the clay, and opened his eyes. Then again the Pharisees also asked him how he had received his sight. He said unto them, He put clay upon mine eyes, and I washed, and do see. Therefore said some of the Pharisees, This man is not of God, because he keepeth not the sabbath day. Others said, How can a man that is a sinner do such miracles? And there was a division among them. They say unto the blind man again, What sayest thou of him, that he hath opened thine eyes? He said, He is a prophet. But the Jews did not believe concerning him, that he had been blind, and received his sight, until they called the parents of him that had received his sight. And they asked them, saying, Is this your son, who ye say was born blind? how then doth he now see? His parents answered them and said, We know that this is our son, and that he was born blind: But by what means he now seeth, we know not; or who hath opened his eyes, we know not: he is of age; ask him: he shall speak for himself. These words spake his parents, because they feared the Jews: for the Jews had agreed already, that if any man did confess that he was Christ, he should be put out of the synagogue. Therefore said his parents, He is of age; ask him. Then again called they the man that was blind, and said unto him, Give God the praise: we know that this man is a sinner. He answered and said, Whether he be a sinner or no, I know not: one thing I know, that, whereas I was blind, now I see. Then said they to him again, What did he to thee? how opened he thine eyes? He answered them, I have told you already, and ye did not hear: wherefore would ye hear it again? will ye also be his disciples? Then they reviled him, and said, Thou art his disciple; but we are Moses' disciples. We know that God spake unto Moses: as for this fellow, we know not from whence he is. The man answered and said unto them, Why herein is a marvellous thing, that ye know not from whence he is, and yet he hath opened mine eyes. Now we know that God heareth not sinners: but if any man be a worshipper of God, and doeth his will, him he heareth. Since the world began was it not heard that any man opened the eyes of one that was born blind. If this man were not of God, he could do nothing. They answered and said unto him, Thou wast altogether born in sins, and dost thou teach us? And they cast him out. Jesus heard that they had cast him out; and when he had found him, he said unto him, Dost thou believe on the Son of God? He answered and said, Who is he, Lord, that I might believe on him? And Jesus said unto him, Thou hast both seen him, and it is he that talketh with thee. And he said, Lord, I believe. And he worshipped him. And Jesus said, For judgment I am come into this world, that they which see not might see; and that they which see might be made blind. And some of the Pharisees which were with him heard these words, and said unto him, Are we blind also? Jesus said unto them, If ye were blind, ye should have no sin: but now ye say, We see; therefore your sin remaineth.

JOHN 9

27. Raises Lazarus from the dead

Now a certain man was sick, named Lazarus, of Bethany, the town of Mary and her sister Martha. (It was that Mary which anointed the Lord with ointment, and wiped his feet with her hair, whose brother Lazarus was sick.) Therefore his sisters sent unto him, saying, Lord, behold, he whom thou lovest is sick. When Jesus heard that, he said, This sickness is not unto death, but for the glory of God that the Son of God might be glorified thereby. Now Jesus loved Martha, and her sister, and Lazarus. When he had heard therefore that he was sick, he abode two days still in the same place where he was. Then after that saith he to his disciples, Let us go into Judaea again. His disciples say unto him, Master, the Jews of late sought to stone thee; and goest thou thither again? Jesus answered, Are there not twelve hours in the day? If any man walk in the day, he stumbleth not, because he seeth the light of this world. But if a man walk in the night, he stumbleth, because there is no light in him. These things said he: and after that he saith unto them, Our friend Lazarus sleepeth; but I go, that I may awake him out of sleep. Then said his disciples, Lord, if he sleep, he shall do well. Howbeit Jesus spake of his death: but they thought that he had spoken of taking of rest in sleep. Then said Jesus unto them plainly, Lazarus is dead. And I am glad for your sakes that I was not there, to the intent ye may believe; nevertheless let us go unto him. Then said Thomas, which is called Didymus, unto his fellowdisciples, Let us also go, that we may die with him. Then when Jesus came, he found that he had lain in the grave four days already. Now Bethany was nigh unto Jerusalem, about fifteen furlongs off: And many of the Jews came to Martha and Mary, to comfort them concerning their brother. Then Martha, as soon as she heard that Jesus was coming, went and met him: but Mary sat still in the house. Then said Martha unto Jesus, Lord, if thou hadst been here, my brother had not died. But I know, that even now, whatsoever thou wilt ask of God, God will give it thee. Jesus saith unto her, Thy brother shall rise again. Martha saith unto him, I know that he shall rise again in the resurrection at the last day. Jesus said unto her, I am the resurrection, and the life: he that believeth in me, though he were dead, yet shall he live: And whosoever liveth and believeth in me shall never die. Believest thou this? She saith unto him, Yea, Lord: I believe that thou art the Christ, the Son of God, which should come into the world. And when she had so said, she went her way, and called Mary her sister secretly, saying, The Master is come, and calleth for thee. As soon as she heard that, she arose quickly, and came unto him. Now Jesus was not yet come into the town, but was in that place where Martha met him. The Jews then which were with her in the house, and comforted her, when they saw Mary, that she rose up hastily and went out, followed her, saying, She goeth unto the grave to weep there. Then when Mary was come where Jesus was, and saw him, she fell down at his feet, saying unto him, Lord, if thou hadst been here, my brother had not died. When Jesus therefore saw her weeping, and the Jews also weeping which came with her, he groaned in the spirit, and was troubled. And said, Where have ye laid him? They said unto him, Lord, come and see. Jesus wept. Then said the Jews, Behold how he loved him! And some of them said, Could not this man, which opened the eyes of the blind, have

caused that even this man should not have died? Jesus therefore
again groaning in himself cometh to the grave. It was a cave, and a
stone lay upon it. Jesus said, Take ye away the stone. Martha, the
sister of him that was dead, saith unto him, Lord, by this time he
stinketh: for he hath been dead four days. Jesus saith unto her, Said I
not unto thee, that, if thou wouldest believe, thou shouldest see the
glory of God? Then they took away the stone from the place where
the dead was laid. And Jesus lifted up his eyes, and said, Father, I
thank thee that thou hast heard me. And I knew that thou hearest
me always: but because of the people which stand by I said it, that
they may believe that thou hast sent me. And when he thus had
spoken, he cried with a loud voice, Lazarus, come forth. And he
that was dead came forth, bound hand and foot with graveclothes:
and his face was bound about with a napkin. Jesus saith unto them,
Loose him, and let him go. Then many of the Jews which came to
Mary, and had seen the things which Jesus did, believed on him.
But some of them went their ways to the Pharisees, and told them
what things Jesus had done.

JOHN 11:1-46

28. Heals the woman with a spirit of infirmity

And he was teaching in one of the synagogues on the sabbath. And,
behold, there was a woman which had a spirit of infirmity eighteen
years, and was bowed together, and could in no wise lift up herself.
And when Jesus saw her, he called her to him, and said unto her,
Woman, thou art loosed from thine infirmity. And he laid his hands
on her: and immediately she was made straight, and glorified God.
And the ruler of the synagogue answered with indignation, because
that Jesus had healed on the sabbath day, and said unto the people,
There are six days in which men ought to work: in them therefore
come and be healed, and not on the sabbath day. The Lord then
answered him, and said, Thou hypocrite, doth not each one of you
on the sabbath loose his ox or his ass from the stall, and lead him

away to watering? And ought not this woman, being a daughter of Abraham, whom Satan hath bound, lo, these eighteen years, be loosed from this bond on the sabbath day? And when he had said these things, all his adversaries were ashamed: and all the people rejoiced for all the glorious things that were done by him.

LUKE 13:10-17

29. Heals a man with dropsy

And it came to pass, as he went into the house of one of the chief Pharisees to eat bread on the sabbath day, that they watched him. And, behold, there was a certain man before him which had the dropsy. And Jesus answering spake unto the lawyers and Pharisees, saying, Is it lawful to heal on the sabbath day? And they held their peace. And he took him, and healed him, and let him go; And answered them, saying, Which of you shall have an ass or an ox fallen into a pit, and will not straightway pull him out on the sabbath day? And they could not answer him again to these things.

LUKE 14:1-6

30. Restores sight to the blind

And as they departed from Jericho, a great multitude followed him. And, behold, two blind men sitting by the way side, when they heard that Jesus passed by, cried out, saying, Have mercy on us, O Lord, thou son of David. And the multitude rebuked them, because they should hold their peace: but they cried the more, saying, Have mercy on us, O Lord, thou son of David. And Jesus stood still, and called them, and said, What will ye that I shall do unto you? They say unto him, Lord, that our eyes may be opened. So Jesus had compassion on them, and touched their eyes: and immediately their eyes received sight, and they followed him.

MATTHEW 20:29-34

And they came to Jericho: and as he went out of Jericho with his disciples and a great number of people, blind Bartimaeus, the son of Timaeus, sat by the highway side begging. And when he heard that it was Jesus of Nazareth, he began to cry out, and say, Jesus, thou son of David, have mercy on me. And many charged him that he should hold his peace: but he cried the more a great deal, Thou son of David, have mercy on me. And Jesus stood still, and commanded him to be called. And they call the blind man, saying unto him, Be of good comfort, rise; he calleth thee. And he, casting away his garment, rose, and came to Jesus. And Jesus answered and said unto him, What wilt thou that I should do unto thee? The blind man said unto him, Lord, that I might receive my sight. And Jesus said unto him, Go thy way; thy faith hath made thee whole. And immediately he received his sight, and followed Jesus in the way.

MARK 10:46-52

And it came to pass, that as he was come nigh unto Jericho, a certain blind man sat by the way side begging: And hearing the multitude pass by, he asked what it meant. And they told him, that Jesus of Nazareth passeth by. And he cried, saying, Jesus, thou son of David, have mercy on me. And they which went before rebuked him, that he should hold his peace: but he cried so much the more, Thou son of David, have mercy on me. And Jesus stood, and commanded him to be brought unto him: and when he was come near, he asked him, Saying, What wilt thou that I shall do unto thee? And he said, Lord, that I may receive my sight. And Jesus said unto him, Receive thy sight: thy faith hath saved thee. And immediately he received his sight, and followed him, glorifying God: and all the people, when they saw it, gave praise unto God.

LUKE 18:35-43

31. Curses the fig tree

And he left them, and went out of the city into Bethany; and he lodged there. Now in the morning as he returned into the city, he hungered. And when he saw a fig tree in the way, he came to it, and found nothing thereon, but leaves only, and said unto it, Let no fruit grow on thee henceforward for ever. And presently the fig tree withered away. And when the disciples saw it, they marvelled, saying, How soon is the fig tree withered away! Jesus answered and said unto them, Verily I say unto you, If ye have faith, and doubt not, ye shall not only do this which is done to the fig tree, but also if ye shall say unto this mountain, Be thou removed, and be thou cast into the sea; it shall be done. And all things, whatsoever ye shall ask in prayer, believing, ye shall receive.

MATTHEW 21:17-22

And on the morrow, when they were come from Bethany, he was hungry: And seeing a fig tree afar off having leaves, he came, if haply he might find any thing thereon: and when he came to it, he found nothing but leaves; for the time of figs was not yet. And Jesus answered and said unto it, No man eat fruit of thee hereafter for ever. And his disciples heard it. And in the morning, as they passed by, they saw the fig tree dried up from the roots. And Peter calling to remembrance saith unto him, Master, behold, the fig tree which thou cursedst is withered away. And Jesus answering saith unto them, Have faith in God. For verily I say unto you, That whosoever shall say unto this mountain, Be thou removed, and be thou cast into the sea; and shall not doubt in his heart, but shall believe that those things which he saith shall come to pass; he shall have whatsoever he saith. Therefore I say unto you, What things soever ye desire, when ye pray, believe that ye receive them, and ye shall have them.

MARK 11:12-14, 20-24

32. Heals the ear of Malchus

When they which were about him saw what would follow, they said unto him, Lord, shall we smite with the sword? And one of them smote the servant of the high priest, and cut off his right ear. And Jesus answered and said, Suffer ye thus far. And he touched his ear, and healed him.

LUKE 22:49-51

33. Enables the second catch of fish

And he said unto them, Cast the net on the right side of the ship, and ye shall find. They cast therefore, and now they were not able to draw it for the multitude of fishes.

JOHN 21:6

CHAPTER 17

CALLED TO DO
THE WORKS OF JESUS

Verily, verily, I say unto you, He that believeth on me, the works that I do shall he do also; and greater works than these shall he do; because I go unto my Father.

JOHN 14:12

You and I are called to do the works of Jesus, but to do them we have to know what works Jesus did and how we can follow His example.

How God anointed Jesus of Nazareth with the Holy Ghost and with power: who went about doing good, and healing all that were oppressed of the devil; for God was with him.

ACTS 10:38

The Spirit of the Lord is upon me, because he hath anointed me to preach the Gospel to the poor; he hath sent me to heal the broken-hearted, to preach deliverance to the captives, and recovering of sight to the blind, to set at liberty them that are bruised, To preach the acceptable year of the Lord.

LUKE 4:18-19

Jesus was led by the Holy Spirit at all times, and He was empowered by the Holy Spirit at all times. He didn't say or do anything without the Holy Ghost. He came to the poor to tell them: "You don't have to be poor anymore."

He came to those who were brokenhearted to tell them: "You don't have to be brokenhearted anymore."

He came to those who were bound to tell them: "'You don't have to be bound anymore."

He came to those who were oppressed to tell them: "You don't have to be oppressed anymore. I have come to set you free."

I've come that you might have life and have it more abundantly.

JOHN 10:10B

Do we really understand what it means to do the works of Jesus?

Jesus came to let mankind out of prison. He's already unlocked the prison door, but people are sitting there, not moving—and many of them are believers. We need to let them know that they are free to go. We've got to tell people what Jesus did, because they're sitting in the jail while the doors are wide open, thinking that they're bound, not knowing that He's set them free.

Jesus has already forgiven. Jesus has already healed. Jesus has already delivered. All they have to do is repent of their sins and accept it.

Everything that you and I need to live and walk in victory has already been done at the cross of Calvary by the blood of Jesus! Through the blood of Jesus and by the name of Jesus we have all authority over the enemy.

For this purpose the Son of God was manifested, that he might destroy the works of the devil.

1 JOHN 3:8B

And having spoiled principalities and powers, he (Jesus) made a show of them openly, triumphing over them in it (the finished work of the cross).

COLOSSIANS 2:15

Jesus destroyed the power of the devil, so the devil has no power over you. The only power that the devil has is the power that you give him. That's why the Bible tells you not to give place to the devil (Ephesians 4:27).

People make out like the devil has all this power. He might be big in their eyes, but there's no one as big as my God. God is a big God, a mighty God, a great God, a righteous God. There's no other god like Him. When He speaks, the heavens shake, the earth trembles, the mountains are brought low, and the valleys are made straight. Nothing is impossible with Him.

You have to realize this, because the Bible says that those who know their God will do exploits in His name. If you and I are called to do the works of Jesus, then how in the world are we going to do the works of Jesus if we think we've got a small God and a big devil? Some Christians act like God and the devil are in the wrestling ring together and the devil's beating up God, who's saying: "Help Me; Church, pray for Me. I need help; I need more strength!"

> And such as do wickedly against the covenant shall he corrupt by flatteries: but the people that do know their God shall be strong, and do exploits.
>
> DANIEL 11:32

I want you to know that that's a lie from the pit of hell! God and the devil are not even in the same category. The devil is a creation, but God is the Creator. The devil has a beginning and an end, but God is the beginning and the ending! Besides that, I read the back of the Book and it tells us that God wins! That's why 1 John 4:4 says that greater is He who is in you than he who is in the world.

> Ye are of God, little children, and have overcome them: because greater is he that is in you, than he that is in the world.
>
> 1 JOHN 4:4

All this means that you and the devil aren't in the same category either! The first two chapters of Ephesians say that God has raised you up together with Christ and He's put you together with Him, seated in heavenly places with all things are under your feet. Matthew 28:18-20 says that He's given you all His power and authority in Heaven and earth, to go into all the world and preach the Gospel.

> And Jesus came and spake unto them, saying, All power is given unto me in heaven and in earth. Go ye therefore, and teach all nations, baptizing them in the name of the Father, and of the Son, and of the Holy Ghost: Teaching them to observe all things whatsoever I have commanded you: and, lo, I am with you always, even unto the end of the world. Amen.
>
> MATTHEW 28:18-20

Remember, two-thirds of God's name is "go." The other two-thirds of His name is "do." Go into all the world and preach the Gospel. The Bible says that one of the signs that will follow a believer in Jesus is that they will cast out devils. When you are doing the works of Jesus, then you are casting out devils—devils are not casting you out!

> And he said unto them, Go ye into all the world, and preach the Gospel to every creature. He that believeth and is baptized shall be saved; but he that believeth not shall be damned. And these signs shall follow them that believe; In my name shall they cast out devils; they shall speak with new tongues; They shall take up serpents; and if they drink any deadly thing, it shall not hurt them; they shall lay hands on the sick, and they shall recover.
>
> MARK 16:15-18

When you *know* your God, you can do exploits in His name. He says to you what He said to Joshua: "Just like I was with Moses, so shall I be with you. Nothing shall stand before you, all the days of your life. Every place in which the sole of your foot shall tread, I have given it unto you. Lift up your eyes and look. From the place where you now stand, to the

North, to the South, to the East, and the West, I've given you all the land. Go in and possess it; it's yours. I have delivered the enemy into your hand. Go in and take the cities; there'll not be one city too big."

Now after the death of Moses the servant of the Lord it came to pass, that the Lord spake unto Joshua the son of Nun, Moses' minister, saying, Moses my servant is dead; now therefore arise, go over this Jordan, thou, and all this people, unto the land which I do give to them, even to the children of Israel. Every place that the sole of your foot shall tread upon, that have I given unto you, as I said unto Moses. From the wilderness and this Lebanon even unto the great river, the river Euphrates, all the land of the Hittites, and unto the great sea toward the going down of the sun, shall be your coast. There shall not any man be able to stand before thee all the days of thy life: as I was with Moses, so I will be with thee: I will not fail thee, nor forsake thee. Be strong and of a good courage: for unto this people shalt thou divide for an inheritance the land, which I sware unto their fathers to give them. Only be thou strong and very courageous, that thou mayest observe to do according to all the law, which Moses my servant commanded thee: turn not from it to the right hand or to the left, that thou mayest prosper withersoever thou goest. This book of the law shall not depart out of thy mouth; but thou shalt meditate therein day and night, that thou mayest observe to do according to all that is written therein: for then thou shalt make thy way prosperous, and then thou shalt have good success. Have not I commanded thee? Be strong and of a good courage; be not afraid, neither be thou dismayed: for the Lord thy God is with thee whithersoever thou goest. Then Joshua commanded the officers of the people, saying, Pass through the host, and command the people, saying, Prepare you victuals; for within three days ye shall pass over this Jordan, to go in to possess the land, which the Lord your God giveth you to possess it. And to the Reubenites, and to the Gadites, and to half the tribe of Manasseh, spake Joshua, saying, Remember the word which Moses the servant of the Lord commanded you, saying, The Lord your God hath given you rest, and hath given you this land. Your wives, your little ones, and your cattle, shall remain in the land which Moses gave you on this side Jordan; but ye shall pass before your brethren armed, all the mighty men of valour, and help them; Until the Lord have given your brethren rest, as he hath given you, and they also have possessed the land which the Lord your God giveth them: then ye shall return unto the land of your possession, and enjoy it, which Moses the Lord's servant gave you on this side Jordan toward the sunrising. And they answered Joshua, saying, All that thou commandest us we will do, and whithersoever thou sendest us, we will go. According as we hearkened unto Moses in all things, so will we hearken unto thee: only the Lord thy God be with thee, as he was with Moses. Whosoever he be that doth rebel against thy commandment, and will not hearken unto thy words in all that thou commandest him, he shall be put to death: only be strong and of a good courage.

JOSHUA 1:1-18

God says to the Church now, "I have placed My power and My anointing on the inside of you and you're called to do the works of Jesus—every one of you."

"Oh Rodney, please pray for me; nothing seems to be working." Nothing's working because you're not working! You need to work. Jesus said: *"I must work the works of Him that sent me"* (John 9:4), and just as Jesus must do the works, you have to do the works. You must make a decision every morning to work the works of Jesus.

"Well, I don't feel like praying for the sick today. I barely feel like getting out of bed!" You've got to get out of bed and go do the works of Jesus, no matter how you feel. If I went by how I feel sometimes, I wouldn't get out of bed myself. You just have to make a decision that it doesn't matter how you feel. It doesn't matter what's going on around you. You must decide that circumstances are not going to stop you from doing the works of Jesus.

You see, too many people are in a position where they're just waiting on God. "Oh, I'm waiting on God. Whatever He wants. I just believe in the Doris Day doctrine, 'Que sera, sera. Whatever will be will be.' You know God's ways are past finding out. His ways are higher than our ways; His thoughts are higher than our thoughts. So I'm just waiting on God."

Well, it's time you get hooked up with the Holy Ghost to find out what His ways are and what His thoughts are! When you do that, you'll get the same message Jesus gave: "Greater works shall ye do." But He's waiting for you. You say that you're waiting for Him, but He's waiting for you. You just have to make a decision! You just have to get off your blessed assurance, shake yourself, and say "I'm going to do the works of Jesus."

> Verily, verily, I say unto you, He that believeth on me, the works that I do shall he do also; and greater works than these shall he do; because I go unto my Father.
>
> JOHN 14:12

Now let me make this clear. If you do the works of Jesus, you're going to have opposition. Opposition will be a truck with your name written on it, coming down the road looking for you. Conflict will come, but that just means you're in the right company. Every time Jesus spoke in public, some folks picked up rocks to stone Him. So when they say you're of the devil, remember that they said Jesus cast out devils by the devil. It doesn't matter what people say, just make sure you are right with God and keep doing the works of Jesus. It doesn't matter how you feel, just keep doing the works of Jesus. It doesn't matter what the circumstances around you look like, keep doing the works of Jesus.

"He that believeth on me, the works that I do shall he do also." What were these works? Jesus walked on water, fed five thousand, raised Lazarus from the dead, raised the widow's boy from the dead outside the city of Nain, raised Jairus' daughter from the dead, opened the eyes of the blind, opened the ears of the deaf, cleansed the leper, and much more. *"And greater works than these shall ye do; because I go unto my Father."* God has invested His power, His name, His blood, and His

Spirit to enable and empower you to do the works of Jesus. I'm telling you, we're living in the day and age where we will see some of those greater works. When the Church realizes this, they will shake nations for Jesus!

The time to do the works of Jesus is now, not just on Sunday morning. Sunday morning is a time to celebrate the works that He's been doing on Monday, Tuesday, Wednesday, Thursday, Friday, and Saturday! You must *always* be doing the works of Jesus.

So what's keeping us from doing the works of Jesus? Folks have a variety of excuses. Some people say, "You know I'm fighting this sickness in my body. If I can just get healed of it, then I'll go get somebody else healed."

I'm telling you, if you'll just get out there and do the works of Jesus and lay hands on the sick, you'll look again for the symptoms and they'll be gone. While you were doing the works of Jesus, your own body was healed.

Somebody else said, "I just have this great financial need, and when it gets sorted out, then I'll be able to go and do the works of Jesus."

No, just start right where you are. If you go out of your way to be a blessing to other people, your own needs will be supernaturally met by the power of the Holy Ghost.

People are always waiting for a time that never comes. They're like a donkey chasing a carrot on a stick. They're looking for the pot of gold at the end of the rainbow. To do the works of Jesus, you've just got to start where you are—as bad as you feel, as tired as you feel, as messed up as you feel. *We shouldn't go by how we feel!*

Don't even go by the way you look. "Rodney, if I can just lose a little bit more weight, then I'll be used of God. Maybe if I was prettier or more handsome, I could have a successful ministry." I've seen plenty of preachers who dress so nice and look so wonderful, but they're not doing the works of Jesus. It doesn't matter how you look. God uses people of all different shapes and sizes to do the works of Jesus.

So what are other things we think hold us back? "Well, I don't really speak that well."

Moses didn't think he was a good speaker either, but he stood up to Pharaoh and led the children of Israel out of bondage. When you're doing the works of Jesus, the Holy Spirit will give you the words to say. You'll be amazed at the wonderful things that come out of your mouth!

> And Moses said unto the Lord, O my Lord, I am not eloquent, neither heretofore, nor since thou hast spoken unto thy servant: but I am slow of speech, and of a slow tongue.
>
> EXODUS 4:10

"Well, I don't really have the education." It's not so much education that you need to do the works of Jesus, as it is the anointing. There are a lot of Bible seminaries that make their students ineffective, so that they never produce anything for the kingdom of God. By instilling the students with religion and tradition rather than the anointing of the Holy Spirit, they instill death in them. Many Bible students, who go into seminary, believers, come out doubters!

I do believe that a Bible education is important, but make sure that you get educated in the commandments of God and not the traditions of man. As long as you have a revelation of the *love* of God and you believe in the *power* of the Word of God and you have the *anointing* on your life, you will be an able minister of the Gospel!

Don't let excuses keep you from working the works of Jesus. Allow the reality of the anointing of the Holy Spirit to empower you to overcome any obstacle. God is looking for a Church that is so full of the anointing of the Spirit of God, it just splashes out of us everywhere we go. The famous British man of God, Smith Wigglesworth, once walked into a train passenger car and two ministers fell out of their seats onto their faces. They said: "Pray for us. You convict us of sin." Wigglesworth never said one word. His very presence convicted them of their sins. Why? Because he did the works of Jesus every day. The anointing was with him wherever he went.

If you realize that Jesus Christ of Nazareth, the Son of the Living God, lives on the inside of you, has come to make His home on the inside of you, and is empowering you by His anointing, what more do you need? All you need to do the works of Jesus is the anointing of the Holy Ghost and the determination to use what's been given you.

Some folks think you need to be an ordained minister to do the works of Jesus. When I started out in the ministry, pastors said to me, "Where are your ordination papers? Where are your credentials?"

I had to say, "I don't have any." They didn't check to see if I had the anointing or if I was doing the works of Jesus. As if they expected me to take ordination papers and put them on a man's head and say, "Rise in Jesus's name." As if I was going to use those papers to cast out devils. I have never heard the devil say: "Oh, no! I'm getting out of here. He's got them papers!"

But one day I was praying, and I said: "Lord, if I could just have an ordination certificate, then I would be welcomed in more churches." In the spirit, the Lord showed me an ordination certificate which said: "This is to certify that Rodney Howard-Browne has been ordained to the Gospel ministry;" and there were three signatures: the Father, the Son, and the Holy Ghost. I didn't worry about papers anymore.

About 18 months later, I did get my ordination papers. I even carried my card with me. When I walked into the next church and showed them my papers, can you believe it, they told me, "Oh, don't worry about the papers. Put them away. We don't need those."

Listen, if you want ordination papers, these are your papers: *"These works shall ye do and greater works than these shall ye do because I go to my Father."* Your papers came on the day of Pentecost when, with a mighty rushing wind, there appeared cloven tongues like as of fire, and they were all filled with the Holy Ghost and began to speak with other tongues. Remember this, man did not call you to the ministry—God did.

> And when the day of Pentecost was fully come, they were all with one accord in one place. And suddenly there came a sound from heaven as of a rushing mighty wind, and it filled all the house where they were sitting. And there appeared unto them cloven tongues like as of fire, and it sat upon each of them. And they were all filled with

the Holy Ghost, and began to speak with other tongues, as the Spirit gave them utterance.

ACTS 2:1-4

This is something to get excited about! You've got marching orders from the Son of the Living God! He said these works shall you do and greater works shall you do. You are called to do the works of Jesus, and it's not about you, your abilities, your liabilities, or your inabilities. If you will yield to His Spirit, He will use you in a mighty way. Please understand that! God's not looking for qualified people. God's not looking for educated people.

God's looking for *available* people.

Will you respond to His call today?

CHAPTER 18

JESUS, OUR GOOD SHEPHERD

The Lord is my Shepherd [to feed, guide, and shield me], I shall not lack. He makes me lie down in [fresh, tender] green pastures; He leads me beside still and restful waters. He refreshes and restores my life (myself); He leads me in the path, of righteousness [uprightness and right standing with Him — not for my earning it, but] for His name's sake. Yes, though I walk through the [deep, sunless] valley of the shadow of death, I will fear or dread no evil, for You are with me; Your rod [to protect] and Your staff [to guide], they comfort me. You prepare a table before me in the presence of my enemies. You anoint my head with oil; my [brimming] cup runs over. Surely or only goodness and mercy and unfailing love shall follow me all the days of my life, and through the length of my days the house of the Lord [and His presence] shall be my dwelling place.

PSALM 23:1-6 AMPC

Most likely, Psalms 23 and 91 are the two most published Psalms. Everybody's praying for God's provision and protection. Christians will have it in their cars, on T-shirts, on coffee mugs, and yet they never seem to live by it. Why would people have something on a card or a coffee mug or a T-shirt and not live by it?

"Well, 'The Lord is my Shepherd' is nice. It looks good on a wall. It looks good on a bookmark. It looks good on the dashboard."

But it's got to come off your dashboard, off your T-shirt, off your coffee mug, and it's got to go *into* your heart. The fact that Jesus is your Shepherd has to become a living reality.

He's the *Good* Shepherd! So many people today gather in churches all over the world thinking that Jesus is against them. They think of Him as a bad shepherd, sitting there with a big club, waiting to beat them in the head for all their sin. Jesus is not the beater of the sheep!

I heard one preacher say that sheep are dumb. Sheep are *not* dumb. They know where the grass and the water are, and they're going to find them. They also know how to find safety. If you see them jumping the fence, it's for a reason. If they're jumping the fence, it's because they're saying, "I ain't gonna take this beating anymore."

Look what Jesus says in John 10:1-5:

> Verily, verily, I say unto you, He that entereth not by the door into the sheepfold, but climbeth up some other way, the same is a thief and a robber. But he that entereth in by the door is the shepherd of the sheep. To him the porter openeth; and the sheep hear his voice: and he calleth his own sheep by name, and leadeth them out. And when he putteth forth his own sheep, he goeth before them, and the sheep follow him: for they know his voice. And a stranger will they not follow, but will flee from him: for they know not the voice of strangers.

Now, not all sheep know the voice of their shepherd, and not all shepherds treat their sheep well. I come from South Africa, born in the city of Port Elizabeth, and lived most of my life in the Transkei. The local indigenous tribe, the Xhosa, had large herds of sheep. But unlike the shepherds of the Middle East who Jesus was familiar with, the Xhosa people use dozens of their youngest children to herd the sheep.

When these kids, just three to five years old, look after the sheep, they act like kids. They'll run home at the sight of an animal that's threatening the flock, and because there's a frequent change of shepherds, the sheep don't get to know who the shepherd is. It could be one little guy or his brother or his cousin. They don't know their shepherd. So when he speaks, they don't listen. When he shouts at them, they don't pay attention. Since the sheep won't listen to their directions, the little shepherd boys whip them with sticks and beat them to drive them from camp to camp.

But if you go to the Middle East, you see a very different picture of what it means to be a shepherd. The shepherds are grown men who *live* with the sheep. The sheep lie down to sleep; they lie down to sleep. After awhile, they smell like the sheep and even look like their sheep. There's never a time that they're not with their sheep. When the shepherd gets up, the sheep get up. When the shepherd moves out ahead, all the sheep just come in behind and follow the shepherd, because they know him and they trust him.

From the time that they're little lambs, the sheep hear that same shepherd's voice, so they know his voice very well. When he speaks, his sheep follow his voice, so that even if two flocks get tangled up together, each will follow the right shepherd by following the voice they know.

What a contrast that is from the little African shepherds that I saw as a kid. And I see the same contrast between shepherds in the Church. I see the shepherds who try to beat the sheep and corral everybody, pushing them around and forcing them into places. "Get over here, you dumb sheep!" And, "Grab him! He's going over the fence!"

If you're a bad shepherd, herding your sheep takes all your time and effort. You have these hundred sheep and you can't sleep at night. You're trying to keep them in the pen. They're jumping out. They don't know who you are. They're constantly trying to run away.

On the other hand, Jesus said: "My sheep know My voice. The voice of a stranger they're not going to follow." When the pastor, the under-shepherd, follows the example of Jesus, the Chief Shepherd, then people can come into church and relax, because there's no coercion, no force. If you have to force people to stay, it's not God.

Did you ever wonder why the Psalm talks about "leading me beside still waters?" It's a picture of how a good shepherd provides a relaxing place for his flock to drink. Sheep can't drink in fast running water. The way their nostrils are situated, the water would splash in and they would drown while trying to drink. So the shepherd—the good shepherd— digs a u-shaped hollow in the bank. Then the water can flow into the little hollow and become still. When he calls the sheep in to drink, they come because they know He's prepared a safe place for them.

Jesus said: "My sheep know My voice. They know My voice! The voice of a stranger *they will not follow.*" I believe that in these last days, Jesus is calling His sheep. He's calling them from all different regions. He's telling them, "It's time to come now. It's time." The Shepherd is giving a clarion call: "Come in! Come in from the cold! Come in from a life of self and sin! Come in to My provision and My safety!" He's calling those who are lost. He's calling those who are dying.

Jesus is calling them to come in and they're hearing His voice. I have never seen so many backsliders coming back to God as in this day and this hour. It's awesome! The Shepherd is calling! The Shepherd is calling for His sheep. Matthew 11:28 says: *"Come unto me, all ye that labour and are heavy laden, and I will give you rest."*

There's a vital difference between a shepherd and a hireling. The shepherd is constantly concerned with the safety of his sheep. The hireling is going to run the moment trouble comes. The shepherd is going to stay. The shepherd will be the calming factor. The shepherd will say, "It's all right. The wolf is coming, but I'll take care of it. Don't worry about a thing."

And there are times when a good shepherd, a good pastor, is going to have to protect his flock from "wolves." We don't want to be suspicious of everybody who comes into revival, into the sheepfold, but we've got to know that it's safe for the rest of the sheep to come and drink at the river. That means that if somebody's out of line in their worship or their manner, we're going stop them. It's not that we're running around like policemen—we're happy and free in our worship, and we love the move of God—but when someone gets out of line, we're going to set them straight.

This has really been a problem in the revival around the world. Pastors who never flowed in revival now suddenly have revival hitting their churches, and because they're afraid to stop the move of God, they're allowing everything. They're afraid to stop all kinds of crazy things that are happening, like people making animal noises, barking like dogs, and roaring like lions—and then calling it revival! If you bark like a dog in our church, you're in the doghouse with us! We thank God for the joy and all the manifestations of the Spirit, but we're not going to allow anything like that.

I know that's my job as the pastor, as shepherd of my flock. When pastors don't stop things as they get out of line, their sheep get concerned. They feel in their heart that *there's something wrong here*. But since the pastor's not doing anything about it, they think it must be right. Nevertheless, they still feel uneasy in their spirit and can't drink at the river and feel safe.

Their shepherd needs to come down and say, "Now stop that. You're out of line. You're in the flesh." As a good shepherd of my flock, I want you to come and drink and feel safe when you come and drink. My flock knows that if there is anything spiritually amiss, we'll be on it like ugly on a monkey!

You might be asking how we can know who is in the Spirit and who is in the flesh when two people are sitting next to each other and they are both making a noise. We stop one person, but we don't stop the other. How do we know which one is in the Spirit?

It's the same way the apostle Paul knew when the woman cried out and said: "These men are servants of the Most High God, which show unto us the way of salvation." In the natural, there was no way of knowing that what she was saying was out of line, because it was the truth. But Paul discerned that it was a spirit of divination, and one day he really got irritated about it and said, "Come out of her!"

> And it came to pass, as we went to prayer, a certain damsel possessed with a spirit of divination met us, which brought her masters much gain by soothsaying: The same followed Paul and us, and cried, saying,

These men are the servants of the most high God, which shew unto
us the way of salvation. And this did she many days. But Paul, being
grieved, turned and said to the spirit, I command thee in the name
of Jesus Christ to come out of her. And he came out the same hour.

ACTS 16:16-18

People probably attacked Paul, saying things like, "Did you see
the apostle Paul cast the devil out of the woman who was affirming his
ministry? Don't ever go to Paul's meetings and affirm his ministry—you
never know what's gonna happen."

When a pastor allows carnality in services, it's like a restaurant owner
allowing total strangers to walk in and start adding mystery ingredients
to the food after his chef has prepared it. No! Any restaurant owner
would walk in and say to the stranger, "Who are you?"

"Well, I just feel called of God to be here today."

"And what's that you're putting in our pot?"

I'm not telling you," they say, while they're putting in all kinds of
stuff.

So you might go to a revival meeting and sit there, tasting strange
stuff in your food, but saying, "This is God. Oh, praise God! Hallelujah!
Oh, glory! Terrible stuff, but hallelujah anyway! Oh, glory to God.
Just keep chewing, it's gonna get better, brother! Praise God! Amen!
Hallelujah!" No! We don't want to eat the imitation food, the fake food,
we want the good stuff—directly from Heaven's table!

He shall feed his flock like a shepherd: He shall gather the lambs with
his arm, and carry them, in his bosom, and shall gently lead those
that are with young.

ISAIAH 40:11

Good shepherds have to follow Jesus closely. Jesus, as the head of
the Church, goes out ahead of us, saying: "Come on." I'm listening for
Him, and I'm saying to you, "Come on. I hear Jesus say: 'Let's go.' I
hear Jesus saying: 'It's time to move.' I hear Jesus saying: 'It's time to
run.'" I'm listening just like you are.

Some pastors think that because they're the pastor, everything they say is of God. "Well I'm the pastor, so when I say it, it's GOD."

No, it's not. I'm not God. Never will be God. I'm just here to feed the flock of God. But if I feel God's telling us to do something, then it's up to the people to follow me. They should know the voice of the Good Shepherd and know in their hearts whether the pastor is leading in the right direction or not.

Problems arise when the pastor doesn't know God's voice and the congregation has no clue either. When people are led astray, it is their own fault, because they should build their own relationship with God and not rely completely on another person for God's wisdom and direction. But when God gives us a godly pastor and we keep ourselves sensitive to God's Spirit, we will stay on the right track with God.

Don't ever believe someone who tells you that they have all the answers for the direction of your life. Whatever anyone tells you should already have been told to you by the Holy Spirit. Otherwise, put it on the shelf—lay it aside. If it *is* God, it *will* happen. *Listen to your conscience.* God will speak to your heart and your conscience will be His guide for your every step.

Psalm 23 goes on to describe what life is like when we follow our Good Shepherd:

> You prepare a table before me in the presence of my enemies. You anoint my head with oil; my [brimming] cup runs over. Surely or only goodness and mercy and unfailing love shall follow me all the days of my life, and through the length of my days the house of the Lord [and His presence] shall be my dwelling place.
>
> PSALM 23:5-6 AMPC

This table is not set for you in Heaven—you have no enemies in Heaven. This table is set for you here and now.

Now, you're sitting at the table with all your enemies around you. They don't like you; they hate you. They're gnashing their teeth at you. But you're protected by your Shepherd, so you can just ignore them and sit there and eat, pray, and have a fun time! Your head is being anointed with oil by your loving Shepherd. And when you get up from the table, guess who's following you? Goodness and mercy!

Your enemy says, "I was gonna attack you, but I can't."

"Why?"

"It's them two big fellows with you! Goodness and mercy. We can't touch you!" And it says that they follow you *all the days of your life*.

He feeds us. He leads us. He guides us. He fills us. He protects us. He's with us! We're never alone! He's with us! He's at our side! He loves us!

Even if you run off and leave the ninety-nine, He knows you by name and He'll seek you out.

"I'll go fetch him. Come here, you. Don't you just love this sheep? He just needs special attention."

Jesus is our *Good Shepherd*! And He loves us so very much. Hallelujah!

CHAPTER 19

THE SWEET PRESENCE OF JESUS

Thou wilt show me the path of life: in thy presence is fulness of joy;
at thy right hand there are pleasures for evermore.

PSALM 16:11

The Church needs to have the sweet revelation of Jesus. So many times when they're trying this and they're trying that, the only thing they really need is His presence. While the world is crying out for the presence of Jesus, because it's only in the presence of Jesus that they're going to find true satisfaction, the Church is often running away from His presence. And if the Church doesn't walk in His presence, how will people meet Jesus?

What separates us from His presence? For the unbeliever, it's sin. It's not big sin or little sin. It's just plain, flat-out, ornery, stinking sin. For the believer, it can be a little more subtle than that. It's still sin, but you don't recognize it as sin, because it's hidden in your heart; it takes place on the inside. But if you really look at your attitude, you will know it is sin. The only ones who know it is wrong are you and God.

It's what I call the *hidden sins of the heart*. That's what separates the believer from God's presence. The blood of Jesus brings a believer into fellowship with God at the new birth, but later he feels like the presence of God is far from him. Why? Because of his hidden sins: pride, bitterness, jealousy, unforgiveness, a critical and judgmental attitude, we can go on and on.

Now don't misunderstand me. A believer can also be separated from the presence of God by outward sin—lying, stealing, adultery, and so on. But most believers have stopped doing those things, so it's easy for them to think everything's okay. If they are not in the presence of God and feel far from Him, they wonder why. It's probably because they are not allowing the Spirit of God to deal with the sins of their heart.

To get into the presence of God and stay there, we've got to stop what we're doing. We've got to make a decision to repent. We've got to turn around and make a 180-degree turn. We've got to flee from the very thing that keeps us from His presence.

You know what it's like. You've gone along in the presence of God, but suddenly you start doing something that you know you shouldn't be doing. His presence starts to leave us. You would think we would learn after one or two or three trips to the Land of No Presence. Even an old dog, when he goes down to a water trough to drink and a brick falls on his head every time, starts to think to himself, "Water, drink, brick, pain." So he quits what he's doing to stop the pain.

We need to be as smart as that old dog. You know perfectly well when you're sinning, when you're stepping outside of God's presence. You know when you're going to do it. You decide to sin, so don't be surprised to find yourself out of His presence.

Don't come tell me, "Well, Rodney, I just don't know how it happened. It just happened. I was serving God and praying in tongues and the next thing I knew I went and I robbed a bank. I don't understand how it happened."

"Rodney, I was just serving the Lord and singing some of the worship tapes and suddenly I found that I had some other woman in my arms. I don't know how it happened. The devil made me do it."

You know the moment that you've missed the mark! You've sinned and departed from God's presence. Do you also know that you keep missing it by doing the same thing? Isn't that a form of insanity—to do the same thing over and over and expect a different result?

"Well, the last time I did this, I got out of His presence. But let's just do it again, anyway."

Surely an alarm needs to go off. "Bwaaahhh, bwaaahhh, bwaaahhh, *You are now leaving the presence of the Lord! You are stepping into the Land of No Presence! Repent! Back up! This is your final warning.*" And then, when you back up and repent, "You are now in the safe zone."

Well, we have that alarm—He's the Holy Spirit. We simply have to respond when the alarm goes off in our hearts. We must not harden our hearts to the alarm of the Holy Spirit. We've got to allow Him to continually do a softening work in our hearts, because over a period of time, our hearts can become hardened. We allow people to get to us. We allow hurts and disobedience to come in, and our hearts become hard and calloused. We need to allow the Spirit of God to come and do a softening work. We must get back into His presence.

Get hungry for more of Jesus.

Get thirsty for more of Jesus.

If you hunger and thirst after righteousness you will be filled. God said: "If you draw nigh to Me, I will draw nigh to you." We must stay in His presence *and not come out!*

We have to make the decision on a daily, hourly, minute-by-minute basis: "I will stay in His presence, and I'm not going to allow anything— the deceitfulness of riches, the cares of this world, the lust of other things— to come in and pull me away from the presence of the Lord Jesus."

Someone said: "Well, I just feel like having an argument. I think I'm going to phone up that individual and just give them a piece of my mind."

You'd better not do that. You might be giving away the last little piece of your mind! You may need it sometime. That's why some people are walking around with no mind. They've given it all away!

You have to consistently make the decision to stay in God's presence.

Every time the temptation comes up, you're going to choose not to be drawn away from Him. Now notice that I'm not looking for a manifestation. I'm looking for His presence. I'm seeking His face and not His hand. You may need a healing miracle, but more than anything, you need His presence.

When you wake up in the morning, say, "This is the day the Lord has made! I will rejoice and be glad in it! I'm going to worship Him! I'm going to praise Him! I'm going to praise Him in the morning! I'm going to praise Him in the noontime! I'm going to praise Him in the evening. As long as I have breath, I'm going to praise Him!"

This revival is about people deciding to get into God's presence, and then deciding to stay there—no matter what.

People are not going to get the presence of Jesus from some religious institution, because religion promotes religion, not Jesus. He wants to be there more than we want Him and more than we allow Him. We've got to open the door. We've got to say, "Come, Lord. Come by Your power. Come by Your anointing and touch the lives of hungry people."

Most people think revival means big meetings and lots of souls being saved, but that is the *result* of revival. Revival is when God's people get hungry for His presence, and He literally takes over their lives and their meetings. Once the church is revived, then it is time for sinners to get saved—which is an awakening. Sinners can't have revival, because they have not yet had "revival"! People come to Jesus—because Jesus is there, they sense His presence, and everything they need is in His presence.

God's presence is everything we need to live and walk in victory. If you look at some of the songs that were written out of revival, you'll see that they had the presence of Jesus, such as that old hymn, "In the Garden," that has the line, "and the joy we share as we tarry there, none other has ever known." Those songs were all written out of encounters with the Lord Jesus Christ in great revival.

If in His presence there is fullness of joy, then I want you to know that in His presence there is healing. In His presence there is provision. In His presence is everything that you and I need. When Jesus walks in the door, something is going to happen. When Jesus walks in the door, the very atmosphere is going to change.

We must never become blasé about the presence of the Lord. We must never come to the place where we say, "Well, we've been there. We've seen that. We've done that. Now we want something else." God doesn't want us to be like the children of Israel when they wandered in the desert. They complained and grumbled over the manna that came from Heaven. When they didn't have it, they complained. When they had it, they complained.

What do *you* want? People don't have the presence of Jesus, and they complain. Then they have the presence of Jesus and they complain. What do you want? I know what I want. I want His presence more than anything that this world has to offer. I want the continuous presence of Jesus.

I don't just want His presence on a Sunday morning. I want His presence on a Monday morning, on a Tuesday, on a Wednesday, on a Thursday, on a Friday, on a Saturday. I want to live and dwell in His presence, because I've found out that His presence is the hiding place for the believer. When the storms of life are raging, where do I go? I go to His presence. I go to the cleft of the rock. I go to the secret place. Psalm 31:19-20 says:

> Oh, how great is thy goodness, which thou hast laid up for them that fear thee; which thou hast wrought for them that trust in thee before the sons of men! Thou shalt hide them in the secret of thy presence from the pride of man: thou shalt keep them secretly in a pavilion from the strife of tongues.

If you're getting arrogant, I know what the cure is. You've just got to get in His presence. The more you're in His presence, the smaller you become and the bigger He becomes. The reason some people are puffed up with their own importance, a legend in their own minds, is because they've been outside of the presence of Jesus. When you come into the presence of Jesus, you realize that you are nothing and He is everything.

When we started our church, a preacher called me, and he was angry. He said: "I just want to tell you right now, you're not an apostle."

I said, "Okay. That's fine."

He said, "You're not a prophet."

I said, "That's fine, whatever you say."

He said, "You're not an evangelist. You're not a pastor. You're not a teacher."

I started to laugh on the telephone. I was laughing so much, tears were rolling down my cheeks. I said, "You're a very funny man."

He asked, "Why?"

I said, "You have blessed me with this phone call."

"What do you mean?"

I said, "For years, I've been praying, 'Lord, I'm nothing. You're everything.' And now you've phoned me to confirm that my prayer has finally been answered!"

Everybody's worried about titles, but I'm not. You can call me what you like—I just want the presence of Jesus. In His presence, there's fullness of joy. In His presence is everything we need. And I want His presence all the time. Someone said, "You can't have it all the time." But I want His presence all the time every day. When I lie on my bed, when I wake up in the morning, and when I drive down the road.

People will notice when you're in the presence of Jesus. Look at Acts 4:13. The people of Jerusalem looked at Peter and John and perceived that they were unlearned and ignorant men, but they marveled and they took knowledge of the fact that they'd been with Jesus. Do people take knowledge that you've been with Jesus?

It's the presence of Jesus that's going to make the difference in your life. It's the presence of Jesus that's going to put you over. It's the presence of Jesus that's going to cause you to rise above the storms of life, to rise above the circumstances of life. And you can have it every day! You can make the decision: "Today, I'm not going to hang around Sister Bucketmouth or Brother Doodad. I'm going to hang around Jesus."

"Well, Rodney, what will people say?" Who cares? They've already said it! It doesn't matter!

I just want Jesus—Jesus in the morning, Jesus in the noontime, Jesus in the evening. Jesus, Jesus, Jesus. It's hard to stay arrogant when you're in the presence of Jesus. When He comes, He overwhelms you. He's so big.

It's hard to grumble when you're in the presence of Jesus. It's hard to gripe when you're in the presence of Jesus. It's hard to complain when you're in the presence of Jesus. It's hard to criticize when you're in the presence of Jesus. It's hard to judge when you're in the presence of Jesus. And it's nearly impossible to sin when you're in the presence of Jesus. To me, it looks like the only place you'd want to be is in the presence of Jesus!

When people enter revival, the things that used to get them down stop getting them down. Why? Because they get into the presence of the Lord Jesus Christ. If you can get into the presence of the Lord for a day, then you can stay there for a week, or you can stay there for a month, or you can stay there for six months. Then, bless God, you can stay there permanently, and you can live there no matter what. Don't let the enemy draw you out! Don't let him take you out of the presence of Jesus. Just say, "No, I'm not going to argue, I'm doing a good work for God. I'm staying in the presence of Jesus. I'm going to do the work of the Lord."

You have to *make a decision to stay* in the presence of the Lord. I hold revival services in some places and the ministers are so busy they can't even come to the service. "Well, Rodney, I've got to take care of business."

I say, "Lord, have mercy! Shut the shop down! We're having revival. Don't you believe what's happening is important? You were running around last week and you're going to be running around next week. Just shut it down."

"Well, there's business to take care of."

"Forget the business. This is bigger business."

You have to make a decision. When you're dealing with the presence of Jesus, you can choose to either be like Mary or you can choose

249

to be like Martha. You can be like Martha, encumbered about with her serving duties, running here and running there. Or you can decide to be like Mary and come and sit at His feet.

> Now it came to pass, as they went, that he entered into a certain village: and a certain woman named Martha received him into her house. And she had a sister called Mary, which also sat at Jesus's feet, and heard his word. But Martha was cumbered about much serving, and came to him, and said, Lord, dost thou not care that my sister hath left me to serve alone? bid her therefore that she help me. And Jesus answered and said unto her, Martha, Martha, thou art careful and troubled about many things: But one thing is needful: and Mary hath chosen that good part, which shall not be taken away from her.
>
> LUKE 10:38-42

Your choice depends on how desperate you are, how hungry you are, and how thirsty you are. Jesus is not going to come and force His presence on you. You've got to come to Him and say, "Lord, I want to be in Your presence. I want to be in Your presence daily. I just want to live there, right on Glory Boulevard, in Presence Place."

It's a hiding place. It's a secret place. When we have revival meetings week after week, sometimes the hardest section of the meeting to break through is the ministers' section. Why? Because half of them are outside handing out their business cards. Or they're sitting there trying to work out what in the world is happening. They're thinking, "How is he doing that? And what is he saying that causes this to happen?"

When we worship, many ministers just sit there. They don't even know how to worship. I've said, "Lord, why is that? Shouldn't preachers be the ones worshipping more than anybody else?"

The Lord told me one time, "They can't worship because they're too used to being worshipped."

When we come into a church or meeting, it doesn't matter who we are and where we're from. The only individual that matters here is Jesus, King of kings, and Lord of lords. That's why revival has a way of equalizing everybody. When everybody is flat on the floor under the power of God, it doesn't really matter who is what! Have you noticed that when you're on the floor, everyone is on the same level?

Remember Psalm 31:20, which says that the presence of the Lord will hide you from the pride of men. If I want to be hidden from the pride of men, I must daily seek to live in His presence. It also says that the hiding place will be a secret place that will keep you from the strife of tongues. Tongues will be wagging and gossiping, but it will not affect you because you're in His presence.

> Thou shalt hide them in the secret of thy presence from the pride of man: thou shalt keep them secretly in a pavilion from the strife of tongues.
>
> PSALM 31:20

I can always tell the moment that I'm starting to get out of His presence. It's when the critical things people say against my ministry start to affect me. Then, the moment I get back in God's presence, what they say doesn't matter. In fact, the effect of His presence is very funny.

Somebody asked me, "Did you read the book attacking you?"

I said, "Yeah, I read the book; it was a good book. I laughed my way through the whole thing. Thank God, He used a critic to verify that this is a genuine revival. It's documented in history and there's nothing they can do to take it out now!"

But that was only because of the anointing of God. If I'd have read the book in the flesh, I'd have gotten mad. But when I read it under the anointing, it was a funny book, because whether my critics agreed with the revival or not, they had documented it. It will go down in history now. When you live in God's presence, He will protect you. People will say critical things, but their words will run off you like water off a duck's back.

The Lord has laid on my heart that people are coming to revival meetings desperate to hear from God, to be in His presence. In our meetings last year, we had people from forty-nine states and forty foreign countries. People are coming to hear from God. And the only way they're going to hear from God is to get into His presence.

Even if I'm not preaching the precise message a person needs to hear, while I'm preaching, God will speak to them directly because they're in His presence. God's presence will go right through the human intellect and touch the heart. God doesn't want to touch heads—there are too many fat heads. He wants to touch, change, and transform hearts.

In my meetings, the power of God is all over the place. And I pray that as you read this, you feel the power of God falling like rain on you.

Fill Your child to overflowing with Your presence, Lord!

It's in His presence that times of refreshing come. Do you need refreshing? Be refreshed. What are you waiting for? Acts 3:19 says: *"Repent ye therefore, and be converted, that your sins may be blotted out, when the times of refreshing shall come from the presence of the Lord."*

I believe you can be healed while reading this book. I believe you can be delivered from oppression and depression, from fear and the control, manipulation, and doctrines of men. You're set free by the power of the Holy Ghost!

CHAPTER 20

LIVING IN THE PRESENCE OF JESUS

Now when they saw the boldness of Peter and John, and perceived that they were unlearned and ignorant men, they marvelled; and they took knowledge of them, that they had been with Jesus.

ACTS 4:13

We often read the Gospels and say to ourselves, "Wouldn't it have been wonderful to have lived in Bible days!" When I was a kid growing up, I thought it would be the neatest thing if I could have lived back then. Just imagine hanging around Jesus all the time. I would never have left His side!

It must have been the greatest fun in the world to be around Jesus, because there was never a dull moment. The Gospels tell of all the miracles He did, but the end of the book of John says that if all the other miracles He did were written down, all the books in the world couldn't contain them.

Miracles in the morning, miracles at noon, miracles in the evening. Miracles of provision, forgiving people of their sin, healing the sick, casting out devils. What fun! Walking on the water, feeding multitudes,

253

waking up in the morning and saying: "I wonder what He's going to do today! Did you see what He did yesterday? *What is He going to do today?*"

But I've got news! We never have to wonder how it might have been to live with Jesus. Why? Because we—the blood-washed, blood-bought Church of the Lord Jesus Christ—are living in the days of Jesus! No, we're not in Israel, and Jesus is not actually walking around physically so we can run up and touch Him, but He has come to live on the inside of each and every one of us. Jesus really is here today, but He's having to wait to stand up on the inside of many people, because they won't give Him first place in their life. They won't allow the life of Christ to come forth.

Jesus said that we would do the works He did and even greater works, because He was going to His Father. He promised the Holy Ghost would come to empower us after He was gone, and the Holy Ghost indeed came on the day of Pentecost. The Bible tells us, *"In him we live, and move, and have our being"* (Acts 17:28a) and *"Out of your belly shall flow rivers of living water"* (John 7:38). What Jesus was saying was that out of our innermost being will flow His presence. So when we think about living in the presence of Jesus, we don't have to think about going to Heaven, going to Israel, or getting a time machine and going back in time. We don't have to go back in time because He has come to us here in the future!

> Verily, verily, I say unto you, He that believeth on me, the works that I do shall he do also; and greater works than these shall he do; because I go unto my Father.
>
> JOHN 14:12

> And when the day of Pentecost was fully come, they were all with one accord in one place. And suddenly there came a sound from heaven as of a rushing mighty wind, and it filled all the house where they were sitting. And there appeared unto them cloven tongues like as of fire, and it sat upon each of them. And they were all filled with the Holy Ghost, and began to speak with other tongues, as the Spirit gave them utterance.
>
> ACTS 2:1-4

Jesus has come to indwell man, to empower man, to anoint man, to equip man, to grace man, to enable man. Where you go, Jesus goes. He is living on the inside of you. He wants to look through your eyes; He wants to touch through your hands. He wants to speak out of your mouth!

Sometimes people are waiting on the lightning to strike and the water to part and a loud voice to say, "Yea, lift thy hand and say, 'Be healed.'" But it's not going to be that way! It's just going to be you, stepping out in faith because the Greater One lives in you. That which is impossible with man is possible with God. He is the God of the impossible. He can make a way where there is no way.

Why don't you just make a decision right now? Decide that you're going to live in the presence of God twenty-four hours a day, seven days a week, fifty-two weeks a year, living and dwelling in the presence of God, because if the same Spirit that raised Christ from the dead dwells in you, it's going to quicken or make alive your mortal body.

> But if the Spirit of him that raised up Jesus from the dead dwell in you, he that raised up Christ from the dead shall also quicken your mortal bodies by his Spirit that dwelleth in you.
>
> ROMANS 8:11

John G. Lake, that great apostle of faith, was very aware of that power in him. He went to South Africa and pioneered 550 churches in five years. While he was in Africa, the bubonic plague broke out, but he went right in amongst the people, praying for them and ministering to them. When plague victims died, they would foam at the mouth, and if you came in contact with that foam, you would catch the plague too. It was very contagious.

Doctors and scientists couldn't understand why Dr. Lake had survived seven years of ministry to these people, so they asked to examine him. He told them to scrape some of the plague foam off a patient and put it under the microscope. They put it under the microscope and saw that it had living disease germs. Then he said: "Put it on my hands." They put it on his hands, and he said: "Now scrape it off and look at it again."

They put it back under the microscope and saw that the plague germs were all dead! They asked him how this was possible. He said, *"The law of the spirit of life in Christ Jesus has made me free from the law of sin and death"* (Romans 8:2).

So why doesn't every Christian walk in divine healing? Some people don't realize what Jesus did for them at the cross of Calvary. Many times believers beg God to do what He has already done.

> Who his own self bare our sins in his own body on the tree, that we, being dead to sins, should live unto righteousness: by whose stripes ye were healed.
>
> 1 PETER 2:24

John G. Lake knew what Jesus had done, that the work of the cross was complete and provided divine health. But Lake also made the daily decision to *live* in God's presence.

God comes to live in us and He wants to do mighty works through us. If you grab hold of this, it'll change your life. We've got to let Jesus rise up big on the inside of us and make a decision *every day* to live in His presence.

The best way that I know to live in His presence is just to worship Him. It's not that you have to cry, "Oh God, I pray that this day I would live in Thy presence." Simply worship Him. Talk to Him, praise Him, and thank Him.

This is why the Church needs revival, because revival brings people back into the presence of Jesus. Hosea 6:2 (NIV) says: *"After two days he will revive us; on the third day he will restore us, that we may live in his presence."* That is what revival is all about: living in His presence.

People say, "Rodney, if you lived happy and free all the time, it just wouldn't be right. You're going to have some bondage and oppression in life. You can't be free and happy all the time. It's not normal. Jesus didn't promise us that life would be easy. He promised us that the way would be *haaarrrddd*." I've heard preachers tell the people as they come to the altar, "Now it's going to be really hard for you now that you've given your life to Jesus." The guy has been serving the devil all of his life, and now they're telling him it's going to be hard? *Give me a break!*

Jesus said: *"Take My yoke upon you, learn of Me, My yoke is easy; My burden is light"* (Matthew 11:29-30). What's this "heavy burden" part? The Bible says, *"the way of the transgressors is hard"* (Proverbs 13:15b). What's really hard is to try to serve Jesus with one foot in the world and one foot in the kingdom! You have one foot in hell and one foot in Heaven and you're miserable. Just make the decision to cut your ties with hell and you'll have Heaven on earth.

The Bible tells us, *"Let God arise and His enemies be scattered"* (Psalm 68:1a). When God arises—when we praise Him—our enemies are scattered. The Bible says in Deuteronomy 28:7 that He will cause our enemies to run from us in seven different directions. I don't know why people have a problem grasping this. It's not complicated.

> The Lord shall cause thine enemies that rise up against thee to be smitten before thy face: they shall come out against thee one way, and flee before thee seven ways.
>
> DEUTERONOMY 28:7

If Jesus walked into our houses right now, we'd never have another problem that could overcome us. Well, the truth of the matter is that He has already walked in our houses! He lives in us, but we don't even realize it! We're so busy looking at our circumstances, talking about our problems, and watching television. We listen to all the lies of the devil. We should be taking our eyes off the wind and waves and putting our eyes on Jesus, the living Word of God:

> Come unto me, all ye that labour and are heavy laden, and I will give you rest.
>
> MATTHEW 11:28

> Then he uttered his oracle: 'Arise, Balak, and listen; hear me, son of Zippor. God is not a man, that he should lie, nor a son of man, that he should change his mind. Does he speak and then not act? Does

he promise and not fulfill? I have received a command to bless; he has blessed, and I cannot change it. No misfortune is seen in Jacob, no misery observed in Israel. The Lord their God is with them; the shout of the King is among them.

NUMBERS 23:18-21 NIV

When the shout of the King is among you, when the Lord is with you, and when you live in the presence of God, no misfortune in your life will faze you. There will be no misery in your life when you're living in the presence of God. In 2 Corinthians 8:2, Paul writes of the Macedonians' sufferings and how God worked miracles in and through their lives:

How that in a great trial of affliction the abundance of their joy and their deep poverty abounded unto the riches of their liberality.

2 CORINTHIANS 8:2

The moment you get outside the presence of God, you get hit. The safest place is the cleft of the rock, the secret place of the Most High. If you don't believe what I'm telling you, then you don't believe Psalm 91:

He that dwelleth in the secret place of the most High shall abide under the shadow of the Almighty. I will say of the Lord, He is my refuge and my fortress: my God: in him will I trust. Surely he shall deliver thee from the snare of the fowler, and from the noisome pestilence...

A thousand shall fall at thy side, and ten thousand at thy right hand: but it shall not come nigh thee.

There shall no evil befall thee, neither shall any plague come nigh thy dwelling. For he shall give his angels charge over thee, to keep thee in all thy ways.

PSALM 91:1-3, 7, 10-11

In the *Amplified Bible, Classic Edition,* it says those angels will *"preserve you in all your ways [of obedience and service]."* In other words, the angels will not keep you in the ways of disobedience and disservice, but they will keep you when you walk in obedience.

God brought them out of Egypt; they have the strength of a wild ox. There is no sorcery against Jacob, no divination against Israel. It will now be said of Jacob and of Israel, "See what God has done."

NUMBERS 23:22-23 NIV

You have to catch it. We're living in the presence of Jesus. God is with us. Emmanuel, "God with us." That's His presence. And when you live in the presence of God, nobody can put a curse on you. Any curse will ricochet and go all the way back to them.

God is not a man, that he should lie; neither the son of man, that he should repent: hath he said, and shall he not do it? or hath he spoken, and shall he not make it good? Behold, I have received commandment to bless: and he hath blessed; and I cannot reverse it.

NUMBERS 23:19-20

No man can curse what God has blessed. Has God pronounced His blessing over you? Then no man can curse you! Whoever curses you will be cursed, and whoever blesses you will be blessed (Numbers 24:9).

The Lord said, "I have indeed seen the misery of my people in Egypt. I have heard them crying out because of their slave drivers, and I am concerned about their suffering. So I have come down to rescue them from the hand of the Egyptians to bring them up out of that land into a good and spacious land, a land flowing with milk and honey—the home of the Canaanites, Hittites, Amorites, Perizzites, Hivites and Jebusites."

EXODUS 3:7-8 NIV

That's what God has done for you and for me! He has brought us into His blessings. This is not something that is going to happen. This has already transpired, and it took place at the cross of Calvary. On the cross! That is where our victory was won! On the cross! The cross is final!

If you look at the Church in America today, you would think we had to pray and ask Jesus to come back and finish up. But He finished it! To live in the presence of God, you've got to grab hold of that fact.

You've got to see it. You've got to come up higher. You've got to come above the clouds. You've got to come up above the storm of the world. You've got to come up and see where the eagles soar. You've got to come up and see all that heaven has for you!

> The Lord your God is with you, He is mighty to save. He will take great delight in you, He will quiet you with His love, He will rejoice over you with singing.
>
> ZEPHANIAH 3:17 NIV

God is rejoicing over you today. He is walking up and down in your house rejoicing over you with singing and with gladness. The Lord your God is mighty in your midst: mighty to save, mighty to heal, mighty to deliver!

Here are some points that will help you. These are principles that I apply in my life on a regular basis as I try to live in the presence of God.

First, never forget that God is your source. The moment you think you have to do it, you replace God as the source and you become dependent upon yourself. When you become dependent upon yourself, you're also dependent on your own limitations. Suddenly you find out that you can't do anything—you question your qualifications or your education. You realize you don't have the answers, so suddenly you don't know what to do.

But as long as you keep God as your source, you know that He knows the end from the beginning. You know that He makes a way where there is no way. Even if you don't know what's going on right now, you know God's going to help you.

James 1:5 says: *"If any of you lack wisdom, let him ask of God, that giveth to all men liberally, and upbraideth not; and it shall be given him."* God's going to give you wisdom; all you've got to do is ask. Just say, "Lord I don't know what to do, but Your Word says if I lack wisdom and I ask of You, You're going to give me wisdom. Lord, I need wisdom." God will tell you the way. Then all you have to do is walk in that wisdom and He'll make a way where there is no way.

I always remember that God is my source. I have never, ever, in all these years, thought I was bringing revival or working miracles. I have always known it was God. I have always known it was His power. All I am is a messenger boy.

Second, act on God's Word as a way of life. Do what He tells you to do! Don't call Him, "Lord, Lord," and then refuse or neglect to do the things He tells you to do. For instance, you can't live in the presence of God and have unforgiveness in your heart. You can't live in the presence of God if you're living in sin. It's impossible to be with Him if you're practicing sin. You have to make a decision to put those things behind you. Act on His Word, walk in the love of God, and obey Him.

And don't say that you don't know when you missed it. You knew before you sinned that you were going to sin. You planned to. You didn't just walk down the road and end up robbing a bank.

"Rodney, I don't understand! I woke up this morning on fire for God. I was serving God, praising God, and the next thing I knew I went to deposit my check, but instead of saying, 'Will you deposit it,' I said, 'stick 'em up,' and pulled out a gun! I don't understand how it happened."

Backsliding does not come overnight. You don't go to sleep on fire for God and wake up cold, not serving God, wanting nothing to do with God. There is a gradual cooling-off process. That's why the Bible says to protect your heart with all diligence, for out of it flow the issues of life (Proverbs 4:23). Protect your heart daily with the Word of God. You're even going to have to protect yourself from some of the people who you hang around, because they'll come and quench the fire in your life.

Third, don't lose the excitement of living for Jesus. Get excited and stay excited. Expect God to move every day, even on an off day, on a day of rest. God never sleeps. That's why I don't like to go to sleep—I might miss some excitement. Since I want to hang around Him and I know He doesn't sleep, I'm concerned that if I go to sleep, I might miss something!

Get excited about serving Jesus. If you get excited about living for Jesus and serving Jesus, there'll never be a morning that you don't want to get out of bed and live life to the fullest. You'll get up with a spring in your step and you'll face every obstacle with joy, because you know that He's with you and that He's going to help you.

Fourth, always give Jesus the glory. For every little thing, give Him the glory. I give Him glory just because I am able to walk outside and see a sunny day. I give Him glory for the palm trees and the grass and the privilege to be alive. When you do this, the presence of God comes on you.

"Well, I've got nothing to be excited about, Rodney. Will you please pray for me? The air conditioner's not working in my house, the TV broke down, and my computer won't work anymore."

Well, are you breathing? Give God the glory! "Lord, thank You for the ability to breathe air. Thank You that I'm alive today. Thank You for the privilege of being alive in this day and this time." When you start doing that, the presence of God just comes in.

Have a thankful heart for the tiniest little things—the water you drink, the air you breathe, the ability to use your hands. There are some people who can't use their hands today. There are some people who can't walk normally, or who are confined to a wheelchair, paralyzed for the rest of their lives. Some of these people have more of a thankful attitude than people who have the use of all their limbs.

We've got young people thirteen years of age wanting to kill themselves because life isn't worth living. Who sold them that lie? As long as you're breathing, as long as you have life on the inside of you, as long as you can depend upon Jesus, there's no problem too great!

God will move the mountains for you, but in order for Him to move the mountains, you've got to thank Him for each little shovelful. You can't just give Him glory when a mountain gets moved. You've got to thank Him when a molehill gets moved. Thank Him for every little molehill, keep a heart that is thankful all the time, and when a mountain gets in your way, the presence of God will blow it away!

Under the old covenant, God inhabited the praises of His people, but under the new covenant God inhabits the people of praise. So when you praise and thank Him, God comes and makes you His sanctuary.

Fifth, think back on your past victories. Think about where He's brought you from and where you could have been. Reflect briefly on your life, then think about the day He saved you. Think about the family He's blessed you with—your spouse, your children. Think about all the failures God turned around. Think about the times it looked like you were never going to make it. You even thought to yourself, *I don't know how I'm going to get through.* Then remember how God brought you through every one of those things!

Well, He's not going to drop you now! He didn't bring you this far to leave you. He didn't teach you to swim to let you drown, either. The Bible says that He who began a good work in you is able to complete it. And Hebrews 12:2 tells us that He's the author and the finisher of our faith. That means if He authored it, He started it, so He'll complete it.

> Being confident of this very thing, that he which hath begun a good work in you will perform it until the day of Jesus Christ.
>
> PHILIPPIANS 1:6

> Looking unto Jesus the author and finisher of our faith; who for the joy that was set before him endured the cross, despising the shame, and is set down at the right hand of the throne of God.
>
> HEBREWS 12:2

Sixth, always testify. Always talk about God's goodness. Talk about His goodness to your children every day when you sit around the table to eat. Talk about the goodness of Jesus, His greatness, and His wondrous works. That's how His presence comes. When you talk about how the Lord first touched you, it just comes afresh to you again. Just try to tell somebody each day. "I want to tell you what happened to me." When you start telling, it comes alive on the inside of you again. You bring His presence.

You know what a lot of Christians are doing? The moment they get together, they say, "Let me tell you what the devil did to me last week. Now Monday, he attacked me here, and Tuesday, that happened, then Wednesday..."

What happens? The presence of God is gone—and I'm gone too! I don't want to hang around that mess. I'd rather be with those who talk about the Lord—His goodness, His grace, His glory, His mercy, His faithfulness, His lovingkindness, and all of the blessings that He's so freely and lavishly bestowed upon you.

Can you think of things to testify about? You could have been in a strait jacket in a mental institution today, but here you are sitting clothed in your right mind. You've got something to shout about! You could still be bound by religious tradition today, but He has delivered you and set you free. You could be sick, dying of a terminal disease, but Jesus has set you free. That's something to shout about! That's something to testify about!

Think about what could have been and think about how God delivered you. If He delivered you once, He'll deliver you again and again! Hallelujah!

Remember, you can consistently live in the presence of Jesus if you:

- Never forget that God is your source.

- Act on God's Word as a way of life.

- Don't lose the excitement of living for Jesus.

- Always give Jesus the glory.

- Think back on your past victories.

- And always testify of His goodness.

CHAPTER 21

PRESSING IN TO JESUS

And, behold, there was a man named Zacchaeus, which was the chief among the publicans, and he was rich. And he sought to see Jesus who he was; and could not for the press, because he was little of stature. And he ran before, and climbed up into a sycamore tree to see him: for he was to pass that way. And when Jesus came to the place, he looked up, and saw him, and said unto him, Zacchaeus, make haste, and come down; for to day I must abide at thy house. And he made haste, and came down, and received him joyfully.

LUKE 19:2-6

"You need to press in to Jesus." That's a statement I make all the time, and people often come to me and say: "What do you mean by press in to Jesus?"

What does it mean to press in? How do you press in, and what is there to press into? Let's look at the story of Zacchaeus in the Gospel of Luke. First of all, Zacchaeus was a wealthy tax collector who wanted to see Jesus, but he was too short to see over the crowd. So he devised this plan: "I've got to see Jesus, so I'm going to climb up in this tree. Then, when He passes by, I'll be able to see Him."

Just picture a wealthy man climbing up and sitting in a tree, waiting for Jesus to come by. He wanted to see Jesus so much, he didn't care what anybody thought of him.

"Well, isn't that old Zach? Hey Zacchaeus, what are you doing up a tree?"

Imagine how Zacchaeus felt when Jesus told Him to come down. He knew his life would never be the same.

When you're desperate, you'll do anything. We've got an individual attending our Bible school right now who drove eight days to get to Florida from Alaska. When you're desperate, you're going to do anything you can to get to the place where you can see Jesus. When you are desperate to see Him, nothing else matters.

A lot of people are facing dire circumstances today because they're just putting up with a situation. "Well, I guess this is my lot in life," they say. "I'm just going to have to put up with this sickness and disease. I'm just going to have to put up with this circumstance at my work. I'm just going to have to put up with this problem in my marriage."

Well, it's time to get up off of your blessed assurance and stop putting up with it! It's time to say, "No more! I'm not going to tolerate this sickness and disease another day in my life. I'm not going to tolerate this lack another day in my life. I'm going to do something! I don't care what it takes! Even if I have to get out of the house and climb a tree, I'm going to get close to Jesus!"

How desperate are you?

I remember going to pray for a person who had emphysema. He could barely breathe, even on an oxygen machine, but he was sitting there smoking a cigarette. He said, "Pastor Rodney, would you pray for me?"

I said, "What's wrong?"

"I've got emphysema."

"Well, how desperate are you to get healed?"

"I need a miracle. Can I get some new lungs?"

This person wasn't desperate enough to live to even quit smoking! How desperate are you?

And again he entered into Capernaum after some days; and it was noised that he was in the house. And straightway many were gathered together, insomuch that there was no room to receive them, no, not so much as about the door: and he preached the word unto them.

MARK 2:1-2

Jesus came into this house, and then everybody started telling the neighbors, "Hey, you know who's in that house? It's Jesus!" People were stuck all over that house—in the living room, in the basement, in the bathroom, in the kitchen! But when you're desperate, the crowd doesn't matter.

And they came unto him, bringing one sick of the palsy, which was borne of four. And when they could not come nigh unto him for the press, they uncovered the roof where he was: and when they had broken it up, they let down the bed wherein the sick of the palsy lay. When Jesus saw their faith, he said unto the sick of the palsy, Son, thy sins be forgiven thee. But there were certain of the scribes sitting there, and reasoning in their hearts, Why doth this man thus speak blasphemies? who can forgive sins but God only? And immediately when Jesus perceived in his spirit that they so reasoned within themselves, he said unto them, Why reason ye these things in your hearts? Whether is it easier to say to the sick of the palsy, Thy sins be forgiven thee; or to say, Arise, and take up thy bed, and walk? But that ye may know that the Son of man hath power on earth to forgive sins, (he saith to the sick of the palsy,) I say unto thee, Arise, and take up thy bed, and go thy way into thine house. And immediately he arose, took up the bed, and went forth before them all; insomuch that they were all amazed, and glorified God, saying, We never saw it on this fashion.

MARK 2:3-12

When you get desperate, you don't care. These four were thinking, "We've got to get in that house! Our friend is sick and there's only one way in—through the roof, so let's climb on top of the house, rip up the roof, and let him down from the top. *We have to get hold of Jesus.*"

Somebody said, "You can't do that. He's preaching!"

"I don't care what He's doing. I'm going to get hold of Jesus."

Somebody said, "But you can't rip up the roof, they'll arrest you. You'll get thrown in prison for vandalism."

"I don't care! I've got to get hold of Jesus. I'm desperate."

How desperate are you?

When people get into desperate situations, they do the most amazing things. I heard about a lady who arrived on the scene of an automobile wreck. Someone was trapped under the automobile and this little lady picked the automobile up and pulled the person out from under it. She did something that she could not do physically. In a moment of desperation, she did something beyond her natural abilities.

That reminds me of a funny story. A drunk decided to take a shortcut home through the graveyard one night. Unfortunately for him, the gravedigger had dug a new grave that day, and it was directly in his path. He fell headlong into the grave, and it was so deep he couldn't get out of it. After an hour of trying, he realized there was no way to get out, so he decided just to sit there and spend the night.

At midnight, a second drunk man staggered out of the bar and decided to also cut through the graveyard. Boom! He fell into the same open grave. He tried to jump out, but to no avail. It was far too deep. The first drunk, who had fallen asleep, was awakened by the noise. He said to the second drunk, who was unaware of his presence in the grave, "You're not gonna get out of this grave tonight!"

But he did!

When you're desperate you can find a way!

How desperate are you? Are you desperate enough to press in to Jesus?

So many of us are living with situations that we're just putting up with—in our job, in our finances, in our marriage, in our physical body. Are we desperate enough to say: "I've had it now! Devil, you've come this far and you can't come any farther!"

Zacchaeus was desperate, and he pressed into Jesus. The way that he pressed in was by climbing a tree. The four men were desperate to help their friend, and they pressed in to Jesus by ripping up a roof. The way you press in might be totally different from anybody else.

Look at this familiar story in Mark 5:25-34:

> And a certain woman, which had an issue of blood twelve years, And had suffered many things of many physicians, and had spent all that she had, and was nothing bettered, but rather grew worse, When she had heard of Jesus, came in the press behind, and touched his garment. For she said, If I may touch but his clothes, I shall be whole. And straightway the fountain of her blood was dried up; and she felt in her body that she was healed of that plague. And Jesus, immediately knowing in himself that virtue had gone out of him, turned him about in the press, and said, Who touched my clothes? And his disciples said unto him, Thou seest the multitude thronging thee, and sayest thou, Who touched me? And he looked round about to see her that had done this thing. But the woman fearing and trembling, knowing what was done in her, came and fell down before him, and told him all the truth. And he said unto her, Daughter, thy faith hath made thee whole; go in peace, and be whole of thy plague.

This woman had desperate faith, so she pressed in through the crowd to touch the hem of Jesus's garment. You've got to have that same kind of desperate faith. Desperate faith will cause you to rise up and grab hold of your miracle.

Desperate faith is when you cry, "That's it!" You need to get mad at the right thing. You've been getting mad at the preacher, at your brother, at your sister. But you need to get mad at the devil and rise up and do something in Jesus's name.

If you're unhappy and desperate enough about the way things are, you can change them. How desperate are you?

Speaking of desperate people, look at the story of Bartimaeus in Mark 10:46-50:

And they came to Jericho: and as he went out of Jericho with his disciples and a great number of people, blind Bartimaeus, the son of Timaeus, sat by the highway side begging. And when he heard that it was Jesus of Nazareth he began to cry out, and say, Jesus, thou son of David, have mercy on me. And many charged him that he should hold his peace: but he cried the more a great deal, Thou son of David, have mercy on me. And Jesus stood still, and commanded him to be called. And they call the blind man, saying unto him, Be of good comfort, rise; he calleth thee. And he, casting away his garment, rose, and came to Jesus.

That last verse is very important. The garment Bartimaeus was wearing signified that he was a blind man, just as blind people today might use a white cane or a guide dog. Bartimaeus cast away the garment that signified he was blind. What was he doing? In his desperation, he was taking off the clothes that attached him to his blindness, saying: "I'm leaving the past behind and I'm going forward. I'm pressing in to Jesus. Doesn't matter what the past has been like. Because I'm desperate, I'm pressing in to Jesus."

And Jesus answered and said unto him, What wilt thou that I should do unto thee? The blind man said unto him, Lord, that I might receive my sight. And Jesus said unto him, Go thy way; thy faith hath made thee whole. And immediately he received his sight, and followed Jesus in the way.

MARK 10:51-52

When you're pressing in to Jesus like Bartimaeus, you've got to leave that old garment behind. Leave that old garment of doubt and unbelief, that old garment of "you're never going to make it," that old garment of "you're going to fail." Take off that old garment of sickness and disease, that old garment of poverty and lack. Cast off those old garments of depression, oppression, fear, bondage, religious tradition, doctrines of men, and doctrines of devils. When you press in to Jesus, you're going to leave them behind, because Jesus has got great things prepared for you.

Listen to what the apostle Paul wrote to the Philippian church:

> Not as though I had already attained, either were already perfect: but I follow after, if that I may apprehend that for which also I am apprehended of Christ Jesus. Brethren, I count not myself to have apprehended: but this one thing I do, forgetting those things which are behind, and reaching forth unto those things which are before, I press toward the mark for the prize of the high calling of God in Christ Jesus.
>
> PHILIPPIANS 3:12-14

I don't know about you, but I made a decision: I'm pressing in to Jesus. Sometimes "casting off the old" might mean getting rid of some of the friends that you've had because they're holding you back. They're holding you in bondage. They are the ones who are telling you that you can't make it. They want you living in the past, on yesterday's bread, eating yesterday's manna. But it's a new day, and you just have to say: "I'm forgetting those things which are behind and reaching forth unto the things which are before."

Do you realize what is before you? History books are waiting to be written about the man and woman of God who will totally, 100 percent, yield themselves to the Spirit of God, forgetting the past and saying: "Those days are over." Will that be you?

Make this day the day you cast off the old garment and press in to Jesus!

In Revelation 1:8, Jesus tells us that He is the Alpha and Omega, the beginning and the end. In this book, I believe I have only scratched the surface of all He was, is, and will be to those of us who love Him.

> I am Alpha and Omega, the beginning and the ending, saith the Lord, which is, and which was, and which is to come, the Almighty.
>
> REVELATION 1:8

To be perfectly honest, I didn't know how or where to end this book, because the more I study, preach, and write about Jesus, the more I see and the more I want to tell you. Finally, to get the book published, I had to stop somewhere!

If there is one thing, I would like you to remember always, it is that Jesus loves you and He is for you. No matter where you are or what you've done, no matter how bad you have messed up—as a believer or an unbeliever—you can come to Him at any time and He will not condemn you. He will forgive you and set you free.

Not only is Jesus the only one who can give you eternal life, but Jesus is the only one who can give purpose and meaning to your life. He is the only one who can tell you who you are and what you are created to be and do. He is the only one who can give you true joy, peace, and love.

Jesus wants to bless you beyond your wildest dreams! He will challenge you to grow up and mature along the way, but He will never push you. He is a gentleman and He respects your will. It's up to you to seek Him—in the Word of God, as you pray, in church, on the job, and as you fellowship with other believers. He will go as far with you as you will allow Him to go. And I can tell you from personal experience that He can take you a long, long way!

Begin this adventure right now, if you haven't already, and see if your life doesn't turn out to be more than you could ever have imagined!

SALVATION PRAYER

Father, I come to You in the precious name of Your Son, Jesus. You said in Your Word that if I confess with my mouth that Jesus Christ is my Lord and my Savior and I believe in my heart that God has raised Him from the dead, I will be saved. I make the decision today to surrender every area of my life to the lordship of Jesus.

Jesus, come into my heart. Take out the stony heart and put in a heart of flesh. I turn my back on the world and on sin. I repent and I put my trust in You. I acknowledge that I am a sinner. I would like to thank You for dying on the cross for my sin and shedding Your blood for me so that I might be forgiven of my sin. Thank You that You rose from the dead and that one day, You are coming back for me.

I confess that Jesus Christ has come in the flesh and that He is my personal Lord and Savior. Thank You, Lord Jesus, for saving me. I accept by faith the free gift of salvation. Amen (so be it).

Dear Friend, if you just prayed this prayer, I would like to welcome you into the family of God! Your sins are forgiven! This is the good news of the Gospel of the Lord Jesus Christ. You are now a child of God and you will live with Him forever. I encourage you to do several things to get to know Him. Read your Bible and pray every day (talk to Jesus about everything in your life). Find a Bible-believing church that believes in the lordship of Jesus Christ. Be around strong believers who will encourage you and lift you up in your walk with God. Tell someone about your new-found faith and joy that only Jesus can bring. Use this book and my other books and teachings to help you in your new walk with God.

PRAYER OF RECOMMITMENT

Father, I come to You in the precious name of Jesus.

I know I have given my life to You in days gone by. However, I've not been serving You as I should. I took my eyes off Jesus and allowed my heart to grow cold.

I surrender my life to You afresh. Take all of me. I want all of You.

Restore my first love. Let me fall in love with Jesus all over again. Restore the joy of my salvation.

From this day forth, I promise to run the race until I see You face to face.

Thank You for Your blood that cleansed my soul. I receive Your forgiveness.

Take out my stony heart and put back a soft heart. Thank You, Father, for Your grace and mercy.

Amen.

About the Author

DRS. RODNEY AND ADONICA HOWARD-BROWNE are the founders of Revival Ministries International, The River at Tampa Bay Church, River Bible Institute, River School of Worship, River Bible Institute Español, and River School of Government in Tampa, Florida.

Rodney and Adonica have been called by God to reach out to the nations—whilst keeping America as their primary mission field. Their heart is to see the Church—the Body of Christ—revived, and the lost won to Christ. They have conducted a number of mass crusades and many outreaches, but their heart is also to train and equip others to bring in the harvest—from one-on-one evangelism to outreaches that reach tens, hundreds, thousands and even tens of thousands. Every soul matters and every salvation is a victory for the kingdom of God!

In December of 1987, Rodney, along with his wife, Adonica, and their three children, Kirsten, Kelly and Kenneth, moved from their native land, South Africa, to the United States—called by God as missionaries from Africa to America. The Lord had spoken through Rodney in a word of prophecy and declared: "As America has sown missionaries over the last 200 years, I am going to raise up people from other nations to come to the United States of America. I am sending a mighty revival to America."

In April of 1989, the Lord sent a revival of signs and wonders and miracles that began in a church in Clifton Park, New York, that has continued until today, resulting in thousands of people being touched and changed as they encounter the presence of the living God! God is still moving today—saving, healing, delivering, restoring, and setting free!

Drs. Rodney and Adonica's second daughter, Kelly, was born with an incurable lung disease called Cystic Fibrosis. This demonic disease slowly destroyed her lungs. Early on Christmas morning 2002, at the age of eighteen, she ran out of lung capacity and breathed out her last breath. They placed her into the arms of her Lord and Savior and then vowed a vow. First, they vowed that the devil would pay for what he had done to their family. Secondly, they vowed to do everything in their power, with the help of the Lord, to win 100 million souls to Jesus and to put $1 billion into world missions and the harvest of souls.

When Drs. Rodney and Adonica became Naturalized Citizens of the United States of America, in 2008 and 2004 respectively, they took the United States Oath of Allegiance, which declares, "I will support and defend the Constitution and laws of the United States of America against all enemies, foreign and domestic..." They love America, are praying for this country, and are trusting God to see another Great Awakening sweep across this land.

Believing for another Great Spiritual Awakening, Drs. Rodney and Adonica conducted Celebrate America DC, a soul-winning event. They preached the Gospel of Jesus Christ for thirty-five nights in Washington, D.C. at the Daughters of the American Revolution Constitution Hall, just 500 yards from the White House, from 2014-2018. Through the evangelism efforts on the streets, in the halls of Congress, and the nightly altar calls, 57,498 individuals made decisions for Jesus Christ.

With a passion for souls and a passion to revive and mobilize the Body of Christ, Drs. Rodney and Adonica have conducted soul-winning efforts throughout sixty nations with Good News campaigns, R.M.I. Revivals, and the Great Awakening Tours. As a result, over 21,570,000 precious people have come to Christ and tens of thousands of believers have been revived and mobilized to preach the Gospel of Jesus Christ. For more information about the ministry of Drs. Rodney and Adonica Howard-Browne, please, visit www.revival.com.

Connect

Please, visit revival.com for our latest updates and news. Many of our services are live online. Additionally, many of our recorded services are available on Video on Demand.

For a listing of Drs. Rodney and Adonica Howard-Browne's products and itinerary, please, visit revival.com. To download the soul-winning tools for free, please, visit revival.com and click on Soul-winning Tools.

Like us on Facebook:
Facebook.com/rodneyadonicahowardbrowne

Follow us on Twitter: @rhowardbrowne

Follow us on YouTube: Youtube.com/rodneyhowardbrowne

Follow us on Instagram: @rodneyhowardbrowne

Other Books and Resources by Rodney Howard-Browne

BOOKS

The Killing of Uncle of Sam: The Demise of the United States of America
The Killing of Uncle Sam Study Guide
The Killing of Uncle Sam Answer Key
Thoughts on Stewardship
The Coming Revival
This Present Glory
The Touch of God
The Gifts of the Holy Spirit
The Reality of Life After Death
Seeing Jesus as He Really Is
The Curse Is Not Greater than the Blessing
How to Increase and Release the Anointing
School of the Spirit
The Anointing
Manifesting the Holy Ghost
What Gifts Do You Bring the King?
Prayer Journal
Sowing in Famine

AUDIO CDS

Prayer Time
Weapons of Our Warfare
Becoming One Flesh
Faith
Flowing in the Holy Ghost
How to Flow in the Anointing
Igniting the Fire
In Search of the Anointing
Prayer that Moves Mountains
Accelerate
The Camels are Coming
Pray Without Ceasing Vol.1
Pray Without Ceasing Vol.2
The Touch of God
Mountain Moving Prayer
Having an Encounter with God
God's Mandate
The Anointing is Transferable
Dealing with Offenses
The Vow and the Decree
Whosoever Can Get Whatsoever
Run to the Water
Demonstrations of the Spirit and of Power
The Double Portion
More Than Laughter
The Hand of the Lord
Running the Heavenly Race
The Holy Spirit, His Purpose & Power
The Power to Create Wealth
Walking in Heaven's Light
All These Blessings
A Surplus of Prosperity

The Joy of the Lord is My Strength
Prayer Secrets
Communion–The Table of the Lord
My Roadmap
My Mission–My Purpose
My Heart
My Family
My Worship
Decreeing Faith
Ingredients of Revival
Fear Not
Matters of the Heart by Dr. Adonica Howard-Browne
My Treasure
My Absolutes
My Father
My Crowns
My Comforter & Helper
Renewing the Mind
Seated in High Places
Triumphant Entry
Merchandising and Trafficking the Anointing
My Prayer Life
My Jesus
Seeing Jesus as He Really Is
Exposing the World's System
Living in the Land of Visions & Dreams
Kingdom Business
Taking Cities in the Land of Giants
Spiritual Hunger
The Two Streams

MP3 CDS
The Killing of Uncle Sam Audio Book
The Touch of God: The Anointing
Knowing the Person of the Holy Spirit
The Love Walk
How to Hear the Voice of God
Matters of the Heart
Exposing the World's System
How to Be Led by the Holy Spirit
The Anointing
The Ways of the Wind

DVDS
Mountain Moving Prayer
How to Personally Lead Someone to Jesus
The Fire of God
Vision for America
Living the Christian Lifestyle
No Limits No Boundaries
The Curse is Not Greater Than the Blessing
God's Glory Manifested through Special Anointings
Good News New York
Jerusalem Ablaze
The Mercy of God by Dr. Adonica Howard-Browne
Are You a Performer or a Minister?
Revival at ORU Volume 1, 2 & 3
The Realms of God
Singapore Ablaze
The Coat My Father Gave Me
Have You Ever Wondered What Jesus Was Like?
There Is a Storm Coming (Recorded live from Good News New York)
Budapest, Hungary Ablaze
The Camels Are Coming

Power Evangelism
Taking Cities in the Land of Giants
Renewing the Mind
Triumphant Entry
Merchandising and Trafficking the Anointing
Doing Business with God
Accelerate

MUSIC
Nothing Is Impossible
By His Stripes
Run with Fire
The Sweet Presence of Jesus
Eternity with Kelly Howard-Browne
Live from the River
You're Such a Good God to Me
Howard-Browne Family Christmas
He Lives
Anointed—The Decade of the '80s
Live Summer Campmeeting '15
Live Summer Campmeeting '16
Haitian Praise
No Limits

The River at Tampa Bay Church

THE RIVER AT TAMPA BAY CHURCH was founded on December 1, 1996. At the close of 1996, the Lord planted within Pastors Rodney and Adonica's heart the vision and desire to start a church in Tampa. With a heart for the lost and to minister to those who had been touched by revival, they implemented that vision and began The River at Tampa Bay, with the motto, "Church with a Difference."

Over 575 people joined them for the first Sunday morning service on December 1, 1996. Over the years, the membership has grown and the facilities have changed, yet these three things have remained constant since the church's inception ... dynamic praise and worship, anointed preaching and teaching of the Word, and powerful demonstrations of the Holy Spirit and power. The Lord spoke to Pastor Rodney's heart to feed the people, touch the people, and love the people. With this in mind and heart, the goal of The River is:

To become a model revival church where people from all over the world can come and be touched by God. Once they have been not only touched, but changed, they are ready to be launched out into the harvest field with the anointing of God.

To have a church that is multi-racial, representing a cross section of society from rich to poor from all nations, bringing people to a place of maturity in their Christian walk.

To see the lost, the backslidden and the unsure come to a full assurance of their salvation.

To be a home base for Revival Ministries International and all of its arms. A base offering strength and support to the vision of RMI to see America shaken with the fires of revival, then to take that fire to the far-flung corners of the globe.

To break the mold of religious tradition and thinking.

To be totally dependent upon the Holy Spirit for His leading and guidance as we lead others deeper into the River of God.

Our motto: Church with a Difference.

For The River at Tampa Bay's service times and directions, please, visit revival.com or call (813) 971-9999. Location: The River at Tampa Bay Church, 3738 River International Dr., Tampa, FL 33610.

The River Bible Institute

THE RIVER BIBLE INSTITUTE (RBI) is a place where men and women of all ages, backgrounds and experiences can gather together to study and experience the glory of God. The River Bible Institute is not a traditional Bible school. It is a Holy Ghost training center, birthed specifically for those whose strongest desire is to know Christ and to make Him known.

The vision for The River Bible Institute is plain: To train men and women in the spirit of revival for ministry in the 21st century. The school was birthed in 1997 with a desire to train up revivalists for the 21st century. It is a place where the Word of God and the Holy Spirit come together to produce life, birth ministries, and launch them out. The River Bible Institute is a place where ministries are sent to the far-flung corners of the globe to spread revival and to bring in a harvest of souls for the kingdom of God.

While preaching in many nations and regions of the world, Dr. Rodney Howard-Browne has observed that all the people of the earth have one thing in common: a desperate need for the genuine touch of God. From the interior of Alaska through the bush country of Africa, to the outback villages of Australia to the cities of North America, people are tired of religion and ritualistic worship. They are crying out for the reality of His presence. The River Bible Institute is dedicated to training believers how to live, minister, and flow in the anointing.

The Word will challenge those attending the Institute to find clarity in their calling, and be changed by the awesome presence of God. This is the hour of God's power, not just for the full-time minister, but for all of God's people who are hungry for more. Whether you are a housewife or an aspiring evangelist, The River Bible Institute will deepen your relationship and experience in the Lord, and provide you with a new perspective on how to reach others with God's life-changing power.

You can be saturated in the Word and the Spirit of God at The River Bible Institute. Since 1997, The River Bible Institute has graduated over 4,000 students. It is the place where you will be empowered to reach your high calling and set your world on fire with revival. For more information about RBI, please, visit revival.com or call (813) 899-0085 or (813) 971-9999.

THE RIVER SCHOOL OF WORSHIP (RSW) is where ability becomes accountability, talent becomes anointing, and ambition becomes vision. It has been Drs. Rodney and Adonica Howard-Browne's dream for many years to provide a place where men and women of all ages, backgrounds and experiences could gather together to study and experience the glory of God. The River School of Worship is not a traditional music school. It is a training center birthed specifically for those whose strongest desire is to worship in Spirit and in Truth, and where the Word of God and the Holy Spirit come together to produce life, birth ministries, and launch them out.

The Word will challenge those of you attending to find clarity in your calling, and be changed by the awesome presence of God. The River School of Worship will deepen your relationship and experience in the Lord, and provide you with new perspective on how to reach others with God's life-changing power. You can be saturated in the Word and the Spirit of God at the River School of Worship. It is the place where you will be empowered to reach your high calling and set your world on fire with Revival. For more information about RSW, please, visit revival.com or call (813) 899-0085 or (813) 971-9999.

The River School of Government

Moreover, you shall choose able men from all the people—God-fearing men of truth who hate unjust gain—and place them over thousands, hundreds, fifties, and tens, to be their rulers.

EXODUS 18:21 AMPC

THE RIVER SCHOOL OF GOVERNMENT (RSG) has been founded as a result of the corruption that we see in the current government system and the need to raise up godly individuals with personal and public integrity to boldly take up positions of leadership in our nation. For hundreds of years, the Constitution of the United States of America, the supreme law of the land, has stood as a bulwark of righteousness, to protect the rights of its citizens. However, there have been attacks, from many quarters, all designed to neutralize the Constitution and to progressively remove citizens' rights.

There is a great need to raise up individuals who will run for office in the United States of America, from the very bottom all the way to the highest level of government, who will honor and stand up for both the integrity of the Constitution and the integrity of God's Word. If we are going to see America changed for the good, we have to get back to her founding principles, which were laid out by the Founding Fathers at her inception. This is the heart and soul and primary focus of the River School of Government.

The River School of Government will work to expose the enemies of our sovereignty and Constitution. The students will be trained in every area of governmental leadership and responsibility, and upon successful graduation will be entrusted with specific positions, tasks and responsibilities, each according to their ability and calling. The River School of Government's goal is not to raise up career politicians, who will abuse their positions for personal gain or for personal power, but to raise up people who will govern according to solid godly principles and who will continue to faithfully defend the individual rights and freedoms that are guaranteed by both the Constitution and God's Word.

The River School of Government is non-partisan and has one objective: to raise up people in government, who are armed with a solid foundation in the Constitution, God's Holy Word, and the power of the Holy Spirit—to take America back! We believe that the Lord will help us to accomplish this goal of taking America back, with a well-defined four, eight, twelve, sixteen, and twenty-year plan, springing out of a third Great Spiritual Awakening! For more information about RSG, please, call (813) 899-0085 or (813) 971 9999 or email us at rsg@revival.com.

God Wants to Use You to Bring in the Harvest of Souls!

THE GREAT COMMISSION, "Go ye into all the world and preach the Gospel to every creature," is for every believer to take personally. Every believer is to be an announcer of the Good News Gospel. When the Gospel is preached, people have an encounter with Jesus. Jesus is the only One Who can change the heart of a man, woman, child, and nation!

On the next page is a tool to assist you in sharing the Gospel with others. It is called, "The Gospel Soul-Winning Script." Please, make copies of it, fold it in the center lengthwise, and read it to people. As you read it to others, you will see many come to Christ, because as stated in Romans 1:16, *"For I am not ashamed of the gospel of Christ: for it is the power of God unto salvation to every one that believeth ... "*

Please, visit revival.com, click on Soul-Winning Tools, and review the many tools and videos that are freely available to help you bring in the harvest of souls. It is harvest time!

THE GOSPEL SOUL-WINNING —SCRIPT—

Has anyone ever told you that God loves you and that He has a wonderful plan for your life? I have a real quick, but important question to ask you. If you were to die this very second, do you know for sure, beyond a shadow of a doubt, that you would go to Heaven? [If "Yes"— Great, why would you say "Yes"? (If they respond with anything but "I have Jesus in my heart" or something similar to that, PROCEED WITH SCRIPT) or "No" or "I hope so" PROCEED WITH SCRIPT.]

Let me quickly share with you what the Holy Bible reads. It reads "for all have sinned and come short of the glory of God" and "for the wages of sin is death, but the gift of God is eternal life through Jesus Christ our Lord". The Bible also reads, "For whosoever shall call upon the name of the Lord shall be saved". And you're a "whosoever" right? Of course you are; all of us are.

continued on reverse side—

I'm going to say a quick prayer for you. Lord, bless (FILL IN NAME) and his/her family with long and healthy lives. Jesus, make Yourself real to him/her and do a quick work in his/her heart. If (FILL IN NAME) has not received Jesus Christ as his/her Lord and Savior, I pray he/she will do so now.

(FILL IN NAME), if you would like to receive the gift that God has for you today, say this after me with your heart and lips out loud. Dear Lord Jesus, come into my heart. Forgive me of my sin. Wash me and cleanse me. Set me free. Jesus, thank You that You died for me. I believe that You are risen from the dead and that You're coming back again for me. Fill me with the Holy Spirit. Give me a passion for the lost, a hunger for the things of God and a holy boldness to preach the gospel of Jesus Christ. I'm saved; I'm born again, I'm forgiven and I'm on my way to Heaven because I have Jesus in my heart.

As a minister of the gospel of Jesus Christ, I tell you today that all of your sins are forgiven. Always remember to run to God and not from God because He loves you and has a great plan for your life.

[Invite them to your church and get follow up info: name, address, & phone number.]

Revival Ministries International
P.O. Box 292888 • Tampa, FL 33687
(813) 971-9999 • www.revival.com

THE RIVER AT TAMPA BAY CHURCH
ALTAR CALL

CELEBRATE AMERICA
WASHINGTON, D.C.
57,498 SALVATIONS

WINTER CAMPMEETING AT RMI WORLD HEADQUARTERS

THE GREAT AWAKENING BROADCAST WITH
CHRISTIAN TELEVISION NETWORK
OVER 16 MILLION RECORDED DECISIONS FOR CHRIST

GOOD NEWS NEW YORK - 1999
MADISON SQUARE GARDEN
48,459 SALVATIONS

GOOD NEW SOWETO - 2004
SOWETO, SOUTH AFRICA
177,600 SALVATIONS

GOOD NEWS UMLAZI - 2005
UMLAZI, SOUTH AFRICA
286,750 SALVATIONS

SINGAPORE 1995

THE EARLY YEARS
RODNEY, ADONICA, KIRSTEN, KELLY, & KENNETH

THE EARLY YEARS
RODNEY & ADONICA